DAYANANDA SARASVATI
ESSAYS ON HIS LIFE AND IDEAS

DAYANANDA SARASVATI

Essays on His Life and Ideas

J. T. F. JORDENS

MANOHAR
1998

First published 1998

ISBN 81-7304-244-6

Published by
Ajay Kumar Jain for
Manohar Publishers & Distributors
2/6, Ansari Road, Daryaganj
New Delhi 110002

Lasertypeset by
A J Software Publishing Co. Pvt. Ltd.
305, Durga Chambers,
1333, D.B. Gupta Road,
Karol Bagh, New Delhi 110005

Printed at
Replika Press Pvt. Ltd.
Plot No. A-229, DSIDC Narela Indl. Park
Delhi 110040

To
ANN-MARI
again

Contents

PART IV: ARYA SAMAJ

Preface

In 1978 my book *Dayananda Sarasvati, His Life and Ideas*, was published by Oxford University Press, Delhi. During the years preceding and following that publication I wrote a number of essays on the same topic. Some were published in books and journals in Australia, India and the Netherlands, others were delivered as papers at various international conferences. Those interested in the published essays would find it extremely difficult to acquire them, and the unpublished papers were available only to the few specialists present at the conferences. I therefore decided that in order to make these works more freely available to interested readers, I would publish them in this volume.

I thank those holding the copyright of the various published essays for allowing me to reproduce my work in this form. I have indicated at the beginning of the notes of each chapter when and where the original version was first published. I wish to thank Ramesh Jain of Manohar Publishers & Distributors for his interest and extreme helpfulness, and my wife, Ann-Mari, for her enormous patience and dedication in typing my various papers and essays onto disk.

J.T.F. Jordens

PART I
Biographical

CHAPTER 1

Pilgrimage to the Sources: Dayananda Sarasvati and the Vedas

MOST BIOGRAPHIES of Swami Dayananda Sarasvati give the impression that he received from his guru Swami Virjananda the clear and explicit mission to revive the ancient Vedic religion by the propagation of the Vedas, and that the remainder of Dayananda's life was simply devoted to the realization of that mission. That view is a gross simplification. It was a long pilgrimage that gradually brought the Swami to his final conception of the Vedas, and to the elaboration of practical reform measures that would lead to the eventual restoration of Vedic civilization.

Recent studies have demonstrated how much Mohandas Karamchand Gandhi was influenced by his Kathiawari background. The influence of Kathiawar was equally strong on Mulji (Dayananda's previous name according to the tradition). But the background of Mohandas, a Vaishnavite of the merchant class, was very different from that of Mulji, a brahmin Shaivite. The Shaivites of Kathiawar, who were mostly Smarta brahmins had a very special self-image: they constituted a practically pure brahmin elite whose roots were firmly planted in antiquity. On the one hand there was the glorious past of the Shaiva kingdoms, most aptly symbolized by the ruins of Somnath, on the other hand was their exclusive access to the ancient roots of Hinduism through Sanskrit and the Vedic rites. From his very youth Mulji's eyes were turned to antiquity and the Vedas: He studied Sanskrit and learned by heart the *Yajurveda*.[1]

At the age of twenty-one Mulji ran away from home to escape an impending wedding, and he soon became initiated as a Sarasvati Dandi *Sannyasi* of the Shankaracharya order, receiving the name he would make famous: Dayananda Sarasvati. Then started fourteen years of frantic search by the young *sannyasi:* the search for religious liberation, *moksha*, initially through the study of the great Hindu system of Advaita Vedanta, but for the latter ten years dominated by the practice of Yoga. Dayananda's search for the perfect guru who would guide him to the fulfilment of ultimate realization drove him to the snowy peaks of the land of Kumaon and through the fearful jungles of the Vindhya range. That first arduous pilgrimage ended in frustration and occasionally even despair: the perfect guru was never found, and the 'doors of perception' remained stubbornly closed. In these first fifteen years of the Swami's adult life, the Vedas played no role.[2]

At the end of 1860 the Swami arrived at Mathura. From here another pilgrimage was soon to start. The effect of Mathura and Swami Virjananda on Dayananda was a total redirection of his life; in this chapter our interest is focused on Dayananda's rediscovery of the Vedas. What Dayananda studied with his guru Virjananda was Sanskrit grammar; it seems quite clear that they did not read any Vedic texts together. But the grammarian Virjananda had in the later years of his life discovered a seminal idea that came to dominate his thinking. At a particular serious crisis in his life he went into seclusion in order to quietly examine his life and priorities. When he reopened his grammar school a great change took place: he threw out all the grammar texts he had previously used, such as the *Siddhantakaumudi*, the *Shekar* and the *Manorama*, and replaced them by the one and only *Ashtadhyayi* of the sage Patanjali. The significance and importance of this change becomes clear in the context of Virjananda's new interpretation of the whole of Hindu literature.[3] This concerns the vital distinction he established between *arsha* works, those written by the *rishis*, the real sages of ancient India, and *anarsha* works, those written by others. Virjananda's key idea was that the contemporary degeneration of Hinduism was fundamentally caused by the proliferation and influence of 'spurious' works of a sectarian nature, and aggravated by a parallel neglect of the real sources of Hinduism, the books of the *rishis*. The implication was that the regeneration of Hinduism could only be achieved through a renewal of the study of the works of the *rishis* and the elimination of the works of sectarian origin.

That was the seminal idea Virjananda communicated to his favourite pupil Dayananda. However, it is quite clear that the guru had no definite idea as to exactly which were the books of the *rishis*. He had come no further than to formulate three criteria by the application of which the wheat could be separated from the chaff. These were his criteria: (1) the books written by the *rishis* always begin with the words OM or ATHA, not with the invocation of a particular deity; (2) the works of the *rishis* exhibit a universal character, not a narrowly sectarian one; (3) the commentaries on the works of the *rishis* were all written by recognized teachers such as Shankaracharya and Patanjali.[4]

When Dayananda said goodbye to his guru after nearly three years' study, he set out on the first stage of his second pilgrimage with the aim of finding out for himself which exactly the books of the ancient *rishis* were. This search took him seven years. As frantically as Dayananda previously had sought a guru, he now searched for books. He ransacked the libraries of Agra, Gwalior, Jaipur, Pushkar and Ajmer. The early Hindi biographies reveal how by the progressive elimination of *anarsha* works, the Swami gradually narrowed the list of books possibly written by the *rishis* down to the four Samhitas.[5]

The first work to be struck off was the *Bhagavata Purana*; but at that time the Swami still accepted other Puranas such as the *Devi*, *Kurma*, and *Linga*. It took him about four years to come to the conclusion that all the Puranas and all the Tantras were inauthentic. The next step was his assertion that parts of the *Ramayana*, and of the *Bhagavad Gita* were prone to errors and, therefore unacceptable as revealed, and that the *Upanishads* also strayed from the path of truth.

In 1870 occurred the famous public disputation between Swami Dayananda and the pandits of Varanasi in which he was unfairly and ignominiously declared the loser. By that time he had drastically narrowed down his search for the authentic sources of Hinduism; he now held that these pure sources were to be found in the Samhitas, the four Vedas. But, and this is an important point, he still accepted that the Samhitas included their respective Brahmanas or commentaries. A year later the Swami eliminated the latter and arrived at his definitive doctrine that only the four Vedas, exclusive of their Brahmanas, contained the original divine revelation. Nearly eight years had elapsed since he left his guru Virjananda. During these years the Swami's study of the Vedas had deepened, and a competent and independent witness, Dr Hoernle of Varanasi wrote at that time that Dayananda knew the Vedas 'better than most if not all the great pandits of Varanasi', and that he was also remarkable in that his interpretation was original and free from the dominance of traditionalism.[6]

In fact Dayananda had gone much further than simply answering the original question of Virjananda, 'which were the books composed by the *rishis*?' He introduced a radical distinction between the four Vedas, the original revelation of God transmitted through the passive agency of the *rishis*, and other works composed by the *rishis*, which had only a derivative type of secondary authority. On the one hand there were the Vedas, not composed but only transmitted through them; on the other hand there were various works and commentaries composed by the *rishis* themselves. The authority of the latter depended on their conformity with the former, the four Vedas, which constituted direct divine revelation containing the blueprint of the ideal religion and the ideal social system.

The Swami had also developed further the three criteria used by Virjananda for determining the authenticity of sacred texts. He still accepted the external criteria relating to the opening words, but to him the internal criteria became the really decisive ones. Any text that offended logic or morality could not be the word of God. Miracles were discredited because their physical impossibility offends reason, and so does any form of idolatry, superstition, polytheism or internal contradiction; any hint of immorality, as found in myths and legends, also necessarily relegates a work to human level.

However, at this time the Swami did not yet have very definite ideas as to what exactly the Vedas contained, in what manner they revealed God's message, and what their position was *vis-a-vis* the revelations claimed outside Hinduism by other religions. It was during his visit to Calcutta in 1872 that those issues forced themselves on his attention.

Questions about 'revelation' had been on the mind of the Bengali reformers since the time of Rammohun Roy. They had thought about them in a wide context, pressed on by the challenge of the claims of Christianity and Islam, both religions of the book. The general conclusion of these reformers had been to reject *all* claims to exclusive revelation by any religion; they accepted that different religions presented in their holy writ complementary aspects of a universal religion. From that theoretical premise followed their practical eclecticism: they borrowed freely from different scriptures for their inspiration and their religious services. This practical eclecticism was carried to its greatest lengths by Keshub Chandra Sen.

However, in the 1870s that universalistic and eclectic approach was being increasingly challenged by a newly emerging movement of

Hindu pride and nationalism, according to which Hinduism was not just one among equals in the brotherhood of religions, but was superior to all others. This movement was spearheaded by the Adi Brahmo Samaj under the leadership of Rajnarayan Bose and the Tagore family. The organizational offshoots of this movement were the Society for the Promotion of National Feeling, the Hindu Mela, and the National Society. The aim of all these organs was to counteract Western influence by the promotion of the knowledge and awareness of the greatness of Indian culture, a greatness closely linked to the Hindu religion and heritage according to Nabagopal Mitra's dictum, 'The Hindus are destined to be a religious nation.'[7] That same connection was eloquently proclaimed by Rajnarayan in his famous lecture of 1872, given only a few months before Dayananda's arrival in Calcutta, entitled 'The superiority of Hinduism'. He read this text to Dayananda and presented him with a copy.[8]

Those were the people who were Dayananda's hosts in Calcutta. The Swami met other personalities imbued with that same new spirit of Hindu revival, such as the historian Rajnikanta Gupta and the educator and journalist Bhudev Mukhopadhyay. It has been taken for granted that Dayananda's concept of the superiority of Hinduism was the direct outcome of his Vedic studies. However, before coming to Calcutta, he never thought about Hinduism in comparative terms, or even in nationalist terms. It was in Calcutta that, through the influence of his hosts, his outlook widened so that he started to think of Hinduism in relation to other religions, and more precisely, to think of the Vedas in comparison with the Bible and the Koran.

Calcutta had yet another profound influence on the Swami. He met a significant cross-section of the leading Bengali intelligentsia, and he must have been struck by their extreme individualism. Among those he met, very few would have found themselves in full agreement on the basic question of the relation between religious and social reform, on the issue of Westernization *versus* cultural revival, and on matters of statecraft and political action. Their conceptions of the essence of Hinduism, the sources of true religion and the implementation of religious reform, were amazingly divergent. Perhaps there was only one conviction they all shared: the denial that the Vedas represented the unique and definitive divine revelation. Dayananda diagnosed that refusal as the root-cause of their disagreements. It is in Calcutta that he made up his mind that he himself would write a commentary on the Vedas.[9]

A year after his visit to Calcutta, in 1874, the Swami's theology of revelation reached its full maturity and was clearly enunciated in the first edition of his *Satyarth Prakash*.[10] But his study of the Vedas had still a long way to go. Three years later he started publishing his 'Introduction to the commentary of the *Rig* and other *Vedas*',[11] and began the publication of his Commentary with Hindi translation in monthly fascicules. Only part of his Commentary was thus published during his lifetime: fifty-one fascicules each of the *Rigvedabhashya* and of the *Yajurvedabhashya*. It took the Arya Samaj, after the Swami's death in 1883, another six years to complete the publication of the latter, and no less than sixteen years to complete that of the former. The total output comprises over 7,000 large pages of print, treating the whole of the *Yajurveda* and the *Rigveda* up to *Rigveda* VII.4.60. All this was written out within a span of six years, at an average of 1,200 pages per year. This was a remarkable achievement as it occupied only part of the Swami's time; his other writings and his guidance of the Arya Samaj also demanded much attention.

Such was the long pilgrimage of Swami Dayananda to the sources of Hinduism. From the time he started his study with Virjananda in 1860, it took him ten years to arrive at the doctrine that only the four Vedas strictly speaking were divine revelation. It took him another four years to formulate his doctrine of Vedic revelation. He spent another three years in preparing himself for the writing of his translation and commentary. When death cut short his life in 1883, he had been working on his commentary for only six years, and it was far from complete. It had been indeed a long and arduous pilgrimage to the sources.

In this second part, Dayananda's doctrine of revelation will be described as it was explicitated in his theological works and practically applied in his commentaries.[12]

The Vedas, which henceforth refer exclusively to the *Samhitas* without their commentaries, were directly revealed by god to the *rishis* Agni, Vayu and Aditya. God, present in their minds, taught them the texts and their meaning; the *rishis* 'heard' them 'like a voice from the sky', and that is why revelation is called *shruti*, that which was heard'. These *rishis* then passed their knowledge on to others. The Vedas, as the wisdom of God Himself, are eternal and perfect as He is; as recitation or as books, they are created and non-eternal, co-extensive with the cosmos, originating and disappearing in conformation with its periodic creation and dissolution.

The Vedas are by essence universal, and that is why they were not revealed in the language of a particular people or country. Their language was Sanskrit, the sacred language which is nobody's mother tongue, the universal language, the perfect language that is able to subsume a wide range of meanings within even a limited ambit of text.

The Vedas, as expression of the wisdom of God, are universal also in another sense; they contain, at least in germinal form, the totality of knowledge. That means that we can find in them not only answers to our questions about God and about the religious duties and destiny of mankind; we can also find a blueprint of the perfect society and the ideal state. Moreover, they were also the repository of scientific truth, containing the seeds of the manifold scientific principles which lie at the basis of both science and technology.

The conception of Vedic revelation described above forms the very basis of Dayananda's interpretation of the text in his commentary. Flowing from that conception one can indicate in the commentary a certain number of basic guidelines or theological presuppositions that direct and determine at every step the concrete interpretation of the stanzas of the text.

First of all, since the Vedas are the wisdom of God, they must proclaim a pure monotheism since that is the only logically acceptable conception of the divine. However, many *devas* are invoked in the Vedas and they have their own individual names such as Agni, Varuna, and Indra. Since the Vedas cannot propose polytheism, terms such as 'Agni' need to be carefully interpreted. Dayananda's solution is that the term 'Agni' has two different meanings: either it means 'God', that is the one and only Lord, or, wherever that meaning does not fit with the context, it simply means 'fire'. In no case could it refer to a special divinity called Agni.

A second assumption, also following logically from the Vedas containing the eternal wisdom of God, is that all Vedic statements have to have a 'universal' character. One of the major applications of this principle is the following: what is universal is free from the bonds of time and space. Vedic statements, therefore, never refer to particular places on earth or to particular periods of time. No Vedic statement, in other words, has an actual geographical or historical reference. Dayananda went to great lengths of semantic ingenuity and contortion in order to explain away the names of kings, accounts of battles, and geographical features contained in the Vedas. The Vedas transcend time and history as they transcend space and location. Incidentally, this argument was used by Dayananda to show the superiority of the Vedas over the Bible and the Koran, which are both totally steeped in time and space.

Another necessary consequence of the divine nature of the Vedas is that they could not possibly contain anything that offends reason. The application of this principle evidently depends largely on what one declares to be illogical. For instance to Dayananda all myths and miracles are irrational; it follows that the Puranas which abound in both could not possibly be of divine origin. This also explains why the Swami relentlessly de-mythologized all mythical references of Vedic lore. A striking example is the very prominent myth of Indra and Vritra often referred to in the hymns, which has three levels of meaning, historical, naturalistic, and cosmological. Dayananda, following his principles, accords any texts referring to the Indra-Vritra myth the possibility of only two meanings: either the text explains scientific truths about the interaction of sun and clouds, or it proposes ethical rules for the proper conduct of battle by the king.

Similarly, the Vedas could not possibly contain anything that offends morality. Again, it is of the utmost importance to realize what Dayananda categorized as 'immoral'. He certainly included under that category anything that is in any way connected with idol worship. Any Hindu text, therefore, that recommends idol worship is man-made, and it is impossible that there could be any reference to idol worship in the Vedas. In fact the latter was repeatedly the topic of discussions and public disputations between the Swami and leading orthodox pandits.

This concise exposition of the essentials of Dayananda's doctrine of revelation raises the question if this doctrine diverged from the general concept of revelation in the Hindu tradition.

First of all, Dayananda was quite out of line with the consensus of the tradition when he restricted *shruti* (revelation) to the four Samhitas only. The tradition has always accepted that *shruti*, the collection of authoritative revelation, includes besides the Samhitas, also the Brahmanas, Aranyakas and Upanishads. In fact, the tradition expressed its preference for the Upanishads by calling them Vedanta, the end and the goal of the Vedas. The great Hindu theologians echoed that preference by making the Upanishads the preferred subject of their commentaries.

There was another way in which Dayananda's concept of Vedic

revelation diverged significantly from traditional ideas. To the Swami the revelation contained in the Vedas was 'total': they contained the fullness of all truth; theological, ethical, social, governmental, scientific and technical. This idea of totality contains two elements. First, all truth revealed in the Vedas is definitive, final, true for all places and all times, and secondly, it is comprehensive, encompassing all possible knowledge.

Neither of these conceptions is to be found in the traditional understanding of the Vedas. In fact, the Hindu tradition itself provides explicitly for the fact that the revelation of *shruti* needs supplementation. The tradition has fashioned two mechanisms which express that conviction and show a way of coping with the incompleteness of *shruti*. The concept of the *kaliyuga* features importantly in the Hindu Dharmashastras. The *kaliyuga*, the fourth of the cycles which start with the Golden Age, is the age of darkness, degeneration, weakness and chaos. In the Dharmashastras, written long after the Vedas, it always refers to contemporary times. The ideals described in *shruti* belong to the Golden Age. In the *kali* age, man is too weak and stupid to live up to them, and for that reason the Shastras proclaimed a new *dharma* different from Vedic *dharma* and called it *apad-dharma*, a *dharma* adapted to the needs of an age of degeneration. In other words, the injunctions of the Vedas were not considered totally definitive and unalterable; strictly speaking they were meant only for the Golden Age; the *kali* age needs a different *dharma* which is expounded in the Shastras.[13]

There is another traditional Hindu concept that also provides a method of coping with the passing of time, the changing of the era, and the inadequacy or incompleteness of Vedic revelation, the concept of the 'fifth Veda'. Over the centuries new religious movements arose in Hinduism, the most penetrating and widespread of which were *bhakti* and *tantra*. These movements produced their saints and prophets, their poets and theologians, and, inevitably, their own sacred religious lore. These texts were accepted as revelation that was additional to that of the Vedas. They did not supplant the Vedas, but they supplemented their message; that is precisely why they were called 'the fifth Veda'. [14] Revelation, therefore, was not seen as totally finished with the Vedas, but rather as a continuous process. The *Bhagavata Purana* is a good example: to many sects of Krishna *bhakti*, it represents the highest revelation of Lord Krishna, much more illuminating and spiritually effective than what is found in the Vedas.

These two instances show that Dayananda's contention that Vedic revelation was definitive and total, was not part of the Hindu tradition, which accepted post-Vedic supplementary revelation overriding the earlier one. In the particular case of Dayananda, the spokesmen of the Hindu tradition did in fact denounce what they thought was wrong with Dayananda's theories about Vedic revelation.

On Saturday, 22 January 1881, a special meeting was convened in Calcutta at the University Senate Hall.[15] Three hundred pandits participated, and some two hundred notables attended. The objective of this gathering was to give authoritative answers to four questions relating to doctrines of Dayananda Sarasvati about the Vedas 'which had aroused considerable doubt among Hindus'.[16] This was a most extraordinary, in fact an unprecedented event in the history of Hinduism. It was not the convening of a group of pandits in order to make authoritative statements which was unusual. There was a very long tradition for that measure, as P.V. Kane writes in his authoritative *History of Dharmashastra*: 'For over 1,500 years before the Shankaracharya, the *parishad* of learned brahmanas was the acknowledged authority for settling doubtful points of dharma.'[17]

The next chapter in this volume discusses in detail that famous gathering of pandits in Calcutta, and indicates how it both related to and diverged from the traditional Hindu institution of pandit councils. The council attacked Dayananda's doctrine of the exclusive revelation-value of the four Vedas proper, which constituted a radical reduction of the traditional sources of Vedic reference and authority. They saw his translation into Hindi as an attempt to freeze every Vedic stanza into a single meaning, thus depriving the text of many possible different interpretations. They condemned the way he proceeded from there to declare many traditional Hindu rites invalid and worthless. They were convinced that by these actions the Swami attempted to deprive the brahmin pandit, the living representative of ultimate Vedic authority, of that authority.

Dayananda took many years to decide what the authentic and authoritative sources of Hinduism are. But at the end of the quest he overshot the mark: he presented Hinduism as a religion of the book, which it never was. By translating the Vedas with a commentary he was seen as taking away their essential polyvalence and undermining the pandits' authority. He certainly deserves to be called the Luther of India because he brought the Vedas to the people by translating them into Hindi. But the pandits accused him of trying to ossify the texts that were the living, adaptable, ever renewable sources of Hindu authority. In fact, Dayananda went too far because he wanted the Vedas to be viewed as the perfect revelation in contrast with the very inferior Bible. In this process he took a leaf out of the Christians' book by attempting to change Hinduism into a religion of the book. But the pandits with their instinct for orthodox tradition knew that this was not in accordance with Hindu tradition, and they proclaimed it loud and clear. Dayananda Sarasvati's arduous and stubborn pilgrimage to the sources, they declared, had led him beyond the pale of Hinduism.

NOTES

[This chapter was originally published as 'Pilgrimage to the Sources: Dayananda Sarasvati and the Vedas', *The Journal of the Oriental Society of Australia*, vols. 18-19, 1986-7, pp. 50-63.]

1. For a detailed study of Dayananda's Kathiawari background, cf. J.T.F. Jordens, *Dayananda Sarasvati, His Life and Ideas*, Delhi, 1978, ch. 1.
2. Cf. ibid., ch. 2.
3. Cf. Devendranath Mukhopadhyay, *Virjanandacharit*, translated into Hindi by Ghasiram, Agra, 1918; especially the document *Sarvabhauma Sabha*, on pp. 201-15.
4. Ibid., pp. 108-11.
5. For details, cf. Jordens, pp. 39-45.
6. Dr Rudolf Hoernle's article about Dayananda in the *Christian Intelligencer* of March 1870, has been reproduced in Lajpat Rai, *A History of the Arya Samaj*, revd. edn. by Shri Ram Sharma, Mumbai, 1967, pp. 28-38.
7. B.B. Majumdar, *History of Indian Social and Political Ideas from Rammohan Roy to Dayananda*, Calcutta, 1967, p. 116.
8. Rajnarayan Basu, *Hindudharmer Shreshtata*, Calcutta, 1872; Ghasiram, *Maharshi Dayananda Sarasvati ka Jivan-Charit*, vol. 1, Ajmer, 1957, p. 259.
9. For the detailed study of the impact of Calcutta on Dayananda, cf. Jordens, ch. 4.
10. Dayananda Sarasvati, *Satyarth Prakash*, 1st edn., Varanasi, 1875.
11. Dayananda Sarasvati, *Rigvedadibhashyabhumika*, published first in sixteen fascicules, from 1877 onwards, by the Lazarus Press, Varanasi. The best edition available now is that by Y. Mimamshak, Amritsar, 1967.
12. For detailed references, cf. Jordens, pp. 102-4, 157-9, 177-8, 270-1.

13. Cf. P.V. Kane, *History of Dharmashastra*, vol. 3, Pune, 1973, ch. 34 *Kalivarjya*, especially p. 967.
14. Cf. P.V. Kane, vol. V, part 2, pp. 913ff.
15. Full report in Lekhram, *Maharshi Dayananda Sarasvati ka Jivan Charitra*, transl. into Hindi by Kaviraj Raghunandansingh 'Nirmal', Delhi, 1972 (first and only Urdu version was published in Lahore, 1897), pp. 671-701. For a detailed study see J.T.F. Jordens, 'Orthodoxy and Heresy: Reflections on the 1881 Calcutta Pandit Council' in Ganga Ram Garg (ed.), *World Perspectives on Swami Dayananda Sarasvati*, New Delhi, 1984, pp. 239-52.
16. Lekhram, p. 672, quoted from the *Hindu Patriot*.
17. P.V. Kane, vol. II, p. 967.

CHAPTER 2

Orthodoxy and Heresy: Reflections on the 1881 Calcutta Pandit Council

THE AIM OF THIS chapter is to closely analyse the purpose and meaning of the famous meeting of pandits that took place in the Calcutta University Senate Hall on Saturday 22 January 1881, in which four doctrines held by Swami Dayananda Sarasvati were condemned. In order to fully understand this event it is necessary to put it in the perspective of the traditional usage of *pandit-parishads*. Moreover, in order to bring out most clearly the very special nature of the Calcutta meeting, a short reference will be made to two other occasions in modern times when committees of pandits were established for a special purpose.

'For over 1500 years before the great Shankaracharya, the *parishad* of learned brahmanas was the acknowledged authority for settling doubtful points of dharma.'[1] This statement of P.V. Kane in his massive *History of Dharmashastra* is the strongest authority one could present for indicating the traditional vital function of the *pandit-parishad* in matters of orthodoxy. The rules that governed the composition of the *pandit-parishad* were very clearly prescribed from the time of Manu, and all authorities agreed on the basic principles. The people involved had to be brahmins learned in the Shastras. Kane stresses this very strongly and incidentally disapproves of a modern tendency to consult the Shankaracharya of a famous *math* in questions of *dharma*. The tradition never gave him any authority in such matters. The proposed number of pandits constituting a *parishad* varied between ten and three, and they were urged to arrive at a unanimous decision. In special cases, even one person may be accepted as authority, as long as he was a pandit learned in the Shastras.[2]

What then was the traditional view of the function of these *pandit-parishads*? They were called upon to give a decision when doubts arose whether a particular course of action was in conformity with the *dharma*, the overriding code of social and ritual duty. It is immediately obvious that these *parishads* had absolutely nothing to do with what we could call questions or doubts in matters of doctrine. Naturally, the Hindu tradition has had 'doctrinal' concerns for two millennia. Indeed, it coined a special word to categorize those who fundamentally erred in doctrine: that of *nastika*. It clearly refers to those who deny the authority of the Veda, such as Buddhists, Jains, and materialists, and who are consequently outside the pale of Hinduism. Within Hinduism, however, the freedom of doctrine and theology was practically unlimited. Sects may even proclaim their holy texts as a 'fifth Veda' for the *kali* age, but that name itself implied the acceptance of the Vedas. Great theological battles were fought with enormous vigour, but in Hinduism, 'heresy' was not a valid category as long as the fundamental framework was not challenged.[3]

The Dharmashastras repeatedly discuss the question of what constitutes proper authority in Hinduism. However, in this context, the authority refers to matters of *dharma*, and not to matters of doctrine. Notwithstanding differences of opinion, some fundamental principles were generally agreed upon. The Veda, or *shruti*, which included the four Vedas, the Brahmanas and the Upanishads, were the final authority. Next came the Dharmashastras, a literature of which some ten thousand specimens survive. Their authority, however, was firmly believed to be rooted in and derived from the Vedas: the authors were steeped in the Vedas with which they had penetrated their intelligence and their life. Third in line was the specialist in the *smriti* texts, the pandit, *sabhya*, or *shishta*. His authority was based on his intimate knowledge of the Shastras and, very importantly, on his knowledge of the Vedas.[4] This system of authority assured that every decision in matters of *dharma* had a transcendental reference in the Vedas, 'key to ultimate legitimation',[5] and that this key was used by the only qualified person: the brahmin, living representative of the Vedas.[6]

Authoritative decisions in matters of *dharma* often justified themselves by references to Vedic texts. The concrete interpretation of particular Vedic texts gave rise to great variations among Dharma-shastras and among pandits. This is not surprising considering the fact that Vedic texts not only dealt primarily with matters of a ritual nature, but were moreover couched in a difficult and cryptic idiom: the texts themselves invited a variety of interpretations. This flexibility made it possible for Hinduism to continuously adapt itself to new circumstances and yet create a Vedic justification. To the Hindu tradition the value of the text itself far exceeded that of its literal worth. As Derrett put it forcefully: 'A historical and literal interpretation of the actual "original" meaning of a Vedic or *smriti* text was not permitted. The texts meant what, at any time or place, the referees said they meant.'[7] The fluidity, variety, and adaptability of Vedic texts constituted an essential condition for the very permanence of the transcendental Vedic reference. The withholding of the sacred texts from the ordinary people was but a natural consequence of that situation, and an insurance that the interpretation of Vedic texts remained the exclusive concern of those specialists who were its living representatives.[8]

It was within that general frame of reference that the *pandit-parishads* operated. Before considering the Calcutta Pandit Gathering that condemned Dayananda, we will consider two other pandit gatherings in modern times. The first example of a modern *parishad* was called the *Dharmanirnayamandala* (committee for deciding cases of *dharma*), and founded by Swami Kevalananda Sarasvati of Wai in 1934.[9] The organization comprised 14 original founding members, mostly experts in the Dharmashastras, including P.V. Kane. This body held eleven sessions between 1934 and 1959, and passed in all 82 resolutions.

The particular purpose and slant of this body is clearly expressed in its original name *Tattvanishta-parivartanvadi-parishad*, 'committee of people who favour the introduction of changes based on fundamental principles', and in one of its very first resolutions which reads as follows, 'Usages have been changed from time to time by former learned men (*shishtas*) and the learned men of the present have the authority to introduce changes in usages as the present circumstances may require.' This body, therefore, saw itself as a reform body with the function of introducing changes; but at the same time it held that these changes of usage should be in conformity with fundamental principles of the tradition. This attitude expresses in practice a powerful theme that runs right through Kane's *History of Dharmashastra*: that the laws and regulations that have directed the Hindu's *dharma* through over two millennia were never conceived as static and immutable, but always changeable and adaptive, and that the very composition of the Dharmashastra literature was not a continuous attempt to ossify the law, but rather a continuing re-interpretation and adaptation of the law to new circumstances with the aim of helping the Hindu to cope with the present in an effective way without losing the roots of his tradition.

A survey of the resolutions passed by this *parishad* indicates quite clearly how it conceived the scope of its decisions on *dharma*. All resolutions deal with questions of caste laws and inter-caste relationships. Here are some of the principal ones.

— Untouchability of certain castes should be abolished, and untouchables should be entitled to study the Vedas and have the *upanayana* performed.
— *Jatis*, with similar usages, sacraments and food regulations should merge.
— Interdining is lawful as long as vegetarians are served vegetarian food.
— Any Hindu who was converted to another religion should be allowed to come back into the Hindu fold after proper expiation.
— Divorce should be allowed in all castes in the case where one spouse had converted to another religion.
— Intermarriage should be allowed on a much wider scale, excluding only *sapinda* relationships.

All these resolutions concern usage and behaviour but none of them ever touch upon questions of doctrine. Secondly, they all tend to be of an extremely radical nature.

On 24 August 1923, the Hindu Mahasabha at its Varanasi session considered the question of *shuddhi*, the reacceptance of Muslims and others into Hinduism. This discussion was held in the context of a very crucial contemporary agitation concerning the Malkana Rajputs, who were being readmitted into Hinduism, a movement that caused an immediate counter-agitation by the Muslims. The following resolution was passed at the conference: the executive committee should appoint a subcommittee of men learned in Hindu Shastras to consider with due regard the needs of the present time, how and to what extent this idea (of *shuddhi*) could be translated into action and to report to the subcommittee.[10] The movers of the resolution and the supporters of the motion comprised very learned orthodox pandits such as Mahamahopadhyayas Hathibhai Shastri of Jamnagar, Jaidev Mishra of Varanasi, Harinarain Shastri of Delhi, Pandits Satya Saran Shastri, and Harihar Swarup Shastri, and Babu Bhagavan Das of Varanasi. Only two people spoke against the resolution, Pandit Kedarnath of Kanpur and Mr Jaramdas of Lahore.[11]

This resolution was adopted unanimously. The following day the Mahasabha considered the question of untouchability, and decided to refer this also to the committee of pandits in order 'to frame rules and regulations to secure for the members of the so-called untouchable classes access to public meetings, drinking wells, temples and public schools'.[12]

The purpose and brief of this *pandit-parishad* was again clearly limited to matters of social *dharma* without any reference to questions of doctrine. We are in for considerable surprise, however, when we hear the composition of this body reported as follows: 'A Vidvat Parishat consisting of nearly 75 Sanskrit scholars and religious heads from all parts of India including Buddhist, Jain, Sikh and Arya Samaj representatives, with Pandit Madan Mohan Malaviya as convener, was appointed.'[13]

In view of this extraordinary composition, one is confronted with an even greater surprise when reading the extremely conservative decisions of this *parishad*, which can be gathered from the report of the Special Session of the Hindu Mahasabha held at Allahabad on 5 February 1924. As for untouchability, the original resolution recommended efforts for educating the untouchables, giving them access to public schools, to temples and to public wells. The sting was in the last paragraph: 'that it was against the scriptures and the tradition to give the untouchables "yajyopavit", to teach them Vedas and to interdine with them, and the Mahasabha hoped that workers in the interest of unity would give up these items of social reform'. In the matter of *shuddhi*, the decision was 'that any non-Hindu was welcome to enter the fold of Hinduism, though he could not be taken into any caste'.[14] It is quite clear that in the convocation of those two *pandit-parishads* in modern times, the Hindus involved were conscious of the fact that such *pandit-parishads* were sanctioned by a centuries-old tradition, and somehow derived their authority from that tradition. Looking back at the general simple directives of the tradition, the question may be asked in how far these two *pandit-parishads* conform with those directives. Some conclusions become immediately obvious.

As for the composition of the committee, the Maharashtrian

Dharmanirnaya-mandala in which Kane participated comes closest to the traditional norm, both in its numbers and the qualifications of the participants. The *pandit-parishad* constituted by the Mahasabha breaks away from that norm in blatant fashion: the huge number of 75 is excessive, but more importantly the inclusion of Buddhists and Jains is totally against the tradition, which consistently refers to those as *nastikas.*[15] The numbers were inflated to project an impression that the decisions of the committee had wide support among the leaders of Hinduism. The tradition was never concerned with that, but only with the scholastic reputation of the committee members.[16]

As for the issues considered, both the Maharashtrian *Dharmanirnayamandala* and the *pandit-parishad* of the Mahasabha concerned themselves strictly with matters of social *dharma*, as directed by the tradition. However, there are two matters in which there is innovation. The traditional *parishad* was constituted to give a decision in doubtful cases and pronounce what rule applied, or did not apply, or how new circumstances warranted a new usage, or how a new usage may be justified. The *Dharmanirnayamandala* gave itself a much wider brief; it was intent on promoting social reform, and actively involved itself in changing custom and law in a particular direction. In other words, whereas the traditional *parishad* always remained a good distance behind changes in society and dealt with case-law to handle these changes within a Hindu context, the modern *parishad* made itself an instigator and leader in social reform.

The *pandit-parishad* of the Mahasabha shared to a lesser extent that same concern of directing the Hindus towards social reform. It was also innovative in another direction. There was a definite concern to present an image of Hindu solidarity and unanimity. It should be remembered that the Mahasabha sessions of this period were very much preoccupied with Hindu Sangathan.[17] The composition and deliberations of the *pandit-parishad* were slanted in that direction. It is true that the traditional *parishad* was directed to try to arrive at unanimous decisions. This, however, had nothing to do with projecting the image of a consolidated Hindu community. The Mahasabha had that concern, and was disappointed when in its deliberations the decisions of the *parishad* had to be somewhat circumscribed so as to pacify the strong Arya Samaj contingent.[18]

Having set the traditional context, and considered how two other modern *pandit-parishads* fitted within that context, and yet diverged from it, the time has come to closely consider the Calcutta meeting.

On Saturday 22 January 1881, a very special meeting took place in Calcutta at the University Senate Hall.[19] About 300 pandits were present. The organizer was Pandit Maheshchandra Nyayaratna, Principal of Sanskrit College, and among the most prominent and active participants were Pandits Taranath Tarkavachaspati, Jivananda Vidyasagar, Bhuvanchandra of Navadvip, Ramdhan of Jessore, Banke Bihari Vajpeyi of Kanpur, Jamna Narayan Tiwari, Sudarshanacharya of Vrindavan, Ramsubrahmanyam Shastri of Tanjore. Several of these had previously clashed with Swami Dayananda Sarasvati.[20]

This meeting, attended also by some two hundred notables, had a very clear objective. Some doctrines of Dayananda Sarasvati about the Vedas had aroused considerable doubts among a good number of Hindus.[21] The pandits had been brought together in order to provide an authoritative answer to the following four questions, each of which concerns doctrines quite openly advocated by Dayananda and the Arya Samaj:

1. Are the Brahmanas as valid and authoritative as the four Samhitas, and are the other Smritis as valid and authoritative as that of Manu? The answer was affirmative.
2. Are the *puja* of the gods, *shraddh*, and pilgrimages sanctioned by the Shastras? The answer was yes.
3. Does the word *Agni* in the *Rigveda* mean 'fire' or 'god' (Ishwar)? The answer was: its primary meaning is 'fire'.
4. Is the *yajna* performed for purifying the air or for securing salvation? The answer was: for securing salvation.[22]

It is immediately obvious that the questions considered in Calcutta were substantially different from those faced by the bodies previously mentioned. The latter confined themselves strictly to problems of social *dharma*, basically questions relating to caste duties and privileges, asking what type of actions one was allowed to engage in as a person belonging to the Hindu community. The Calcutta meeting, on the other hand, directed itself first of all to the question of the extent of scriptural authority. Dayananda had preached since his famous Varanasi disputation that ultimate religious authority was vested exclusively in the four Samhitas, and that all other Shastras had authority only in those matters where they conformed with the four Vedas.[23] The Calcutta council asserted, on the basis of exegetical proof, that the later texts were equally authoritative as the four Vedas. A second concern was of particular Vedic interpretation of the term '*agni*'; the pandits in fact accused Dayananda of misinterpreting Vedic texts.

The other two questions refer to religious rites of Hinduism. Dayananda was preaching that the rites of *puja*, *shraddh*, and *tirtha-yatra* were not sanctioned by the Vedas, were later inventions that had no religious value and should be rejected. The pandits declared that these rites were sanctioned by the Vedas and the other Shastras and, therefore, proper Hindu religious rites. In a similar vein, the pandits condemned Dayananda's interpretation of *yajna*, the sacrificial offering of clarified butter in the fire. The Swami declared that its purpose was purification of the atmosphere. The pandits declared its purpose was the achievement of salvation.

All these questions, therefore, deal with specifically religious topics: the respective authority of sacred texts, and the religious validity and efficacy of particular rituals. They do not directly consider questions of dogma as such, of theological tenets. Basically, what this gathering of pandits wanted to proclaim with a show of authority was the following: Dayananda Sarasvati's doctrine of the exclusive authority of the Vedas, his interpretation of the Vedas, his denunciation of certain Hindu rituals as un-Vedic and futile, should all be rejected by the Hindus because they go against the texts and the accepted authorities of Hinduism. In other words, what he preaches is un-Hindu.

It is quite obvious that the issues considered by the Calcutta council of pandits fall outside the brief of the traditional *parishads*, which was limited to matters pertaining to social and ritual laws, rules, and mores. In considering basic questions of scriptural authority and the validity and meaning of certain rites, this council's deliberations were a new phenomenon in the history of Hinduism. Did these pandits attempt to brand Dayananda as unorthodox, and did they thus take a step usually associated with other traditions such as the Christian one, but basically alien to the Hindu tradition? It appears that the answer to these questions has to be in the affirmative.

How can that extraordinary action of the Calcutta council be explained? The only way this can be done is by demonstrating that the pandits considered that the Swami was introducing into Hinduism a novel kind of dissent that threatened its accepted framework. At the beginning of this chapter this frame of reference was described. The basic living authority of Hinduism lay in the transcendental reference to the Vedas. This continuous reference within centuries of change remained possible by the support of two presuppositions: the essential flexibility and interpretative adaptability of the Vedic texts themselves, and the living authority of brahmin and pandit for interpreting these texts and for showing their concrete relevance for historical situations. Through these two, the Vedas could constantly remain the key to ultimate legitimation.

Dayananda's doctrines were seen as threatening that basic framework. First of all, the Swami restricted the absolute authoritative quality of *shruti* to the four Samhitas proper, excluding Brahmanas and Upanishads. Similarly, he accepted a thoroughly edited Manu only as a secondary authority, and relegated all other Shastras to a very much lower place. This restriction was compounded by another factor. The Swami was in the process of translating the Vedas into Hindi with his own commentary. Although he never claimed his was the final word, many of his followers considered it as such, and other Hindus were convinced that was his purpose. On the basis of this restriction of *shruti* and of the definition of individual texts, the Swami proceeded to declare invalid and worthless a host of Hindu rites and practices; he rejected all forms of image and temple worship, pilgrimages, *shraddh*, and the myriad of taboos in matters of diet, marriage, and ritual purity. Another effective corollary of his teaching was to deny the authority of the brahmin pandit, the living representative of ultimate Vedic authority. In other words, Dayananda was seen as undermining the millennial authority structure of Hinduism by eliminating the very possibility of continuous justification of right behaviour by the pandits' free interpretation of *shruti*.

A contemporary commentator, the editor of the journal *Sar-Sudhanidhi*, clearly expressed that concern. Reflecting on the deliberation of the Calcutta council he tried to explain exactly in what manner Dayananda's dissent differed from that of many sectarian dissenters within Hinduism. He wrote that whereas other sectarians 'had not tampered with the basic life-force of our *dharma*', Dayananda 'had attacked that very base (*muladharma*), which is established by the total and equal recognition of all *shruti* and *smriti*'. Dayananda had, therefore, 'inflicted a wound on the very life-power of Hinduism'.[24] The Arya Samajists themselves were also aware of the complete novelty of the action of the Calcutta Pandit gathering, 'an example of which cannot be found in the history of India'.[25]

Although the pandits were aware of the 'dangerous' doctrines of the Swami, they may not have taken too much notice if Dayananda had been satisfied with gathering a minor sect within the world of

Hinduism. Such minor sects come and go; they either disappear without a trace, or get absorbed back into the whole. But by 1880, it was clear that the Swami's ambitions were much wider than that. The most ominous sign of his intent was the growing dissemination of his Hindi translation and commentary of the *Rigveda* from 1878 onwards. It appeared in monthly fascicules which were efficiently distributed in many hundreds right across north India. Some thirty towns in the U.P. are mentioned in subscription lists, twenty in the Punjab, a dozen in western India, and ten each in the Central Provinces, Bihar, Bengal and Rajputana.[26]

The Swami had scored his first considerable success in the Punjab in 1877-8, and when he came down into the U.P. his new fame preceded him, and his efforts redoubled. He loudly heralded his aim to reform the whole of Hinduism, and his impact started to show itself. The number of Arya Samaj branches in the U.P. jumped to twenty, and, for the first time, the number of brahmins joining up became significant.[27] As the Swami acquired his own press, the distribution of his Vedic commentary became more efficient.[28] Arya Samaj journals and pamphlets started to appear in the Punjab and the U.P. and professional preachers and also itinerant *sannyasis* became roving missionaries of the Arya Samaj.[29] The Swami gained prestige by his alliance with the very newsworthy Theosophical leaders, and by his forceful appearance at the great pilgrimages at Hardwar and Pushkar.[30]

Dayananda's last stay in Varanasi, from November 1879 to May 1880 was so eventful that the *Pioneer* referred to him as 'a second Luther'. This period was full of events that kept his presence in the forefront of the news: the ban, subsequently lifted, imposed by a local magistrate on his lectures; the visit of Madame Blavatsky and Colonel Olcott and their joint appearance on the public rostrum; the Swami's widely-advertised but frustrated challenge to the local pandits for a public disputation; the ceremonial establishment of Dayananda's very own Vedic Press, inaugurated with a long series of lectures; the foundation of a local branch of the Arya Samaj; a public written challenge by the famous Varanasi identity Raja Shivaprasad, answered by the Swami in a special pamphlet entitled *Bhramochhedan*. During those six months Varanasi, the centre of orthodoxy, was not allowed to forget the presence of the Swami.[31]

Moreover, the Swami started giving more attention to and lecturing about the subject of cow-protection, an issue very dear to most

Hindus. Then came the case of Munshi Indramani. He was brought to court by Muslims for his offensive writings about Islam, and a fund was started for his defence.[32] The case attracted great publicity and the Swami steered his Arya Samajists into close collaboration with other Hindus.[33] All these facets of the Swami's public activity made it very clear by the end of 1880 that his stance was not that of a minor sectarian guru, but of one whose aims were much wider, namely to involve his Aryas with all other Hindus into a reformist movement that would redirect Hinduism towards his conception of Arya Dharma.

Our conclusion is that the august gathering of pandits in Calcutta in January 1881 did want to declare the Swami unorthodox. It was the combination of two factors that prompted them to do so. First of all, they were of the opinion that his teachings tended to undermine the age-old authority structure of Hinduism; secondly, they felt that the Swami's message was starting to have too widespread an impact. Dayananda Sarasvati represented a very novel phenomenon in the history of Hinduism; that was why he had to be fought by a novel method.

NOTES

1. P.V. Kane, *History of Dharmashastra*, vol. II, Pune, 1973, p. 967.
2. On *pandit-parishads*, cf. Kane, vol. II, pp. 966-71; vol. IV, pp. 85-6.
3. Cf., e.g. Kane, vol. V, p. 1624; S. Radhakrishnan and C.A. Moore, *A Source Book in Indian Philosophy*, Princeton, 1957, pp. 14-15; J.D.M. Derrett, *Religion, Law and the State in India*, London, 1968, p. 60; W. Norman Brown, *Man in the Universe*, Berkeley, 1970, pp. 41-2.
4. Kane repeatedly discusses these issues in his work. Cf. vol. 1, chs. 1-10; vol. 3, ch. 32; vol. 5, ch. 30.
5. J.C. Heesterman, 'Veda and Dharma', in W.D. O'Flaherty and J.D.M. Derrett (eds.), *The Concept of Duty in South Asia*, London, 1978, p. 93.
6. Cf. Derrett, ibid., pp. 38-40.
7. Ibid., p. 41. Harischandra Bharatendu, an avowed opponent of Dayananda and strong supporter of many traditional ideals and practices as a devout Vallabhacharya, expressed that same idea in his essay *Shrutirahasya*, 'The Secret of Revelation', as follows: 'The words of the Veda are like the cow that grants all wishes (*kamadhenu*). For that very reason the different meanings given to them by the great teachers

of all sects are all to be accepted. If even one is rejected, then those denying it are considered to be *nastikas* on account of their censure of the ancient great teachers.' This statement is followed by a series of ten different interpretations of a particular text, which he considered all valid in their own way. *Bharatendu Granthavali*, ed. by Vrajaratnadas, vol. 3, Varanasi, p. 779.

8. Derrett, ibid., p. 41.
9. Kane, vol. V, part 2, pp. 1705-7.
10. *The Leader*, 24 August 1923. For the Malkana question, cf. G. Thursby, *Hindu-Muslim Relations in British India, a study of controversy, conflict, and communal movements in Northern India, 1923-1928*, Leiden, 1975.
11. *The Leader*, ibidem. The title 'Mahamahopadhyaya' was conferred on those who were outstanding experts in Hindu law.
12. *The Leader*, 25 August 1923.
13. Ibid., 23 December 1923.
14. Ibid., 8 February 1924.
15. The laws of Manu use the term frequently (e.g. II. 10-16, IV. 163, VIII. 22, XI. 66-7); other terms are used with the same meaning: *haitukas*, 'those who use logic against the Vedas' (e.g. IV. 30), and *pashanda*, 'heretical' (e.g. IV. 61, V. 90, IX. 225).
16. Large numbers were sometimes used by kings in special cases, 'where the problem was difficult and the penance might be severe, sympathy might be excited, and evasion or faction evoked: numbers were evidently a refuge here'. J.D.M. Derrett, 'The Concept of Duty in Ancient Indian Jurisprudence: The Problem of Ascertainment', in W.D. O'Flaherty and J.D.M. Derrett (eds.), *The Concept of Duty in South Asia*, London, 1978, p. 32.
17. About the Mahasabha and its involvement in Hindu Sangathan, cf. J.T.F. Jordens, *Swami Shraddhananda, His Life and Causes*, Delhi, 1981, ch. VI.
18. *The Leader*, 8 February 1924.
19. Full report in Lekhram, *Maharshi Dayananda Sarasvati ka Jivan Charitra*, translated into Hindi by Kaviraj Raghunandansingh 'Nirmal', Delhi, 1972 (the first and only Urdu version was published in Lahore, 1897), pp. 671-701.
20. M. Nyayaratna had clashed with Dayananda in Calcutta, when he mistranslated some of the Swami's words (Lekhram, p. 230), and in 1878 the Swami published his pamphlet *Bhrantinivarana* as an answer to Nyayaratna's objections to his *Vedabhashya*. Pandit Ramsubrahmanyam is reported to have written a booklet against the Swami (Ghasiram, *Maharshi Dayananda Sarasvati ka Jivan-Charit*, vol. I, Ajmer, 1957, p. 259). Seth Narayandas of Mathura was said to be an agent for Seth Lakshmandas of Mathura, who had tried to have

Dayananda evicted from the house he occupied at that time in Agra (Lekhram, p. 672).

21. Lekhram, p. 672, quoted from the *Hindu Patriot.*
22. Ibid.
23. For the evolution of this idea, cf. J.T.F. Jordens, *Dayananda Sarasvati, His Life and Ideas*, Delhi, 1978, p. 278 and *passim.*
24. Lekhram, pp. 696-7. The *Indian Evangelical Review*, vol. 7, April 1881, p. 499, states that pandits had even come from Chennai because they were 'much vexed by the heterodox opinions of Dayananda regarding the Vedas'.
25. Ibid., p. 683.
26. This estimate has been calculated from the lists of subscribers that regularly appeared in the first twelve monthly fascicules of the *Vedabhashya*.
27. An analysis of the names of subscribers in those twelve fascicules referred to in the previous note gives the following approximate caste distribution: 22 per cent from the trading castes, 23 per cent brahmins, 45 per cent from the writers' castes, and 10 per cent kshatriyas. This distribution was very different from that in the Punjab, where the Arya Samaj was overwhelmingly dominated by the khatris and allied castes.
28. The Vedic Press was established in Varanası on 12 February 1880, and was shifted to Allahabad in March 1881.
29. For details cf. Jordens, *Dayananda Sarasvati*, pp. 201-2.
30. Cf. ibid., ch. 9.
31. Cf. Ghasiram, vol. 2, pp. 221-36.
32. Cf. ibid., vol. 2, pp. 219, 227, 236, 260.
33. Cf. Jordens, *Dayananda Sarasvati*, pp. 216-17.

CHAPTER 3

Dayananda and Christian Missionaries

THE FUTURE Swami Dayananda Sarasvati grew up in an orthodox Shaivite brahmin family in Kathiawar, and left home at the age of twenty-one to become a *sannyasi*. He spent the next fifteen years studying and searching for a perfect guru, whom he finally found in Swami Virjananda at Mathura. There the lone searcher for perfection underwent a radical transformation. His passionate goal was no more his individual perfection, but the reform of what he saw all around him as corrupt Hinduism. He now went in search of 'authentic Hinduism' which he gradually decided was enshrined in the four Vedas. It was during the first years of this search, in 1866, at the age of forty-two, that Dayananda had his first contact with Christianity, which until then had remained a completely unknown world to him. Seventeen years later, in 1883, the year of his death, he included in his final work, the second edition of his *Satyarth Prakash*, a chapter of criticism of Christianity, bequeathing to his Arya Samaj a spirit of aggressive controversy with Christian missionaries. This chapter proposes to enquire how and why this development came about.

Between 1866 and 1873 Dayananda is recorded as having talked to seven missionaries. From the accounts it is clear that they took the initiative, and conversed with the Swami through an interpreter, because he spoke only Sanskrit. Three of these meetings, with the Reverend J. Robson of Ajmer, with the Reverend T.J. Scott of Bareilly, and with Dr Rudolf Hoernle of Varanasi, were recorded by the missionaries themselves and are very important to the historian, as they present independent contemporary accounts of the Swami's ideas at that time.[1] None of these meetings were meant to be or turned into, confrontations. They came about because the missionaries were curious about this extraordinary and impressive *sannyasi*. In fact, in the first half of this period Dayananda was mainly studying, and in the latter he was essentially a rural reformer. He preached and held discussions along the banks of the Ganga, and was primarily addressing himself to the local leaders of orthodox Hinduism, pandits, brahmins, and kshatriyas. He was in fact rather unsuccessful in his endeavours, except for a limited achievement in Farrukhabad, the only larger city he frequented. To the missionaries he posed no threat, nor did they to him.

In 1873 the Swami spent four months in Calcutta, a very crucial stage in his development.[2] There is no record of him meeting any missionaries, and yet this stay represented a very important turning point in his attitude to Christianity. The evidence is indirect and inferential, drawing on two main sources. First of all, we have a record of many meetings of Dayananda with Calcutta *bhadralok* and reports of conversations. Secondly, the ideas expressed by the Swami immediately after his visit to Calcutta contain a number of statements about Christianity not to be found in the previous period.

The central new concept that came to the fore was that the religion enshrined in the Vedas was superior to all other religions and revelations, specifically the Christian. Before Calcutta, the Swami did not think in those terms: he was then totally immersed in the world of Hinduism and preoccupied with his quest for the essence of his *dharma*. Christianity occasionally appeared and disappeared at the periphery of his vision. In Calcutta it was constantly brought to his attention, not by missionaries, but by the beliefs and attitudes of the Bengalis he met. It is significant that the Swami's hosts were the Adi Brahmos, whose current President was Rajnarayan Bose. Under his inspiration a group of Adi Brahmos were leading the newly-emerging movement of proud Hindu nationalism, which was reacting to both the inroads of Westernization into Bengali society and the flirtation with Christianity of the followers of Keshub Chandra Sen, whose controversial 'Lecture on Inspiration' took place during Dayananda's stay.[3] Rajnarayan Bose showed the Swami his own lecture on 'The Superiority of Hinduism',[4] and thus he and his collaborators brought the claims of Christianity and the Bible to his attention. This concern had been foremost in the mind of Bengali reformers since Rammohun Roy, but to Dayananda it was a new discovery.

There was another aspect to this interaction. To the Swami the greatness and superiority of Arya Dharma was firmly founded in Vedic revelation. He welcomed his Bengali friends' claim as to the superiority of Hinduism, but soon discovered that his own claim for the uniqueness of Vedic revelation was rejected by them. He wanted to prove his claim, and this could only be done by demonstrating the complete truth of the Vedas and the deficiencies of the Bible. This became the central argument whenever he dealt with Christianity. This is clearly illustrated by the fact that it was in Calcutta that he decided to write a commentary on the Vedas,[5] and that shortly afterwards he wrote a special chapter on the Bible in his first *Satyarth Prakash*.[6] It is also confirmed by his first recorded conversation with a Christian missionary after his stay in Calcutta, in which he declared that Max Mueller's interpretation of the Vedas was wrong on account of his Christian bias tending to discredit Hinduism, and ridiculed the biblical story of the Tower of Babel.[7]

For the next three years, from mid-1873 to mid-1876, Dayananda had practically no contact with missionaries. However, very important changes took place in his style of life which were to change the attitude of the missionaries towards him. After Calcutta he transformed himself overnight from a Sanskrit-speaking rural reformer seeking out leaders of orthodoxy, into a modern urban reformer. Clad in urban attire, he now spoke Hindi on the public platforms of the cities, reaching out to the educated. His presence and his lectures were intensively advertised and attracted great attention. In 1874 he dictated his first book, the *Satyarth Prakash*, which was published a year later. Then he went back to western India, where he spent eighteen months. There he founded his Arya Samaj, stirred the orthodox and the reformers by his lectures and public disputes, and wrote another six books.

The Swami who entered once more the towns of the U.P. in early 1876 was very different from the naked *sannyasi* whom the Reverend Scott had sought out on the banks of the Ganga eight years earlier at the great Kakora fair. He was now a famous lecturer, debater, author, and founder of a new reform society. He travelled from town to town with his retinue and library, proclaiming everywhere in the best available halls the superiority of Arya Dharma. Nobody could ignore him any longer. During that year he had several long discussions with missionaries, and two public disputations. Whereas previous contacts had been prompted by courteous curiosity, now they usually involved a clash of irreconcilable claims. When the missionaries said that Christ was the only Saviour, the Swami retorted that Krishna and Shankaracharya were men of better calibre, and that belief in salvation through the intercession of a man was worse than idolatry.[8]

In March 1877 the Swami took part in a three-cornered public disputation, usually referred to as the Chandapur Mela. The Muslims' main protagonist was the famous Maulana Muhammad Qasim Nanawtawi; Christianity was represented by T.J. Scott and B.W. Parker, and the Arya viewpoint was defended by Dayananda. For two days they discussed the topics of creation and salvation. The extant report has its limitations, because it is the one published by the Aryas. Although it records the Swami's contribution at great length, and the others' rather succinctly, it does not appear to misrepresent the latters' views. The main method of the Swami's attack was again the literal interpretation of a biblical passage. Although there were minor disagreements on procedure, the disputation was held in a generally decorous and amiable atmosphere. In fact, the Reverend Scott came and chatted with the Swami afterwards at his quarters.[9]

That same month, March 1877, the Swami entered the Punjab, where he was to remain for sixteen months. His first stop was Ludhiana. A missionary came to see the Swami, and declared that it was against reason to call Krishna a *mahatma* since he had committed such bad actions. The Swami retorted that these accusations about Krishna were lies, as he never did those things, and he caustically added that an intelligence that was able to accept that the spirit of God came down on a man in the form of a dove, should have no difficulty in accepting Krishna's behaviour. The local missionaries employed a brahmin teacher, who had become attracted to Christianity and after instruction had decided to receive baptism. The local Hindus were extremely upset and asked the Swami in his turn to instruct that brahmin. He did so, and turned the potential convert away from his desire for baptism, whereupon the missionaries sacked him.[10]

The contrast with the previous period is striking and this example is given because it was typical of the Swami's stay in the Punjab. Firstly, a great number of meetings with missionaries took place: some twenty are explicitly referred to in the sources, and they included some of the most prominent clergymen of the province.[11] The conversations often led to caustic replies by the Swami (one should note that these conversations were mostly held in public, and eagerly listened to by bystanders). The Swami also gave, for the first time, special lectures on Christianity, focusing on the Bible. How did this drastic change come about? The answer lies in the peculiar communal atmosphere of the Punjab, which was a totally new experience for the Swami.

There was significant religious ferment among educated Punjabi Hindus in the 1870s. This had been brought about by a combination of two main factors: the strong upward thrust of the Hindu Khatris as a result of the introduction of British administration, and the parallel rapid expansion of missionary activity.[12] The latter engendered in many Hindus the feeling of a Christian threat, especially since the missionaries tried their best to reach the educated community, and seemed to receive strong support from the British administrators. The first reaction to this threat was the founding of a Brahmo Samaj, followed by its offshoot, the Sat Sabha. But as both were dominated by Bengalis, they found but little success among the Punjabi Khatris, who resented the near-monopoly of administrative posts by imported Bengalis.[13] At Firozpur and Gujarat the Hindus had found it necessary to form a Hindu Sabha to defend themselves, but these were purely local associations.[14]

So, when the Swami entered the Punjab, he encountered a situation totally new to him: amidst a hive of missionary activity, the Hindus were fearful of the progress of conversion in their community. On his very first stop in the Punjab he was asked to prevent such a conversion. Other circumstances reinforced that initial impact. The orthodox leaders of Lahore, who were from the beginning suspicious of the Swami on account of his close association with the outspoken publicist and reformer Kanahiyalal Alakhdari,[15] soon became very distressed about the influence of Dayananda. As an observer remarked, he quickly divided the city into two camps, the old traditional champions of orthodoxy, and the younger educated group in favour of reform.[16] Their anxiety became near panic when some Hindus actually threw their idols out.[17] As their intellectual level was rather low, and they could not even attempt to face the Swami on the public rostrum, they resorted to other means to counteract his influence. They started a campaign of vilification, the major theme of which was that the Swami was actually in the pay of the Christians, and that he tried to turn Hindus away from their religion in order to make them ripe for conversion to Christianity. Influenced by these allegations, Divan Bhagavandas, who had provided quarters for the Swami, asked him to vacate them.[18] Such rumours followed the Swami throughout the Punjab for the first nine months of his stay.[19] This campaign, which on occasion led to rowdy disturbances at lectures,[20] made it all the more imperative for the Swami publicly to demonstrate that he was not an admirer of Christianity.

This confrontation was exacerbated by another important event, when orthodoxy joined the Christians in snubbing the Swami. He had by now started his major work of writing a commentary on the Vedas. He arranged a meeting with J. Griffith, Secretary to the Lieutenant-General of the Punjab and Director of Public Instruction, and asked him if the government would consider subsidizing the publication of his Vedic commentary and its inclusion in the syllabus of the Punjab colleges. He presented a sample of his work, which was circulated for comment to R. Griffith, Principal of Banaras Sanskrit College, C.H. Tawney, Principal of Calcutta Presidency College, and three Sanskrit pandits of Lahore. Their adverse comments somehow came into the hands of the Aryas, and two letters in defence of the commentary were sent to the government, one by the Swami, the other by the Lahore Arya Samaj, but the government stuck to its refusal. In the eyes of Dayananda and his Aryas, Christians and orthodox Hindus had conspired to reject his commentary primarily because in their opinion the interpretation of European scholars was superior.[21]

One is not surprised that the Swami was elated when he received during his stay in the Punjab the first letter of the American Theosophists, which contained the words:

> A number of Americans and other students who earnestly seek after spiritual knowledge . . . finding in Christianity nothing that satisfied their reason or intuition . . . turned to the East for light, and openly proclaimed themselves the foes of Christianity. . . . We place ourselves under your instruction.[22]

This combination of circumstances and events radically changed the Swami's attitude, and led him to consider for the very first time the question of *shuddhi*, purification or reacceptance into Hinduism of ex-Hindus. After six months he gave his first lecture on *shuddhi* at Jalandhar, and is said to have reconverted a Christian there.[23] Pandit Khan Singh of Amritsar, a convert of the Reverend Clark, also became an Arya;[24] and in Gujarat the Swami prevented pupils of the Christian school from receiving baptism.[25] By the end of his stay, the missionaries must have started to consider him a threat. At Amritsar, a group of students of the mission school were attracted to Christianity, called themselves 'Unbaptized Christians', and formed their own society, the 'Prayer Meeting'. Dayananda's teaching diverted them from that path, which considerably upset the local clergymen. It is reported that some reconversions of Christians ensued.[26]

In the following year, from August 1878 to August 1879, the Swami spent the first three months in the U.P., then two months in Rajputana, followed by another stay in the U.P. Once he left the Punjab, the encounter with missionaries became much less frequent: during that year only three meetings are recorded. In Ajmer in November 1878, a disputation took place with the Reverend Grey and the Reverend Husband, the topic of which was the story of creation in Genesis. By this time the Swami had laid down such strict and minute rules about the procedure of public disputations, with impartial judges and verbatim accounts, that progress was excruciatingly slow, and the missionaries withdrew in frustration after two days.[27] At Dehradun, in April 1879, the Reverend Morrisson became very upset over the Swami's lecture on the Bible; and the Swami not only prevented the conversion of a *rais's* son to Christianity, but actually performed the *shuddhi* of a Muslim.[28] It is worth noting here that Dehradun is close to the Punjab. And, finally, at the close of this period, the Swami had a three-day discussion at Bareilly in August 1879 with his old friend the Reverend Scott. Their long-standing friendship made this into a decorous and amicable occasion.[29]

At this stage, there were four years of the Swami's life left, which he spent in the U.P., Bombay, and Rajputana. For these year, we find only half a dozen short talks with missionaries recorded: contact or confrontation with Christians formed no part of the last years of the Swami's life. The first circumstantial reason, naturally, was that he never went back to the Punjab. But there were other compelling reasons. During this time the Swami was fully occupied with the two objectives that he now considered of absolute prime importance. The first was his writing, to which he devoted increasingly more time. The second concern was to prevent his Samaj from slipping into sectarian isolation by bringing it into closer contact and collaboration with the wider world of Hinduism.[30] Christianity was outside his immediate concern, and when his followers wrote to him of their worries about Christian conversions, he gave them the advice that they should avoid disputations, and instead distribute as widely as possible a pamphlet attacking Christianity.[31]

Reviewing the conversations and discussions of the Swami with missionaries, particularly in the crucial three years 1876-8, one notices some recurring topics. On a more theoretical level, there is that of creation. By the mid-1870s the Swami was arriving at his final doctrine of *traitavada*, the eternity of three realities, God, the souls, and nature.[32] The usual position of the opponents was that creation must have a beginning in order to safeguard the essential distinction between creator and creature. This was mostly a fruitless and dispassionate scholastic exchange with both sides firmly ensconced in their positions. Another frequent subject was similarly theoretical, the question of the forgiveness of sins. To the Swami this was a false concept, as he held firmly to a mechanical retribution system of *karma*.[33] To the missionaries this touched the very core of their faith and was linked with the incarnation of the Saviour. As long as the discussion remained philosophical, it remained composed, but the exchange tended, of necessity, to move into questions of biblical interpretation. Then the Swami attacked and condemned the story of Adam, the concept of original sin, and the very idea of God becoming man.

A second area of dispute arose from specific attacks from one or other side on the Vedas or the Bible respectively. The missionaries found it very hard to cope with the Swami's method of giving literal interpretations which he then showed to offend both reason and morality. The missionaries similarly attacked Hindu doctrines and myths, such as the behaviour of Krishna, the incest of Brahma, and cow-sacrifice in the Vedas. On this level the exchange mostly led to justifications, denials, and counter-accusations, and on both sides acrimony was never far away, as both were defending what was dearest to them. Chapter 7 discusses in detail Dayananda's interpretations of Christianity.

There were two decisive episodes in the development of the Swami's attitude to Christianity. The first was his Calcutta experience. There Dayananda learned to see Hinduism in a large comparative context, and to affirm its utter superiority. To him that superiority was based on the Vedas, but his idea of the superiority and uniqueness of Vedic revelation found no response at all among the Calcutta intelligentsia, to most of whom Veda, Bible, and Koran each had but a relative value as a partial expression of a more universal truth. This attitude bitterly disappointed the Swami, and he saw it as the root-cause of the manifest divisiveness among the local intelligentsia. He decided there and then that he himself had to write a commentary on the Vedas. In Calcutta the Swami did not become an active antagonist of Christianity, but he learnt that the superiority of the Vedas was not taken for granted, and had to be demonstrated. Doing so would of necessity include proof of the inferiority of the Bible. This proof he set out to give shortly afterwards in his first *Satyarth Prakash*.

The second decisive episode was the Swami's stay in the Punjab. The basic question that arose in Calcutta remained unchanged, namely the superiority of the Vedas and the Arya Dharma *vis-a-vis* Christianity and the Bible. However, the circumstances in which these issues emerged were totally different, and, therefore, elicited a different response from the Swami. Whereas in Calcutta the arena was essentially intellectual, in that the Hindu intelligentsia had been influenced by Christian ideas, in the Punjab the arena was intensely practical. Missionaries were very active and effective in converting Hindus to an extent that the Punjabi Hindus felt that their community was seriously threatened. Here the Bible was not a mere book-challenge, but had become a powerful, concrete weapon, wielded in preaching and publications, and in schools, to demonstrate the superiority of Christianity in order to convert Hindus. No wonder that the Swami's answer was also practical: he loudly proclaimed in the market-place the superiority of the Vedas and the inferiority of the Bible, and he inaugurated the concrete countermeasure of *shuddhi*.

His belligerent attitude was encouraged by an enthusiastic reception on the part of the Khatri intelligentsia and by the rapid growth of the Punjab Arya Samaj. The sly tactics of vilification and occasional violence used by the orthodox leadership only added fuel to the Swami's fire. The rejection of his Vedic commentary by a combination of orthodox pandits and Christian scholars touched the Swami to the quick, and his conviction that he had been unjustly treated was strengthened by the revelation of the Theosophists that many Westerners were deeply disappointed in Christianity. The circumstances and events in the Punjab made the Swami into a belligerent opponent of Christianity and of missionary conversion work. Whereas one could scarcely have called him a nationalist even in the broadest sense at the time of his Calcutta visit, in the Punjab the Swami became a promoter of nationalist feelings, which were aggressive and had strong anti-British and anti-Christian overtones. That is the nationalism we find expressed over and over again in the second *Satyarth Prakash*, his testament to the Arya Samaj.

One may ask if Dayananda's thought was in any way influenced by Christianity. There seems to have been some influence of a rather indirect nature in two cases. In this chapter we limit ourselves to indicating these areas without further elaboration. Dayananda took a long time to arrive at the final formulation of *traitavada*, his doctrine about the three eternal substances that constitute the totality of being: God, the souls, and nature. In particular his doctrine of creation, of the causal relation between God and the other substances, had been revised several times. It appears that its evolution and clarification were in some way influenced by the repeated attacks by missionaries on some logical weaknesses in the system. However, this influence is counterbalanced by Dayananda's study of Samkhya and Nyaya-Vaisheshika which also helped him to clarify his thoughts. A second area of indirect influence was, surprisingly, Dayananda's concept of Vedic revelation. His final doctrine that Hinduism was 'a religion of the book', possessing in the four Vedas proper (the Samhitas) a total and definitive corpus of revelation, was not as such part of the Hindu tradition: this tradition interpreted *shruti* in a much wider sense, and also accepted the importance and validity of post-Vedic revelation. The way Dayananda limited the corpus of revelation, excluded any post-Vedic revelation, and affirmed the all-comprehensiveness of the content of the four Vedas, is in fact more reminiscent of the way the missionaries he met (all belonging to the protestant tradition) tended to view the Bible.[34]

NOTES

[This chapter was first published as: 'Dayananda Sarasvati and Christianity', *Indian Church History Review*, vol. 15, no. 1, 1981, pp. 34-47.]

1. Cf. J. Robson, *Hinduism in its relation to Christianity*, London, 1893; T.J. Scott, *Missionary Life among the Villages in India*, Cincinnati, 1876; A.F.R. Hoernle's article in the *Christian Intelligencer* of March 1870 was reprinted in Lajpat Rai, *A History of the Arya Samaj*, revd. edn. by Sri Ram Sharma, Mumbai, 1967, pp. 28-38.
2. For an analysis of the total impact of Calcutta on the Swami, cf. J.T.F. Jordens, *Dayananda Sarasvati, His Life and Ideas*, Delhi, 1978, ch. 4.
3. Cf. P.S. Basu, *Life and Works of Brahmananda Keshav*, Calcutta, 1940, pp. 295-300.
4. Cf. Y. Mimamshak (ed.), *Rishi Dayananda Sarasvati ke Patra aur Vijnapanon ke Parishisht*, Amritsar, 1958, p. 53, and Ghasiram, *Maharshi Dayananda Sarasvati ka Jivan-Charit*, vol. I, Ajmer, 1957, p. 259.
5. Ghasiram, p. 261.

6. The first *Satyarth Prakash*, published in Varanasi in 1875 did not contain chapters on Christianity or Islam. It has now been firmly established that he wrote these chapters, which are held by the descendants of the patron of the publication, Raja Jaikishendas, and of which the Paropkarini Sabha of Ajmer has a photocopy. They were excluded because of the great rush to see the manuscript through the press. Cf. Y. Mimanshak, *Rishi Dayananda ke Granthon ka Itihas*, Ajmer, 1949, pp. 21-3; and Y. Mimamshak (ed.), *Rishi Dayananda Sarasvati ke Patra aur Vijnapan*, 2nd edn., Amritsar, 1955, pp. 20-4.
7. Cf. Ghasiram, vol. 1, p. 313.
8. For these meetings, cf. Ghasiram, vol. 2, pp. 2, 3, 11.
9. For a full text of this disputation, cf. B. Bharatiya (ed.) *Dayananda Shastrarth-Samgraha*, Sonepat, 1969, pp. 76-104; cf. also Ghasiram, vol. 2, p. 23.
10. Cf. Ghasiram, vol. 2, pp. 36-7.
11. Rev. E.N. Wherry, Dr W. Hooper, Rev. C.W. Forman, Father Robert Clark.
12. Cf. Jordens, ch. 7; K.W. Jones, 'The Arya Samaj in the Punjab: a study of social reform and religious revivalism, 1877-1902', unpublished Ph.D. thesis, University of California, Berkeley, 1966.
13. Cf. K.W. Jones, 'The Bengali Elite in Post-Annexation Punjab: an example of Inter-Regional influence in 19th Century India', *The Indian Economic and Social History Review*, 3, 1966, pp. 376-95.
14. Ghasiram, vol. 2, pp. 72, 81.
15. Cf. Ghasiram, vol. 2, pp. 18, 66; Lekhram, *Maharshi Dayananda Sarasvati ka Jivan Charitra*, translated from the original Urdu by Kaviraj Raghunandansingh 'Nirmal', Pandit Harischandra Vidyalankar (ed.), Delhi, 1972, p. 341.
16. Lekhram, p. 342.
17. Ibid., p. 349.
18. Ibid., p. 343.
19. Ibid., pp. 357, 361, 383, 387, 400, 405, 415; and Ghasiram, vol. 2, pp. 40, 66, 80, 85.
20. Cf. Ghasiram, vol. 2, pp. 64, 75, 95, 87, 90, 104; and Lekhram, pp. 342, 345, 397, 398, 400, 413.
21. For an account of this episode cf. Ghasiram, vol. 2, pp. 43-7; the Hindi version of the documents is available in Lekhram, pp. 827-35; and the English version in Lala Jivan Das (ed.), *Papers for the Thoughtful*, no. 3, Lahore, 1902, pp. 45-53.
22. For this letter, cf. Har Bilas Sarda, *Life of Dayananda Saraswati, World Teacher*, 2nd edn., Ajmer, 1968, pp. 522-3.
23. Cf. Ghasiram, vol. 2, p. 71; and Lekhram, p. 371.
24. Ghasiram, vol. 2, p. 106.

25. Ibid., p. 84.
26. Ibid., p. 106.
27. Ibid., pp. 138-40.
28. Ibid., pp. 169-71.
29. Ibid., pp. 183-90; for the full text of this disputation, cf. B. Bharatiya, pp. 129-71.
30. This change in the Swami's attitude is fully discussed in Jordens, ch. 9.
31. Cf. Y. Mimamshak, *Rishi Dayananda Sarasvati ke Patra aur Vijnapan*, pp. 435, 438, 446.
32. For an account of this development, cf. Jordens, pp. 275-7.
33. Cf. ibid., pp. 280-2.
34. Cf. ibid., pp. 272-3.

PART II
Doctrinal

CHAPTER 4

Dayananda Sarasvati and Vedanta

ONE OF THE MOST important sources for the study of the growth and dynamics of Dayananda Sarasvati's thought is the first edition of his most comprehensive work, the *Satyarth Prakash*, published at Varanasi in 1875. This edition is so rare that even the latest major study of Dayananda, James Reid Graham's Yale Ph.D. of 1943, entitled 'The Arya Samaj as a reformation in Hinduism with special reference to Caste', does not consider it. A meticulous preliminary word-to-word comparison of the two editions has resulted in pinpointing a number of issues on which Dayananda's thinking changed between 1875, the date of the publication of the first edition of the *Satyarth Prakash* and also of the foundation of the Arya Samaj, and the year of his death 1883, when the revised edition was published.

Apart from particular issues, two broad working hypotheses have emerged. Firstly, Dayananda was much more flexible and influenceable than previously thought. However, no change was allowed to remain fragmentary or adventitious: Dayananda's basic pursuit of rationality saw to it that change in one area found its logical consequence in the total structure of his thought. Secondly, Dayananda was also tenaciously loyal to those aspects of Hinduism which influenced him deeply in his formative years.[1] Shaivism for instance had such an impact on him: he was brought up in a devout Shaivite brahmin family, and the order of the Dandins he joined was a Shaivite order. These influences created a loyalty not easily shaken off. We see Dayananda in 1866, that is three years after his study under his guru Virjananda, at the age of forty-two, still preaching Shaivism, and even converting a raja to it, whilst by then he had been solidly attacking Vaishnavism for about three years. A year later his denunciation of Shaivism starts.

My contention in this chapter is that a similarly deep influence affected Dayananda from Advaita Vedanta, and that it was only in the second edition of his principal work, at the very end of his life, that all aspects of Advaita were eradicated from his thinking. This does seem to postulate that during his last ten years, the most public of his life, continuing strong influences kept pressing him on to this total eradication. The historical question as to what these influences exactly were is a study we are now engaged upon, but which lies outside the scope of this chapter. What we are here directly concerned with is the question: what were the significant differences as far as Advaita ideas are concerned between the first and the second editions of the *Satyarth Prakash*?

It is necessary to first sketch very quickly what contacts Dayananda had with Vedanta[2] prior to his writing of the *Satyarth Prakash*. After he ran away from home at the age of twenty-one to become a *sannyasi*, he was engaged for at least two years, from 1846 to 1848, in the study of Vedanta with Brahmananda and other teachers near Baroda. As he says in his autobiographical account, 'It was Bramhanand [sic] and other holy men who established to my entire satisfaction that Brahma, the deity, was no other than my own Self—my Ego.'[3] This study of Vedanta was continued for at least another year at Chanoda Kanyali, a centre not far away, and was followed by his initiation into the order of the Dandis, when he was given the name Dayananda Sarasvati. His initiator was a Vedantin, and the study of Vedanta was probably continued for sometime. So, it is quite clear that the first deep study Dayananda engaged upon for quite a few years was that of Vedanta.

These studies were then followed by his wanderings over north India, during which he concentrated on Yoga, and probably also for at least a short period became involved in Tantra, which he then totally rejected. In 1860 he finally found his guru in the blind Virjananda, under whom he studied mainly grammar, although there is some vague suggestion that he might have read some Vedantic texts with him. This concludes the stage of Dayananda the self-centered wandering *sannyasi*, and in 1863 starts the period of the wandering preacher. Gradually he came into greater prominence, and twelve years later, in 1875 he published his *Satyarth Prakash* and founded the Arya Samaj; the same year he published a pamphlet against Vedanta.[4] However, this was not the end of Vedantic influence on his thought, as our comparative study will show.

A comparison of the pamphlet with the first edition of the *Satyarth Prakash* shows full agreement between the two. We, therefore, limit our quotations to the first edition of the *Satyarth Prakash*. This has a great advantage in assessing the change: this was the text Dayananda had constantly in front of him as he wrote his second edition, so that all omissions and changes can be taken as made advisedly and deliberately.[5]

On reading through the first edition one notices that Dayananda's criticism of Vedanta is only incidental, and limits itself to two particular tenets, namely the identity of *Brahman* and *jiva*, and the illusory nature of the world. The second edition, on the other hand, contains no less than five lengthy explicit refutations of Vedanta, all running to between four and six pages, in chapters 7, 8, 9 and 11. In these passages Dayananda covers a lot of ground: he gives a reinterpretation of many Upanishadic texts, and he sets out to prove by his interpretation of the Vedanta-Sutras that they did not contain the false Vedanta doctrines. Moreover, he analyses in detail the concepts of *upadhi*, *adhyaropa*, *maya*, *chidabhasa*; he criticizes the doctrine of causality, and refutes the interpretation of dream and illusion. About Shankara, whom he greatly admired, he says: 'If the doctrines of the identity of the soul and *Brahman* and of the illusion of the world were really Shankaracharya's own belief, then it was not a good one; but if he assumed it only to refute the Jains, then it did have some virtue' (N.E. 272).[6]

Dayananda's leanings to Vedanta also clearly manifest themselves in the frequent use he makes of the Upanishads in his first edition. In his chapter on the existence and attributes of God, the first edition gives, under the heading *shabda*, or proofs from revelation, fifteen quotations, fourteen of which are from the Upanishads. The new edition discards ten of these fourteen Upanishadic quotations and replaces them by ten Vedic ones. In the chapter on creation of the old edition we find altogether only ten quotations, two from the *Rigveda*, two from the *Yajurveda*, four from the Upanishads and one each from the *Brahmasutras* and the *Samkhyasutras*. The new edition uses in the same chapter no less than fifty texts, and twenty of these are from the Vedas, and fifteen from the Sutra literature, whereas only twelve Upanishadic texts are mentioned. In the second edition there is in general a heavy reduction of the references to the Upanishads, a great increase in Vedic material and also a very marked increase in Sutra material, with a proportionate decrease of the importance of the Brahma-Sutras. All this is obviously but a symptom of Dayananda's freedom from Vedanta.

In both editions Dayananda replies twice to the objector who states that the six *darshanas* are mutually contradictory, and, therefore, do not warrant that one should regard them as an authority, which is what Dayananda does. There is a significant shift in the refutation of this objection. In the first edition Vedanta is considered as the school that gives the most complete and penetrating, in fact the final answer in contrast with the partial and incomplete answers given by the other schools. Vedanta speaks of 'the ultimate' causes of existence, whereas the others deal only with secondary causes (O.E. 80-3). The text also distinguishes two kinds of *pralaya*: there is *mahapralaya*, a partial dissolution that stops short at subtle matter. That is the *pralaya* the other systems talk about, whereas Vedanta speaks of *atyanta pralaya*, the total dissolution where even subtle matter is dissolved in the ultimate *Brahman* (O.E. 271-2).

The second edition deprives Vedanta of this place of prominence, as all *darshanas* are put on the same level: 'There are six causes of the creation of the world. Each of these is explained by each author of the *darshanas*. Therefore, there is no contradiction between the *darshanas*' (N.E. 67). In other words, causality when referring to the world as a whole is a very complex matter, and the different systems specialise in different aspects. Whereas Vedanta says that 'nothing would have been able to originate without the action of an efficient cause', Samkhya says that all origination presupposes a material cause (N.E. 208). In this way the second edition reduces Vedanta from being the ultimate one, to be just one among the six sources of philosophical argumentation.

This introduces us to the heart of our topic: the essential doctrinal shifts that occurred between the two editions. All these pivot around one central problem, that of creation and dissolution, and of man's origin and destiny within that cosmic rhythm. The differences between the two editions can succinctly be put as follows. The first edition affirms that there is *adisrishti* (absolute creation), that there is *atyanta pralaya* (absolute dissolution) and that *moksha* is irreversible. The second edition explicitly denies everyone of these propositions.

According to the first edition there is an absolute beginning and an absolute end of the world: *adisrishti* and *atyanta pralaya*. Between these two absolute points plays the intra-cosmic rhythm of relative or partial creations and dissolutions. The partial *pralaya* is called *mahapralaya*, and in it the dissolution does not go beyond the state of subtle matter (O.E. 171-2). But dissolution can reach further. Dayananda says, 'When *prakriti-laya* happens, then the one Lord and cause of the world, namely the Lord's potentiality (*samarthya*), will remain, nothing else' (O.E. 262-3). This concept of *samarthya*, potentiality, also enters the discussion of *adisrishti*: this potential is the material cause out of which in the beginning the Lord fashioned the world. 'In the making of the world the material cause was the Lord, because besides Him there existed nothing from which to make the world. Therefore, he made the world from his own natural potential (which has the form of a quality), and so the Lord himself is in fact the material cause of the world' (O.E. 257). It is quite clear that this concept of absolute beginning was clearly fixed in Dayananda's mind. It makes him put the following question in the mouth of the objector: 'God is partial because at the beginning he made some beings human and others animal'. The answer is that 'when *adisrishti* happened, at that time there was no distinction human-animal: that differentiation arose later on' (O.E. 284).

The correlate of *adisrishti* in the first edition is *atyanta pralaya*. It is that final *pralaya* where even *prakriti* is dissolved and all matter disappears completely in the potential of the Lord. Dayananda's meaning is quite clear and unambiguous: *prakriti* itself is made subject to a final dissolution into the pure divine potential out of which it emerged (O.E. 262). The first edition, therefore, clearly and in several places affirms the reality of an absolute beginning and an absolute end of the cosmos.

These are both emphatically and repeatedly denied in the second edition. Here *prakriti* is unbeginning (as in the Samkhya system), it has not been created by God, it is, with God and the *jivas*, the third eternal beginningless and uncaused substance (N.E. 196). There never was a first *srishti* when *prakriti* emerged from the Lord. In fact, *srishti* is now defined as 'the first association of those subtle elements that in the *prakriti* are in perfect equilibrium' (N.E. 208). Similarly, there cannot be an absolute end of the world:

> Creation is preceded by destruction, destruction is preceded by creation, or creation is followed by destruction, that is to say, the rhythmic cycle of the world proceeds with regularity and constancy from all eternity. There is neither beginning nor end of it. The beginning and end of creation and destruction are like those of day and night. Just like the Supreme Spirit, the *jiva* and the *prakriti* are three substances eternal by nature, similarly are the

creation, preservation and absorption of the world eternal by *pravah* (that is by rhythmic flow). (N.E. 211)

In two places Dayananda makes it absolutely clear that the doctrine of absolute beginning and end he is refuting is in fact a doctrine of the Vedantins. 'The Neo-Vedantins say that at the beginning of creation there was no world, and at the end of dissolution no world will be left' (N.E. 199). And elsewhere: '. . . they believe in origination from *Brahman* and dissolution into *Brahman*. . . . That doctrine of beginning and end of the Vedantins is false' (N.E. 281).

As we saw, Dayananda accepted in his first edition the Lord to be the material cause of the universe; in his second edition he not only denies this emphatically, he also enumerates the many contradictions inherent in that proposition (N.E. 200).

Dayananda's concept of man, even in his first edition, has an essential quality that differentiates it from the Advaita concept: man is essentially an active cosmic being. This would need further elaboration, but here it should be sufficient to indicate one aspect of it: man needs his subtle body to be able to enjoy *moksha*. This cosmic conception of man entails that Dayananda's concept of *moksha* will have essential links with his concept of cosmic cycles. Therefore, if our theologian is logically consistent, and that is one thing he always tried to be, then there should be some important differences between the two editions in the conception of *moksha*, since, as we have seen, there are important differences in his conception of cosmic cycles.

In the first edition Dayananda states that the soul, once it has reached *moksha*, never again returns to the wheel of rebirth: *moksha* is definitive, without possibility of reversal (O.E. 168, 294). He specifies this by the following expressions: '*avidya*, the root of death, is destroyed by knowledge' (O.E. 294), '*moksha* is the complete cessation of all sorrow' (O.E. 294), and 'all karma is shed with its very root' (O.E. 296). The very root, the very possibility of all sorrow, death, and *karma* is thus completely destroyed.

However, this does not mean that *moksha* is without end. The question is indeed explicitly put: 'This *jiva* who has gained *moksha*, will he now remain forever, or will he also some time be destroyed?' Dayananda answers that they will persist as long as there is no *atyanta pralaya*, 'because, when total and final *pralaya* happens, then no one will remain, only the Lord and his infinite potential' (O.E. 295).

We see Dayananda here caught in the logic of his Vedantic framework: if absolute beginning and absolute end are accepted, then the *jiva* too must be subject to it. And also: if man is by essence a cosmic being, then the end of the cosmos must spell the end of man. He tries to soften the impact of his answer by adding: 'This *atyanta pralaya* will not happen until all souls have been liberated, not before. It is, therefore, very far off. . . It is only "possible" that there will be an *atyanta pralaya*; in the meantime there will be many times partial creation and dissolution' (G.E. 296).

In the second edition there is no framework of total beginning and end any more, and, therefore, the question if the soul will ever be destroyed does not even arise. But in the very passage where in the first edition he asked the previous question, Dayananda now asks a different one: 'The *jivas* that have gained *moksha*, do they ever again return to the round of birth and death?' (N.E. 226). The answer is in the affirmative. This answer goes against the whole of the Hindu tradition. Nowhere, to one's knowledge, can one find a precedent to this statement. Only the long forgotten doctrines of the Ajivikas ever affirmed this in their doctrine of *mandala-moksha*.[7] The arguments put forward by Dayananda for his position constitute in themselves a most interesting study. Here we only want to indicate how the new assertion neatly fits into his post-Vedantic doctrinal position.

Dayananda's ideological framework in his second edition is dominated by some basic principles, the most important of which is that 'what is, has always been, and will always be'. This applies first of all to the three eternal substances, God, *jiva*, and *prakriti*: these are eternal by nature. But eternity can have another form: eternity by *pravah*, or by rhythm. Creation and dissolution possess that type of eternity, and so does the rhythm of bondage and liberation, of *bandha* and *moksha* (N.E. 407). Although any one *srishti* or *pralaya* arises and disappears, their alternation is without beginning or end. Similarly, although one *jiva* is now bound, then liberated, the alternation of bondage and liberation is also eternally rhythmic. It is evident how much these ideas are in contradiction of the basic Advaita ideas of the identity of *brahman* and *atman* and of the illusory nature of the cosmos.

We saw how in the first edition *moksha* entailed the complete eradication of ignorance, *karma*, sorrow and death. The radical transformation is no more acceptable to Dayananda. In fact he says that the connection of the *jiva* with *karma* is an eternal and essential one. Just as bondage is the result of action, so is emancipation: 'The same causes that are operative in removing dirt are also operative in causing it' (N.E. 407). So we come to the extraordinary situation that the *jiva* in the state of *moksha* remains connected with action, and action entails freedom, a freedom that may bring back sin and ignorance, and thus bondage. Bondage and liberation succeed each other in an eternity of rhythm. This conception would make any Vedantist turn in his grave.

Those then are the important shifts in doctrine between the two editions of the *Satyarth Prakash.* To these can, finally, be added a change of a more practical nature, but intimately connected with Vedanta: it concerns the view of *sannyasa*. Within a Vedantic framework, the *sannyasi* is the person who devotes his energies completely to the highest religious concern, that of realizing his identity with *Brahman* and thus reaching liberation. In the pursuit of this aim the *sannyasi* becomes free from all social and ritual obligations: he is beyond rite and caste, beyond the ethical framework they constitute, in a sense beyond good and evil: he is the supreme individualist, for whom only *moksha* counts.

Although Dayananda even in his first edition rejected the doctrine of the identity *atman-brahman*, there lingered on a Vedantic flavour in his concept of the *sannyasi.* When speaking of the important duty of the Vedic 'five great sacrifices', he says that he who has reached full knowledge, performs these sacrifices only 'inwardly', 'and it is not necessary for him to perform the external actions' (O.E. 123). In his chapter on the *sannyasi* he explicitly says that he should 'give up the *agnihotra* and other external rites . . . because they are useless to him' (O.E. 158); he also 'should give up all external rites and be intent on his only work: *moksha*' (G.E. 172). 'When the *sannyasi* has become filled with proper knowledge, then he is no longer bound by works'. (O.E. 166). We see that Dayananda retains in his portrait of the *sannyasi* those Vedantic traits of freedom from everyday *dharma*, and exclusive concentration on the personal search for *moksha*.

Each of these affirmations just quoted is substantiated by a reference to Manu, and in every case the new edition omits them. This deliberate omission in four different places cannot be without definite purpose. Indeed, in the second edition Dayananda uses one of his favoured procedures to negate these ideas by putting them in the mouth of the objector: '*Sannyasis* say that they have no duties to perform . . . that sin and merit do not affect them . . . that it is not the business of the wise to be ensnared in the affairs of the world . . . that whatever sin or virtue there is, that is a matter only for body and senses, not for the *atma.*' Dayananda exclaims in answer:

What, they do not think they have the duty to perform good works? Manu said that Vedic duties, deeds of truth and dharma, have to be performed by *sannyasis* too. . . . If they do not work at the propagation of the truth, then they are a useless burden on the earth. Whatever deeds are done by the body, they are in fact the actions of the soul, and it is the soul that enjoys their fruit. (N.E. 123.4)

To the question, 'What is the *dharma* of the *sannyasi*?', Dayananda answers that it is the same as that of all men, with the addition of some special duties (N.E. 119). And in his very much rewritten chapter on *sannyasa*, Dayananda's main new emphasis is on the paramount duty of the *sannyasi* to teach and advise. His duty, in other words, is not limited to his own search for *moksha*, but it is a duty towards mankind. In fact, that is the prime *raison d'être* of his very existence: if he does not fulfil that duty, he is nothing but a worthless parasite. Here Dayananda indicts the host of gurus, saints, *sannyasis*, whom he has observed during his travels through India. Perhaps he also thinks of himself: for, during those long years between the age of twenty-one when he ran away from home and the start of his preaching career at the age of forty, his own only concern was, by his own admission, the single-minded, individualistic search for *moksha*.

Those, then, are the changes that occurred in Dayananda's position *vis-a-vis* 'Vedantic' tenets between the first and second editions of his *Satyarth Prakash*. For a full understanding of their import they need to be connected with other facets of his theology: his view of man as a cosmic being, and his view of God's role in the process of bondage and liberation are two most important areas that need further investigation. However, some clear lines of development already show up in this partial study. Dayananda continuously strengthened his view of man as cosmic and active. Activity and relation to the cosmos are not accidental and, therefore, destructible qualities of man: they belong to his very essence. They both imply involvement, deep and lasting, in the world. Whereas a strong strain of Hinduism tends to draw man away from both the world and active involvement, Dayananda was prepared to go further and further in accentuating precisely those aspects of man that entail active involvement: the *sannyasi* is not excused, and not even *moksha* is allowed to escape. As his thought developed he increasingly put the full burden of man's destiny, both as an agent of civilization and as a seeker for *moksha*, squarely on the shoulders of man alone. His repeated attacks on Vedanta were motivated by his view that Vedanta, as he knew it, tended to draw man away from action, world, and society, and thus from the very centre of human life itself. This message of activism and involvement was one of Dayananda's most central ones. And somehow it is not surprising that it was in Lahore among the practical, energetic, down-to-earth Punjabis that Dayananda found instant and enthusiastic response.

The explicitation of Dayananda's gradual theological development brings up the question what the influences were that kept pushing him in those years between 1875 and 1883. As we have only started this investigation, only general lines of enquiry can be indicated here. The detailed biographies frequently mention three groups of people who regularly discussed with Dayananda precisely the issues we have considered. There were the Christian missionaries, whose theological tenets Dayananda vigorously refuted, in particular their doctrine of *creatio ex nihilo*. Then there were the Neo-Vedantins, as Dayananda calls them, who keep appearing and seem to have had an influential following at the time; conversations and discussions with them, conversions of some, and speeches directed against their doctrines occur quite often. At the beginning of this period Dayananda was also in constant close contact with many members of the Prarthana Samaj. Whereas he had no time for the vague deism they shared with the Brahmos, their extremely practical and active approach to social reform must have influenced him considerably. Apart from these three groups there was also the Lahore Samaj group. Although Dayananda visited the Punjab only once in 1877-8, he was from then on in constant close contact with the Lahore leaders. As they prevailed upon him to replace his long and detailed 28-point Bombay creed of 1875 by the concise 10-point Lahore creed, it seems that from the very start Dayananda took their counsel seriously. This contact cannot but have strengthened the development of his theology in a man for whom nothing was purely theoretical. All doctrine was essentially related to his vision of active Hindu man, and of a new Hinduism and a new India, purified, vital, progressive, that he wanted to see reborn on the model of the one that he was convinced reigned supreme in the Vedic Golden Age.

NOTES

[This chapter was first published as 'Dayananda and Vedanta: a comparison of the first and second editions of his Satyarth Prakash', *The Indian Economic and Social History Review*, IX (1972), pp. 367-79.]

1. Recent studies have revealed a similar deep influence on Gandhi, from his Kathiawar background. Dayananda too was a Kathiawari, but the influences were very different. The family, religion, and society in which he grew up were markedly different from those in which Gandhi grew up. For a detailed study, see ch. 8.
2. Dayananda in his works persistently uses the term 'Vedanta' in the narrow sense of Advaita Vedanta. To make his and my terms tally more easily, I will from now on use the term Vedanta in the same restricted sense. In this chapter, I do not try to establish if all the doctrines Dayananda calls Vedantic did in reality form part of the system of Shankara or of his followers. Dayananda was attacking in the main the contemporary exponents of Vedanta, whom he frequently refers to as Neo-Vedantins.
3. *The Theosophist*, vol. 1, October 1879, p. 12.
4. *Vedanta-dhvanta-nivaranam*, Mumbai, 1875.
5. Dayananda's first edition was dictated in Sanskrit to pandits who then put it into Hindi, and there was obviously no proper proof reading by Dayananda. This leaves the door open for corruption of Dayananda's ideas by the pandits. Our study takes this possibility fully into account. The changes and differences we deal with occur in several places, and entail close argumentation: they are not of the type that could have been slipped into the text by the translators.
6. I will refer to the first edition of the *Satyarth Prakash* by putting (O.E.) followed by the page number after the quotation. For the second edition, I will use (N.E.) followed by the page number. For the latter, the following is the edition referred to: *Satyarthaprakashah*, Ajmer, 1966. All translations are mine.
7. Cf. A.L. Basham, *History and Doctrine of the Ajivikas*, London, 1951, p. 259.

CHAPTER 5

Dayananda Sarasvati's Concept of the Vedic Golden Age

TOO OFTEN THE modernizing process in South Asia has been studied in the context of an opposition of tradition and modernity, where 'modern' tended to be equated with 'Western'. Social change and new ideas not only arose from the impact of outside forces on established traditional systems, but may have sprung from alternatives contained in the tradition. As Milton Singer wrote, 'While extreme "modernists" and extreme "traditionalists" sometimes speak of irreconcilable conflict, there is, in fact, a mutual dependence.'[1] The way to correct the perspective of the study of tradition and modernity is, in the words of Rudolphs, 'to accord tradition a higher priority in the study of modernization'.[2] In other words, one has to dig deeper into the traditional sources and bring to the surface the complexity of their different perspectives. Only after that can the question of modernization be asked in a valid way.

Dayananda Sarasvati was steeped in his tradition. For the first forty-eight years of his life he lived within the bosom of traditional society and was largely isolated from outside influences. Yet he became a 'modern' reformer. His key concept of the Golden Age of Vedic times exhibits characteristics which would usually be called 'modern', such as the concept of man-made progress, the refusal of fatalism, the sense of history, the urge to demythologize, and the importance given to technological advance. The idea of a Vedic Golden Age had been advocated by the early British orientalists under the influence of current European ideas propounded by influential thinkers such as Voltaire and Gibbon.[3] On the other hand, the Hindu tradition also contained the concept of a Golden Age, the *krita yuga*. A study of the various factors that influenced Dayananda may throw some light on the process of modernization.

The most important primary sources for the traditional concept are the three great collections of the Dharmashastras, the Puranas, and the *Mahabharata*. We are here not interested in the historical evolution of the idea, which began to take shape at least in the fourth or fifth century BC and had been fully developed in the first centuries of the Christian era, but in the various facets of the idea presented in the tradition. A difficulty that comes straight to mind here is the question how one can satisfactorily cope with the immense amount of source material. An excellent starting point is the voluminous work of P.V. Kane, *History of Dharmashastra*,[4] wherein the bulk of the Dharmashastra literature is surveyed, plus a fair amount of the *Mahabharata* and the Puranas. Its extensive indices refer back to a wealth of primary sources. We have supplemented the references of Kane by scanning eight of the most important Puranas[5] and the two most important books on ethics and politics in the *Mahabharata*, the Shanti and Anushasana Parvans. We feel sure that very little of importance would have slipped through that net, and the few secondary studies on the topic confirmed that feeling.

The following is the scheme that became generally accepted. A *mahayuga* is a period of time divided into four segments called the *krita* (Golden), the *treta*, the *dvapara*, and the *kaliyugas*, following one another in fixed periods of diminishing length and totalling 4,320,000 years. If this time span seems vast, it was subsumed under the immensely greater cosmogonic scheme of the *kalpa*. 'a day of Brahma', which encompasses one thousand *mahayugas* and lasts 4,320 million years. These *kalpas* are divided into fourteen secondary cycles called *manvantaras*, each comprising seventy-one *mahayugas*.[6] That is the broad scheme which in its historical evolution absorbed and adapted elements from astrology and mythology, and incorporated dynastic histories.

The total structure is a cosmogonic myth subsuming human history under the vast umbrella of the emanation and re-absorption of the cosmos by the creator, Brahma. This myth affirms that human life and history are part of an eternal cyclic movement in which night follows day, winter follows summer, death follows life, *kali* age follows Golden Age, dissolution follows creation in a perpetual rotation which itself is in the last instance nothing else than a theophany. The primary purpose of that cyclic cosmogonic myth, which recurs in many civilizations, is to give sense to the vagaries of history welling up out of the darkness of the past and moving into the even more disturbing void of the future. History finds a meaning because it is a theophany, not wedged between two unknowns, but organically part of an ever-returning cycle; every age repeats a necessary pattern which has occurred before under divine guidance and leads to the predictable reenactment of a future also divinely ordained. History and the enigma of time thus lose their terror.[7]

This level of explanation, however, subsumes the Golden and Dark Ages under an immensity where they lose their actuality. One has to make abstraction of the cosmogonic cycle, and look more closely at the description of the eras. This is not an unwarranted procedure. In fact the traditional writers do exactly that. When they speak specifically about the *yugas*, then cosmogony becomes irrelevant. Whenever the *kali* age is mentioned, it has two basic characteristics: it is a time of decadence, and it is the contemporary age of the writer. Kane summarizes it as follows:

> From the Mahabharata, Manu, Narada, Brhaspati and the Puranas it is clear that they all believed in the existence of an ideally perfect community in the dim past, followed by a gradual degeneracy and decline in morals, health and length of life. But they also believed that a cycle of decline would be followed in the far distant future by another of moral perfection. The only pity is that all works that are extant think that they are in the midst of a very sinful age and there is not a single work which thinks that the era of perfection may dawn in the very near future.[8]

The decadence of the *kali* age is characterized by the following:

> the break-down of the system of classes, of sexual mores, and of health and longevity; the predominance of heretical sects; the reign of Shudra and Mleccha (foreign) rulers; a rebellion of nature by famine and floods. All these could be described as the collapse of *dharma* in its broadest sense.[9]

Whereas the texts abound in descriptions of the ravages of the contemporary *kali* age and revel in that of worse catastrophes to come, the references to the *krita* or Golden Age tend to be rather schematic. *Dharma* reigned everywhere, and there was no sin or fickleness of opposites like love and hatred; the stages of life and the duties of classes were clearly distinguished and universally observed; men were equal in every respect, possessing the same happiness, beauty, and longevity (up to 4,000 years in some texts); disease did not exist nor sorrow; human reproduction did not involve sexuality; nature spontaneously produced abundance without toil. The formulas used in the texts to describe the Golden Age are often identical, and it is clear that they do not pretend to portray a historical reality, but rather a theoretically ideal one, constructed as a contrast to the *kali* age.

What explanatory use do the texts make of the *yuga* scheme? The authors of the law-books, which kept being composed from 500 BC to AD 1000, were faced with a great number of conflicting statements in the older texts. A particular problem was that some of the oldest works allowed certain actions which contemporary society no longer permitted. In order to justify their prohibition of deeds permissible in Vedic texts, the authors introduced the category of *Kalivarjya*, 'a thing to be avoided in the *kali* age'.[10] Thus they accommodated *dharma* to changes that had in fact occurred in the ideas and practices of the people. The argument put forward to justify the prohibition was that in the *kaliyuga* 'there was an absence of good people'.[11]

The *yuga* theory was used in a similar fashion in the following argument. As people were naturally good in the Golden Age, there was no need for a king or for the codification and administration of the law. In the *kaliyuga*, however, where evil abounds, there is a pressing need for a powerful king backed by a strong administration and extensive legislation.[12] Thus, the *smriti* writers used the *yuga* scheme to justify the enormous detail of their laws and their divergence from ancient prescriptions, and also to legitimize the extensive royal powers they supported.

The laws of Manu suggest in one verse an extension of that principle to a wider religious sphere: '*Tapas* (asceticism) was the highest goal (deemed to yield great results) in the *kritayuga*, knowledge (of the self) was the highest in *treta*, *yajna* (sacrifice to God) in *dvapara*, charity (*danam*) alone in *kali*'.[13] Here Manu suggests that man's basic approach in religious matters varies between ages, justifying thus the very fact that in contemporary society asceticism, knowledge, and sacrifice did not have the same prevalence they had in olden days. The Puranas took up this idea and made it their main emphasis. They were concerned with legitimizing their preaching of the absolute superiority of *bhakti* over all other means to secure merit and *moksha*. For that purpose they used the *yuga* theory, proclaiming that in fact the *kali* age was superior to any age because it brought with *bhakti* the most powerful religious method:

> A man secures in a single day and night in Kali age as much reward of tapas, celibacy and japa as is obtained in ten years in the Krita age, in one year in

Treta and a month in Dvapara; therefore I spoke of Kali as good; in Kali age man secures merely by the glorification or incessant repetition of the name of Keshava what he would secure by deep meditation in Krita, by sacrifice in Treta, and by worship in Dvapara; I am pleased with Kali because a man secures a great eminence of dharma with a little effort.[14]

The *Mahabharata* repeats in detail the *yuga* scheme given by Manu, and reinforces the uses of it noticed in the Smritis and the Puranas. The Shanti Parvan shows how 'many new kinds of duty or religious observance are brought about in each *yuga*', causing great confusion: 'When the Shrutis and the Smritis contradict each other, how can either be authoritative?' The question of 'righteous action' becomes very complicated and confused if one only refers to what is written. Therefore, man needs to resort to more general ethical principles such as *ahimsa*, non-violence, in order to make a proper choice.[15] The same book also uses the *yuga* scheme to show how throughout the ages the religion of *bhakti*, devotion to Krishna, was transmitted by generations of sages. The *yuga* scheme becomes a backdrop to the glorification of Narayana-Vasudeva and *bhakti*.[16]

But the *Mahabharata* also contains a series of texts where the *yuga* scheme is used differently. All these texts occur in the long section on *rajadharma*, kingship. Yudhisthira asked Bhishma the question, 'There is the science of kingship, there is the king, and there are the subjects. Tell me how one of these is of advantage to the others.' Bhishma answered: 'As to the question whether the king makes the age or the age makes the king, You should have no doubt. The king makes the age. When the king rules with full and strict application of the science of government, then the best age called the Golden Age sets in.'[17] This is not a casual observation. The Shanti Parvan repeats the idea several times using the following clear expressions, 'the king is the cause of the *yugas*'; 'the king is the creator of the Golden Age'; 'all *yugas* have their root in the king'.[18]

All these texts have the same message: that it is within the power of the king to bring about a Golden or a Dark Age. They all occur within the special context of *rajadharma*, where the duties and powers of the king are explained and glorified. In this particular context the larger background of the inevitable cycle of *yugas* recedes into insignificance, and royal action which exerts itself on a much smaller time-scale becomes the immediate focus. On that time-scale *raja-dharma* is all-powerful and able to draw the Golden Age out of its cyclical distant future into historical immediacy. In these *Mahabharata* texts we find a view of the *yuga* scheme basically deviant from the rest of the tradition, affirming the possibility of the dynamic of short-term progress.

Dayananda had a profound personal knowledge of Manu and the Smriti literature, of the Puranas, and the Shanti Parvan of the *Mahabharata* was one of his favourite texts.[19] From 1873 onwards he was increasingly aware of the modern ideas current in nineteenth century India through his contacts with the Bengali, Maharashtrian and Punjabi intelligentsia, through his reading, and his discussions with foreign missionaries and administrators. To what extent was his central concept of the Vedic Golden Age influenced by the tradition, and to what extent did it incorporate modern ideas of his times?

First of all, Dayananda accepted the great cosmogonic scheme of the rhythmic emanation and absorption of the cosmos, but he purged it of its properly mythological dimension and presented it as a philosophical scheme, using Samkhya and Nyaya categories in its elaboration. This scheme is only occasionally referred to as a backdrop to particular discussions about the problem of creation, but most of the time it remains in fact invisible and without influence in the discussion of religious matters, just as it does in the tradition itself.[20]

Dayananda also accepted the scheme of the four ages in its classical form as presented by Manu. But he is very concerned with dating exactly the four ages of the current cycle. The contemporary *kali* age started about 5,000 years ago with the great *Mahabharata* war, and it is to run for another 400,000 years. The Swami traced the degeneration of Hindu religion, society, economy, and politics historically to the disruption caused by that war. The basic reason for this upheaval was the neglect of the Vedas, which led to the collapse of the social order, the degeneracy of the state, the corruption of religion, and the destruction of economic prosperity. In his description of the *kali* age the Swami was always careful to refer to historical phenomena, and studiously avoided the fanciful flights of imagination into yet vaster catastrophes to come, which are part of many traditional accounts.[21]

Whereas the tradition used the *kali* age as an excuse for justifying new developments in society and religion which diverged from the Vedic injunctions, and thus legitimized new customs and practices, Dayananda rejected this procedure. To him the Vedic injunctions alone were intrinsically valid, and the Vedas were the supreme touchstone of truth. Thus he proved the admissibility of some of the famous *Kalivarjyas* such as the journey across the seas, intercaste marriage, the *niyoga* contract, and the employment of shudras for cooking.[22] The claim of the Puranas that the *kali* age justified the advent of a new all-powerful religion of *bhakti* that superseded the Vedas was also anathema to the Swami. To him, only moral action had religious effectiveness, and Puranic religion was a perversion.

Throughout Dayananda's works we find incidental references to the Golden Age, when the *varnashrama dharma* worked effectively, when marriage by choice prevailed, when women were equal to men, highly educated and occupying important positions, when people interdined and intermarried without restrictions: it was an era wherein the religious and social orders were ideal. In a couple of passages where the Swami explicitly wrote about the Golden Age, he stressed two aspects. The Golden Age was when the wise kings of Aryavarta ruled as universal emperors according to the perfect Vedic statecraft. Moreover, that age not only abounded in wisdom, but it was also far advanced in science and technology: both wisdom and science spread over the world from the centre of the Vedic land of Aryavarta.[23]

Dayananda, therefore, agreed with the tradition that the Golden Age possessed both the perfect social organization and the best kind of statecraft, the basic conditions for fulfilment and prosperity. However, the tradition went much further than that, affirming that in fact there was no vice or sin or evil, no disease or early death, no widowhood, that the seasons were perfect, the crops always plentiful, and that each man's cup of life, happiness, and beauty was equally overflowing. Never did Dayananda's description of the Golden Age include any of these fanciful embellishments.

One of the reasons why the traditional sources let their imagination run riot about the Golden Age was that none of them thought that the next Golden Age was to dawn in the near future. Only the *Mahabharata* suggested the possibility of a Golden Era independent of the cyclic necessity, when it stated that it was the king who created the Golden Era. Dayananda forcefully supported the idea, putting it succinctly and sharply as follows in one of his parables:

SAGE: When all wise men teach the same, then there will be no delay in the establishment of one religion.

OBJECTOR: Today is the *kaliyuga*. Do not aspire to things that belong to the Golden Age.

SAGE: *Kaliyuga* is but the name of a period of time. Since time itself is actionless, it is not a factor in the promotion or the prevention of *dharma* or *adharma*. It is you who are yourselves incarnations of the *kaliyuga*.[24]

Dayananda's whole programme of reform was founded on the conviction that the Golden Age could be brought back; he usually called it the 'future regeneration of Aryavarta', or the 'recapturing of the conditions of that ancient time'. However, the Swami did not follow the *Mahabharata* when it put the creation of the Golden Age squarely into the hands of the king, neither did he conceive that regeneration to be a quick process. The study of the Vedas was to be the key; this would lead to universal education, the reestablishment of the Vedic social order, and the emergence of an ideal state. Although the king was to play a significant role, the most important factor would be the multiplication of wise and moral men across the spectrum of society. These were the elite out of which an Aryan kingship would reemerge, not autocratic but controlled by that very elite. The Vedas were the key to everything because they were the 'book of revelation' containing not only the totality of theological wisdom, the perfect moral code, and the perfect idea of statecraft, but also the scientific and technological concepts that make for universal prosperity.[25]

Thus, Dayananda incorporated into his own conception many facets of the tradition, and carefully omitted others. The basic elements have deep roots in the tradition. However, there are three important aspects to his theory of the Golden Age which *as such* seem to be absent in the traditional accounts, namely:

1. the Swami's stress on the historicity and the non-mythical character of the Golden Age;
2. his contention that it was an age of scientific and technological eminence;
3. his idea that the four Vedas contain a complete blueprint for the reconstruction of the Golden Age.

These three aspects need closer investigation to determine their exact origin. Historicity linked with a concern for chronology was definitely a 'modern' idea prevalent in nineteenth-century India. The first concept of a Vedic Golden Age was constructed by the early British orientalists in the subcontinent, such as John Zephaniah Holwell, Alexander Dow, Nathaniel Brassey Halhed, Charles Wilkins,

Sir William Jones, and Colebrooke. Their concern for chronology was the result of contemporary European thought. When European thinkers were faced with the discovery of the ancient religious cultures of China and India, the question of the superiority of Christianity was hotly debated. If these great Eastern religious contained the basic religious and ethical doctrines of Christianity, and yet antedated Moses, how could the claims of Christianity be upheld? Chronology and historicity were at the very centre of the debate, and that concern communicated itself to the budding new intelligentsia of the subcontinent, firstly in Bengal.[26]

Before Dayananda went to Calcutta in 1872, he lived completely within traditional society and was not concerned with comparing the claims of various religions. The Bengali intelligentsia, who had been involved in controversy with Christianity since the time of Rammohun Roy brought that question to the Swami's attention. One such occasion deserves special mention. Rajnarayan Bose, leader of the Adi Brahmo Samaj, was a pioneer of the movement of Hindu nationalism reacting against the influential attitudes of Utilitarians and Evangelicals for whom all history was a dark age and salvation was only to be found in the new dogma of progress, which meant Westernization. He read to the Swami his lecture on 'The Superiority of Hinduism'. There he argued that for twelve reasons Hinduism was in every way superior to all other religions. One of these reasons is of particular interest: whereas other religions such as Christianity, Islam, and Buddhism derived from a relatively recent historical figure, Hinduism pre-dated them all in its hoary antiquity.[27] We can date Dayananda's preoccupation with the superiority of Vedic religion from his stay in Calcutta. The chronological argument always loomed large among his proofs.

The influence of modern thought via the Bengali intelligentsia is incontestable. Yet even in this case one should not overlook the part played by traditional elements, because chronology and historicity were part of their concern in two ways. The texts declared that one of the characteristics of the *kali* age was the advent of Shudra and Mleccha kings and they often attempted to incorporate the dynastic tables of Aryan kings into the scheme of the *yugas*.[28] Part of the stress on historical authenticity was Dayananda's total refusal of myth and miracle. One may wonder if this 'urge to demythologize' was a result of Western rationalist influence. This is not so. The Swami's rationalism clearly antedated his contact with Western ideas, and was firmly rooted in the rationalistic stream of Hindu philosophy, in particular of Samkhya and Nyaya.

The second 'modern' element in Dayananda's reconstruction of the Golden Age was that he ascribed to it scientific and technological superiority. Here again we may refer to Rajnarayan Bose's lecture, which gave as another reason for the superiority of Hinduism the fact that it contained within its scope the fulness of human knowledge, including the political and economic sciences. Hinduism was 'like an ocean containing gems without number'.[29] The germ of the idea was there. Dayananda filled it out by including science and technology.[30] For this one can discern two contributing factors. The first was his admiration for technological and scientific advance and his conviction that they were an essential part of the progress and welfare of the nation. Proof of this lies in his own desire to found a technological institute with machines and even teachers from Germany.[31] The second was his knowledge of ancient texts on astronomy, mathematics, and medical science, and of the epic texts referring to flying machines and magical science-fiction weaponry. All these elements somehow combined in his affirmation that the Vedas contained indications of considerable scientific and technological sophistication.

The third conception of Dayananda which, in our view, is alien to the tradition is that the four Vedas constitute a definitive corpus of revelation given once and for all time, of the total wisdom of God, and that they, therefore, present the blueprint of the Golden Age. No doubt tradition extolled the Vedas as the revealed supreme religious authority, but throughout the ages Hinduism has accepted new revelations, through *avatars* and through new books, such as the Puranas, the Tantras, and the hymns of the saints, which complemented and even superseded Vedic revelation. This new concept of the Swami certainly did not come to him via the Bengali intelligentsia, who totally rejected his claims for the Vedas.[32] However, after his visit to Calcutta, Dayananda was frequently in contact with Christian missionaries, many of whom were fundamentalist in their approach to the Bible. To them Christianity was *par excellence* the religion of the book, which once and for ever had been handed by God to mankind for its salvation. Dayananda transferred this idea to the four Vedas, making them into a definitive corpus of total revelation, recipe for all mankind's ills, be they religious, social, political, economic, or scientific.

Dayananda's concept of the Golden Age was, therefore, far from simplistic, and certainly not caused simply by the process of a clash between traditional and modern ideas or by superficial borrowing. The basic idea of a Golden Age was available in the tradition, and was generally presented as a fatalistic, necessary episode in a preordained rhythm of eternal return on a vast time-scale. However, the *Mahabharata* provided the idea of a Golden Age achieved by man in the short term outside the cycle of necessity, in other words it contained the idea of man-made progress. No doubt Dayananda inherited from modern thought his concern for chronology and historicity. But the process was intricate, and greatly influenced by two other elements. First of all, chronological tables were already part of the traditional lore and of the *yuga* theory itself; these data were used by the Swami as historical proof. Secondly, his concern for demythologization was not a modern borrowing, but had firm roots in the uncompromising rationalism of Nyaya and Samkhya.

The idea that a perfect age of progress and prosperity would of necessity entail scientific and technological advance certainly was a modern one, as such absent from traditional lore. However, even here the ancient texts, particularly the *Mahabharata*, with their wondrous vehicles and war-machines, gave a fundamentalist the opening he needed. Moreover, there was ample evidence of theoretical sophistication in astronomy, mathematics, geography, and medicine in the ancient literatures.

Dayananda's concept of the Vedas as the definitive deposit of all knowledge was influenced by Christian ideas of revelation. However, in this matter tradition offered the Swami the basic elements to build on. The preexcellence of the Vedas over all Hindu texts was amply affirmed, and generally accepted as a sign of orthodoxy. He took that idea and universalized it in one direction: the Vedas were superior to *all* religious scriptures. In another direction he made it more exclusive by denying the claim of revelation to *any* other Hindu text.

At this stage one may ask a further question. In the elaboration of his idea of the Vedic Golden Age the Swami made many choices. Were they prompted by some basic principles, or was his final system a mere eclectic amalgam of disparate elements? We have no time to elaborate, but our answer is that three fundamental principles came to dominate the Swami's thought and were decisive in his elaboration of the Vedic Golden Age. These principles took many years to mature, and basically they were independent from outside (Western) influences.

The first of these principles was that there existed an original revelation with an authority that took precedence over the whole tradition. The second was the touchstone of rationalism: whatever offended reason (the miraculous, the contradictory, the physically impossible, the morally unsound) had to be rejected. The third principle was that among the wide range of religious practices available within (and without) Hinduism, only moral action as such had religious efficacy. This principle excluded the acceptance of any intrinsic power of *bhakti*, ritual, mystical experience, *mantra*, *prasada* (grace), diet, etc. It could be demonstrated that these three principles were decisive at every turn in the Swami's elaboration of the Vedic Golden Age.[33]

The detailed analysis of Dayananda's total concept of the Golden Age demonstrates in one instance how intricate the process of modernization really was. Only a close investigation into the various facets of the total tradition can help to determine the exact areas of modern influence. The study of the interaction of tradition and modernity must cautiously avoid any simplistic assumptions and generalities about traditional India. Milton Singer was right when he said that in the relationship of tradition and modernity, 'the appearance of each face is illumined by the light reflected from the other'.[34]

NOTES

[This chapter was originally published as: 'Tradition and Modernity: Dayananda Sarasvati's concept of the Vedic Golden Age', *Religious Traditions*, vol. 4, no. 2, 1981, pp. 1-10.]

1. Milton Singer (ed.), *Traditional India: Structure and Change*, Philadelphia, 1958, p. xviii.
2. L.I. and S.H. Rudolph, *The Modernity of Tradition*, Chicago, 1967, p. 10.
3. Cf. P.J. Marshall, *The British Discovery of Hinduism in the Eighteenth Century*, Cambridge, 1970.
4. P.V. Kane, *History of Dharmashastra*, 5 vols., Pune, 1930-62.
5. The Puranas consulted were the following: *Agni*, *Bhagavata*, *Garuda*, *Kurma*, *Linga*, *Matsya*, *Shiva*, *Vayu*, and *Vishnu*.
6. For a clear summary of the classical theory, cf. A.L. Basham, *The Wonder that was India*, New York, 1954, pp. 320-2.
7. For a discussion of these ideas, cf. M. Eliade, *Cosmos and History, The Myth of the Eternal Return*, New York, 1959.
8. P.V. Kane, vol. 4, pp. 885-6.

9. For a long description taken from the *Mahabharata*, Vana Parvan, 188, 30-64, cf. Kane, vol. 3, pp. 892-5.
10. For an extensive treatment of the *Kalivarjyas* cf. Kane, vol. 3, pp. 926-68.
11. Ibid., p. 930.
12. Ibid., pp. 4, 33, 244.
13. Manu, I. 86.
14. *Vishnu Purana*, VI, 2, quoted in Kane, 5, 925.
15. *Shanti Parvan*, 231-2.
16. Ibid., 340, 349.
17. Ibid., 12.70.6-7.
18. Ibid., 12.70.6; 12.92.2; 12.13.
19. Cf. J.T.F. Jordens, *Dayananda Sarasvati, His Life and Ideas*, Delhi, 1967, *passim*.
20. Cf. Ibid., pp. 106-7, 251-2.
21. Cf. Dayananda's *Introduction to the Commentary on the Vedas*, ch. I.
22. Cf. J.T.F. Jordens, *passim*.
23. Cf. Dayananda's *Satyarth Prakash*, 1st edn., Varanasi, 1875, pp. 308-9, 373, 219-20; 2nd edn., Yudhisthir Mimamshak (ed.), Sonepat, 1972, pp. 329-34, 407-12.
24. *Satyarth Prakash*, 2nd edn., pp. 591-2.
25. Cf. J.T.F. Jordens, *passim*.
26. Cf. P.J. Marshall, and also D. Kopf, *British Orientalism and the Bengal Renaissance*, Calcutta, 1969.
27. Rajnarayan Basu, *Hindudharmer Shreshtata*, Calcutta, 1872; for a discussion cf. Jordens, p. 78.
28. Cf., e.g. C.D. Church, 'The Myth of the four Yugas in the Sanskrit Puranas; a diamensional study', *Purana*, vol. XVI, no. 1, January 1974, pp. 15-18.
29. Rajnarayan Basu, ibid.
30. This was developed by the Swami in particular in several chapters of his *Introduction to the Commentary on The Vedas*, and frequently referred to in his voluminous Commentary on the *Rigveda* and the *Yajurveda*.
31. Pandit Bhagavaddatt (ed.), *Rishi Dayananda Sarasvati ke patra aur vijnapan*, 2nd edn., Amritsar, 1955, pp. 250, 261.
32. Cf. Jordens, pp. 279-80, 89-91.
33. Ibid., *passim*, especially ch. 12.
34. Milton Singer, p. xviii.

CHAPTER 6

Dayananda Sarasvati's Eschatological Doctrine

Dayananda Sarasvati's final[1] doctrine of *moksha* was startlingly different from that found in the whole Hindu tradition, and he was well aware of that fact. In the ninth chapter of his *Satyarth Prakash*[2] 'the objector' quoted scripture to support his claim that 'once the *jivas* have attained *moksha* they never again return to the misery of the cycle of life and death', and continued that 'such is the belief of all the world and of all authors'. Dayananda did not deny that he was correct in the latter, but firmly stated that such a doctrine was unacceptable.[3] He supported this affirmation by reference to Vedic texts, and by arguments from reason. In this article we want to explore in detail the latter. The Swami referred to the arguments in many places in his *magnum opus*. He tackled it from various angles and was consciously intent on giving his many elaborations an internal logic that was unassailable. The exploration of his various arguments will result in a complete picture of his extraordinary doctrine of eschatology.

The best starting point of this chapter is the careful definition of *moksha* given by Dayananda in his statement of beliefs at the end of his *Satyarth Prakash*:

> *Moksha* means the following: to be delivered from all suffering, and free from all bonds, to move about at one's will in the all-pervading Lord and his creation, and to return back after a definite time to the world of transmigration having enjoyed the bliss of *moksha*.[4]

The most striking element of this definition is that *moksha* is not eternal. In fact, it is of very long duration and extends over a *mahakalpa*, 100 years of Brahma, one day of which lasts no less than 8,640 million years.[5]

The first series of arguments Dayananda put forward to prove the limited nature of *moksha* has to do with the nature of the spirit of man, the *jiva*:

> First of all the powers of the *jiva*, its bodily instruments and its means are all limited; how then can its result be unlimited? The *jivas* do not possess the limitless power, means and activity for enjoying infinite bliss. Therefore they are unable to enjoy infinite bliss. The result cannot be eternal if the means to achieve it are finite.[6]

The basic argument is that the *jiva* is finite. This is then applied in two ways: the *jiva's* power of action is limited, and, therefore, cannot achieve with such limited means an unlimited result; secondly, for the same reason the *jiva* could actually not experience unlimited bliss. There are a number of ramifications to this argument, which will be unravelled as the chapter proceeds.

The question of the activity of the *jiva* is at the core of Dayananda's conception. 'The relation between the *jiva* and activity is one of inseparable inherence.'[7] 'Since this connection with activity is from eternity, the *jiva* can never be released from it.'[8] The power of action was one that was also inherent in the Lord: 'He possesses infinite power, infinite knowledge, and infinite activity. In Him they are natural and innate. If He were without activity, he could not cause the creation, continuation and dissolution of the universe. Therefore, as he is all-pervading consciousness, he also possesses activity.'[9] Since in God and the *jiva* action is innate, it is also eternal. However, there are two ways in which 'eternal' may be understood. God and the soul are both eternal by nature, they are eternal substances. But God's creative activity is eternal *pravah se*, by flow, by rhythm: creation and dissolution follow each other in endless alternation.[10] Although any particular creation has a beginning and an end, the cycle creation-dissolution is an eternal process. 'The *jiva's* activity also is eternal *pravah rup se*, by rhythm.'[11] This rhythm refers to the alternation of bondage and liberation: 'bondage and liberation are essentially correlated, and one always necessarily evokes the other';[12] they follow each other in endless succession.

Dayananda's basic argument (since man's power is limited, his action cannot have an infinite result, and, therefore, *moksha* must be limited) implies that *moksha* is a result of man's actions. What kind of actions does he specifically refer to? He lists them clearly at the end of his *Satyarth Prakash*:

The means to achieve *moksha* are: the worship of God, i.e. the practice of yoga, the performance of acts according to *dharma*, the acquisition of knowledge through the practice of *brahmacharya*, the interaction with wise and learned men, the pursuit of truth, purity of thought, the active striving for the four aims of his life, etc.[13]

The common denominator of this list is that all items referred to describe some kind of moral action. This is confirmed by the longer answer in chapter 9 to the question 'What are the means for obtaining salvation?' The summary answer is *dharmacharan*, the practice of *dharma*, and various activities are listed in detail.[14]

This exclusive stress on moral action alone as the means for attaining *moksha* distinguishes Dayananda's doctrine from other theologies, a fact of which he was clearly aware. In this context he frequently attacked the doctrines of those he called the Neo-Vedantins. The objector put the Vedantic doctrine as follows:

The *jiva* is *brahman*. Hence it follows that in reality it is never veiled, it never is born; it is not really in bondage, it does not use means for its emancipation, does not desire to be liberated, and in fact is never freed. Because, how can there be *moksha* if in final instance it was never in bondage?[15]

Dayananda immediately refuted the very core of that doctrine: that the spirit of man is a pure witness, identical with *brahman*, and that its involvement in the world of bondage and liberation is only an illusion that can be removed simply by the realization that *atman* and *brahman* are identical. The main thrust of the Swami's attack is that the *jiva* is not identical with the absolute, and that it is a doer of deeds. The realization of the identity of *atman* and *brahman* cannot achieve any result, because it is itself only an illusion. 'The *jiva* is not just a witness of deeds, but a doer and enjoyer. Only the Lord is a pure witness of its deeds. The *jiva* is an active agent, it is completely immersed in action.'[16]

Whereas the Neo-Vedantins believed that the identity of *atman* and *brahman* was eternal, the Jains believed, according to Dayananda, that the *jiva* could gradually free itself completely from the contamination of matter and of *karma* and thus attain divinity the same way their Tirthankaras did. Dayananda's retort is simple: 'What is limited in space and in knowledge can never become all-pervading and omniscient. The *jiva's* nature is to be limited in space, in attributes and in activity.'[17] It is in the context of Jainism that Dayananda gives particular stress to his doctrine that even in *moksha* the *jiva* remains active, and, therefore, subject to the consequences of its actions.

> Clothes are soiled by dirt which is removed by washing, and again dirt gets into them. In the same way the *jiva* is affected by the consequences of its actions (of an immoral nature), and it is purified by conduct (of a moral kind). If you believe that the *jiva* becomes contaminated when the causes of contamination are in operation, then you must also accept for certain that a liberated soul may become bound again just like a bound soul may become liberated. Because just like certain causes may cause contamination to be removed, in the same way certain causes will make the contamination take effect again. Therefore, believe that the *jiva* has been eternally subject to bondage and liberation in a rhythmic fashion: neither condition is by itself eternal.[18]

The 'certain causes' that effect both bondage and liberation are the actions (moral or immoral) of man; since man's activity is inherent in his nature, and persists even in *moksha*, the causes of bondage remain present and effective.

The enormous stress Dayananda puts on the doctrine that man's moral action is the only means for obtaining *moksha*, raises the question how the Lord is involved in the process of liberation. As we have seen, activity belongs to God's nature. When on that subject, Dayananda mostly refers to God's activity in the creation, sustenance, and dissolution of the universe and all it holds. He refers to two more activities of God, and these have to do with the process of emancipation. He is the dispenser of the Vedas and the continuous source of justice. Dayananda considered the revelation of the Vedas as necessary for the process of emancipation, because by his own powers man was not able to rise to that knowledge: 'During the period of dissolution the *jivas* became devoid of knowledge, unlike God.'[19] They need revelation, which is bestowed on them by God *kripa karke*, 'out of kindness'.[20] However, nowhere is it suggested that the knowledge of the Vedas by itself causes emancipation; only action illumined by that necessary knowledge, actively acquired, can produce *moksha*.

God is actively involved in the process of emancipation in yet another way, by administering His law of justice. Whatever action man performs must of necessity find its fruit, and the highest fruit of man's activity is the reward of *moksha*. Dayananda fiercely denounced the Jain doctrine that the law of *karma* works autonomously and does not require the existence of the Lord. 'Just as intoxication naturally arises from taking alcohol, so does the fruit of the deed arise from the action. There is no need for another power to cause the effect.'[21] Dayananda answered:

> There is need for a third, namely the Lord, to effect the combination of actions with their results. Inert substances cannot arrange combinations that are according to a strict law. *Jivas* have limited knowledge and cannot by themselves arrange the fruits of their deeds. Thus it is demonstrated that the system of reward and punishment according to deeds cannot operate without the laws of nature established by God Himself.[22]

That law of retribution established and administered by God allows no exceptions. God established the law and consistently operates within it; that is why the very concept of 'forgiveness of sins' was anathema to the Swami. In the thirteenth chapter of his *Satyarth Prakash* he repeatedly branded the Christian doctrine of forgiveness of sin as contradictory to God's infinite justice, and as an incentive for yet more immorality. This concept of divine justice was also used as an argument against the eternity of *moksha*: 'If the Lord bestowed an infinite reward for finite actions, then His justice would be destroyed.'[23] This role of God as dispenser of justice is completely circumscribed by the inexorable law of retribution which he has established and administers: in final instance the just reward will be according to man's moral action only.

Dayananda's concise argument for the limits of *moksha* contained another facet we will now concentrate upon: 'The *jivas* do not possess the limitless power, means and activity for enjoying infinite bliss.'[24] He makes it quite clear that 'even in *moksha* the *jiva*, though purified, remains by nature limited in knowledge, attributes, and activity; it can never become equal to the Lord'.[25] Once it is established that *moksha* does not change the limited nature of the *jiva*, one may ask, 'How does the *jiva* enjoy the bliss of emancipation?'[26] Dayananda's answer is that all its powers remain as before, except that it sheds the physical body.[27] Later on he explains in detail the 'four bodies' that surround the *jiva* like sheaths. The gross physical body is the outermost sheath, composed of matter in its gross form, which disintegrates into its components at the time of death.

The next sheath is the 'subtle body' (*sukshma-sharira*), which is composed of 'subtle matter', constituting the inner senses, and it also contains the natural attributes of the *jiva*. The third sheath is the *karma-sharira*, the causal body, which 'consists of *prakriti*, all-pervading and the same for all the *jivas*'.[28] Dayananda here obviously used the Samkhya categories, wherein the cosmic principles of *buddhi* (mind), *ahamkara* (individuation), and *manas* (sense-coordination) are conceived as universal principles which emerge from the dormant *prakriti* before concrete beings evolve. The two latter sheaths are clearly all still part of the *prakriti* aspect of the universe, and as such represent the natural powers of the *jiva*, carriers of its physical, sensory and intellectual potential.

The *turiya* body, the fourth, is the one 'through which the *jivas* are absorbed in the all-blissful Lord by the trance of *samadhi*. The great power of this pure body, developed by the practice of *samadhi*, is of great help in the enjoyment of *moksha*'.[29] This power or body of trance is again a natural power, which man can refine and develop through the practice of yogic contemplation. Dayananda consistently refused to accept that *moksha* in any way added anything to the natural power of man, or transformed him into a supernatural being. When considering the highest level of *moksha* proposed by the Puranas, namely *sayujya*, 'intimate union with God', he stated, 'that is self-evident; since the *jivas* are inhabited by the all-pervading Lord, they are united with Him'.[30] Elsewhere he stressed that 'Just as one cannot acquire the advantages of knowledge without study, similarly one cannot contemplate the Lord without the practice of yoga and the development of knowledge';[31] and, 'The *jiva* that *makes* its qualities, deeds and nature similar to God's, that *jiva* can speak of its unity and harmony with the Lord.'[32] Dayananda made it thus crystal clear that in his opinion *moksha* did not in any way change the natural powers or nature of the *jiva*. The only differences between the *jiva* in the state of emancipation and in its bondage is that the *jiva* is free from its gross body, and that its purification allows full expansion of its knowledge and bliss.

Dayananda's continuous insistence on the finiteness of the *jiva* and its powers even in *moksha* led him to use an argument that puts the finite nature of the *jiva* in stark perspective. The following is yet another argument for the finiteness of *moksha*:

> Without experiencing misery there can be no experience of joy; just as if there were no bitter flavour how could there be sweetness, and if there were no sweetness what then would one call bitterness. It is by the very opposition of tastes that the experience of both arises. The man who goes on eating and drinking sweet things only, he cannot have as much pleasure as the one who enjoys all kinds of tastes.[33]

In other words, the play of opposites, night-day, hatred-love, misery-joy, is part and parcel of the very nature of *prakriti*; since the *jiva* in the state of *moksha* remains limited and *prakritic*, it remains also subject to that play of opposites. The joy of the liberated soul cannot be perfect, it needs the opposite simply to exist, because however purified it may be, its intimate connection with *prakritic* forces makes it susceptible to the play of the *gunas*.

This brings us to the question what exactly does the bliss of *moksha* consist of? Dayananda gave the following description:

> The liberated *jiva* roams about at will in the boundless all-pervading Lord, contemplates the whole universe with pure knowledge, meets other liberated *jivas*. Aware of all the laws of nature in their orderly operation, he roams about in all worlds visible and invisible. Whatever objects it comes across, it contemplates. The more its knowledge grows, the greater its bliss.[34]

The most striking aspect of this description is the cosmic nature of the experience of *moksha*. Liberated from the confines of the gross body, the *jiva* acquires the freedom to use its subtle bodies to the fullest extent, and finds great pleasure in exploring the universe. It is, however, not all-pervading like the Lord, but moves around at will: there is movement and change. There is also communication with the other emancipated *jivas*. Naturally, as we mentioned earlier, *moksha* also entails the contemplation of the Lord.

This cosmic aspect of *moksha* also transpires from other arguments proposed by the Swami: 'If no *jiva* did return to the world from *moksha*, then this world would become devoid of them.'[35] This problem of the gradual emptying of the world cannot be avoided in a system where a limited number of souls wander through an endless rhythm of creations, from which some keep escaping into *moksha*. The Jains were aware of the problem and had devised their own complex solution of continuous supply.[36] In fact, the Ajivikas had solved the problem by their construct of *mandala-moksha*, which implied a return of liberated souls into the world after *moksha*.[37] Dayananda refused to accept the objector's solution of a regular new creation of *jivas* by God because of his fundamental principle that 'what has a beginning must also have an end', which would mean that the *jivas* became non-eternal.[38] At this stage Dayananda added another argument as follows: 'In the place of *moksha* there will be excessive hustle and bustle because there will be a lot of arrivals but no departures, and there will be no limit to the population growth.'[39] This is a strange argument, but it has a rough logic to it; if *moksha* is a cosmic state, and the emancipated *jivas* are endowed with (even subtle) bodies, and move about in a limited cosmos, eventually problems of space must emerge. A similar logic pertains to the argument that eternal *moksha* would eventually depopulate the world. But both arguments reinforce Dayananda's cosmic approach.

This analysis of Dayananda's eschatology has brought into focus some of his most basic convictions. In his own conception of *moksha* he is constantly intent on avoiding two extremes which he found both in Hinduism and in other religions. On the one hand there was the divinization of man, which he found mainly in the Vedanta and in Jainism. To Dayananda pure monotheism was crucially important and any identification of man and God had to be strictly denied. On the other hand, he rejected those beliefs, Puranic, Christian, and Islamic, which to him seemed to proclaim a limited physical heavenly paradise providing the sinful pleasures of the flesh. He thought this conception to be beyond contempt.[40]

His effort in avoiding these two extremes clarifies his own concept of 'cosmic' *moksha*. Only the continuing cosmic nature of man could guarantee that he would not become divinized, or lose himself in the absolute. The cosmic dimension of his being was the essential limiting factor of his nature. However, cosmic *moksha* should not degenerate into an earthly paradise of physical pleasures. At the time of emancipation man sheds his physical body, and through his subtle body he is able to gain the freedom of the whole cosmos and enjoy it fully through his spiritual powers, at the same time enjoying the intimate knowledge of God. The concept of the essential limitation of man through his cosmic nature was so important to the Swami that he accepted what he saw as its inevitable logical consequence, the limited duration of *moksha* itself, even when it meant contradicting the universal doctrine of Hinduism.

The Swami's eschatological doctrine brings into the limelight another of his most basic convictions. He tirelessly denounced what he saw in other religions as short-cuts to salvation. The faith of Christians and their doctrine of the forgiveness of sins, intuitive realization of the identity of *brahman* and *atman* of the Vedantins, the various *bhakti* practices of the Vaishnavites, were all presented as sure and easy paths to salvation. This was anathema to Dayananda. To him there was only one type of action which could earn that highest fruit of *moksha*: the moral action of man, *dharmachar*, governed by reason and duly assessed by the law of divine justice and retribution. Since to the Swami human action is finite, it could not earn infinite *moksha*: emancipation must needs be temporary, and man's movement from bondage to emancipation and back to bondage must be eternally rhythmical.

Thus Dayananda's eschatological doctrine presents an internally logical structure, and emphasizes his concept of pure monotheism, and also his own view of the essential nobility of man as a being fundamentally involved in the cosmos and capable of achieving the highest goal by dint of moral action.

NOTES

1. For the development of Dayananda's concept of *moksha*, see ch. 4.
2. All references are from the best edition of the *Satyarth Prakash*, Y. Mimamshak (ed.), Sonepat, 1972. All translations are by the author. We will simply quote *S.P.*, p. x.
3. *S.P.*, pp. 356-7.
4. Ibid., p. 923.
5. Ibid., p. 356.
6. Ibid., p. 357.
7. Ibid., p. 659.
8. Ibid., p. 661.
9. Ibid., p. 273.
10. Ibid., p. 330.
11. Ibid., p. 581.
12. Ibid., p. 646.
13. Ibid., p. 623.
14. Ibid., p. 359.
15. Ibid., p. 354.
16. Ibid., p. 346.
17. Ibid., p. 639.
18. Ibid., p. 659.
19. Ibid., p. 299.
20. Ibid., p. 302.
21. Ibid., p. 660.
22. Ibid., p. 661.
23. Ibid., p. 357.
24. Ibid.
25. Ibid., p. 358.
26. Ibid., p. 350.
27. Ibid., p. 351.
28. Ibid., p. 360.

29. Ibid.
30. Ibid., p. 365.
31. Ibid., p. 639.
32. Ibid., p. 283.
33. Ibid., p. 357.
34. Ibid., p. 372.
35. Ibid., p. 357.
36. Cf. S. Radhakrishnan, *Indian Philosophy*, vol. I, New York, 1958, p. 322.
37. The doctrine of the Ajivikas was forgotten for ten centuries, and Dayananda could not have been aware of it. For that doctrine cf. A.L. Basham, *History and Doctrines of the Ajivikas*, London, 1951, p. 259.
38. *S.P.*, p. 357.
39. Ibid.
40. Cf. *S.P.*, chs. 11, 12 and 14, *passim*.

CHAPTER 7

Dayananda Sarasvati's Interpretation of Christianity

IN THE THIRD CHAPTER Dayananda's frequent meetings with missionaries were described and discussed. In this chapter we focus specifically on the Swami's understanding of Christianity, of its doctrines and its claims. Firstly we try to get some idea of the sources of Dayananda's knowledge of Christianity and of the slant they gave to his understanding. In the second part we deal with the Swami's conception of the Bible as scripture, and consider his method of interpretation. In the third part we closely consider those Christian doctrines which Dayananda frequently returned to: the Christian conception of God and His mode of creation; the question of sin and its forgiveness; the view of Christ as redeemer and divine incarnation; the doctrine of salvation by faith in Christ.

The most important published sources for Dayananda's ideas are the following. His conversations with missionaries are reported in the two voluminous biographies of Lekhram[1] and Ghasiram,[2] and in some missionary reports. Another important source is found in the reports of some public disputations, *shastrarths*, conducted between the Swami and missionaries.[3] In March 1977, a three-cornered disputation took place at the Chandapur Mela between the Swami, the famous Maulana Muhammad Qasim Nanawtawi, and the Reverends T.J. Scott and E.W. Parker. In November 1878, a disputation took place in Ajmer with the Reverends Grey and Husband, and in August 1879 the Swami had a three-day discussion at Bareilly with Reverend T.J. Scott. Reports of those three *shastrarths* have been published in the volume *Dayananda-Shastrarth-Samgraha*. The last important source is chapter 13 of the second edition of

Dayananda's main work, the *Satyarth Prakash*, which was completed shortly before his death.[4]

Dayananda came first to know about Christianity through his conversations with missionaries. A certain amount of information about what they told him is available in two sources: the reports of those conversations in the basic biographies of the Swami, and the occasional reports of missionaries themselves. The very first of these meetings, that with the Reverend John Robson in Ajmer in 1866, clearly established a theme that would often recur. Dayananda asked Robson what the Christian doctrine of salvation was, and the following is the gist of the answer. All men are sinners, and Christ has saved men from their sins through his deeds and his teaching, but primarily by his resurrection from the dead.[5] This basic theme was further developed and reinforced in the Swami's conversations with the Reverend T.J. Scott of the Methodist Episcopal Church of North America, whom he met for the first time in November 1868 on the banks of the Ganga not far from Badaun.[6]

The Reverend Scott probably had the most decisive influence on Dayananda's idea of Christianity. He was the first with whom he had long conversations and they talked on four consecutive days on that first occasion. This meeting established a cordial relationship between the two: Scott referred to Dayananda at that time as 'my friend the fakir'. One should remember that at this stage of his career the Swami roamed along the banks of the Ganga clad only in a loincloth. In 1877 and 1878 they participated in public disputations to which detailed reference will be made. In contrast with some other debates with missionaries, these were held in an atmosphere of cordiality and mutual respect. When in 1878 Dayananda spent sometime in Bareilly, Scott's headquarters at that time, the missionary used to attend all his lectures. One day he was absent, and the Swami remarked, 'My friend Scott did not come today.' He was told that it was Sunday and that his friend was conducting a service. Thereupon Dayananda walked to the church with a following, and was invited by Scott to address the congregation.[7] It is quite clear that they liked and respected each other, and had a long association. Reverend Scott's Christian beliefs must have had considerable influence on the Swami's understanding of Christianity.

Scott explained the essence of his belief at their first meetings. The Swami had told Scott his concept of salvation, and how it was to be effected 'by the acquisition of knowledge and the infliction of punishment'.[8] Scott then explained the Christian view, 'that there is no power in human wisdom and learning and legislation to purify the depraved soul. I tried to make plain the fact that, when "the world by wisdom knew not God, it pleased God by the foolishness of preaching to save them that believe" in Christ.'[9]

This doctrine that man is fundamentally sinful and that his sinfulness cannot be removed by himself but only by faith in Christ, was repeatedly communicated to Dayananda by other missionaries, such as the Reverends Anlan, Lalbehari De, J.J. Lucas, and E.W. Parker.[10] In fact, Dayananda refers to Christians as 'those who believe that sin can be removed by faith in Jesus'.[11] In his famous parable about a hundred preachers of different religions, he makes the Christian preacher answer the question, 'What is your *dharma*?', as follows: 'All men are sinners, and they cannot be freed from their sins through their own power. Salvation cannot be attained without becoming purified by faith in Jesus Christ. Christ has revealed his mercy by offering up his own life for the sake of the atonement of the sins of all men.'[12]

It is not surprising that this Wesleyan doctrine of salvation was accepted by Dayananda as the summation of Christianity, because it was in fact the dominant belief of the Protestant missionaries of north India at that time, who were mostly 'evangelicals'.

> During the third quarter of the century, missionaries belonging to these various societies considered themselves 'evangelicals'. The term 'evangelical' was generally used to describe those Protestants (Anglicans, Non-conformists and others) who believed that the essential part of the Gospel consisted in salvation by faith through the atoning death of Christ and who denied that either good works or the sacraments had any saving efficacy.[13]

To Dayananda that was the essence of Christian doctrine. He does not seem to have met or significantly interacted with either Roman Catholic or High Church Anglican missionaries, who would have presented a different approach. This is not surprising because the Catholic effort in north India was minimal at that time,[14] and the activities of High Church Anglicans was also small in comparison with that of other Protestants. It is understandable, therefore, that Dayananda was not aware of the variety among Christians even in fundamental doctrines of salvation. Moreover, whatever differences there existed between various groups, Indian Christians did see themselves as belonging to a single community, and were perceived by outsiders as such.[15]

The second important topic of Dayananda's discussions with missionaries was the Bible. This is to be expected, because on both sides the issue of a unique and universally valid revelation was crucial. Dayananda's central conviction that only the four Samhitas constituted true revelation could not become a convincing argument without disproving a similar claim by Christians about the Bible. On the other side, the 'evangelical' missionaries he communicated with, 'usually believed in the infallibility and overriding importance of the Scriptures'.[16] Webster describes the theology of most missions in the Punjab and the U.P. as very uniformly that of the Princeton school, based on the inerrancy of Scripture. The proof of the latter was to be found in the miracles and fulfilled prophecies of the Bible. This proof was supported by internal evidence: the Bible presented a logically consistent system of truth and morality, and the perfection of the character of Christ was equally convincing.[17] The missionaries with whom Dayananda conversed held such beliefs. Reverend Scott, for example, said in the Bareilly disputation about the Bible, 'That is the very best of books, which proves it comes from God. Whatever is written there is full of wisdom, in accordance with reason, and subject to proof.'[18] Considering such convictions on the part of the missionaries about the Bible, and on Dayananda's part about the Vedas, it was inevitable that much of their conversations would turn to that issue. And in view of the absoluteness of their respective claims, it is not surprising that exchanges about scripture tended to become heated. What Webster says about the approach of the missionaries in such discussions could be said to be equally true of Dayananda, that 'they tended to juxtapose "my scriptures" and "your scriptures", and then to defend the truth of the former and expose the falsity of the latter in an argumentative, scholastic way'.[19]

The other main source of information about Christianity for Dayananda was the text of the Bible itself. The Reverend Scott gave the Swami a copy of the Gospels at the time of their first meeting in 1868,[20] and in 1869 the Reverend Rudolf Hoernle commented, 'He has read the Gospels, though I do not think very carefully. I had some conversation with him about it. But at present his mind is too much occupied with his own plans of reformation to give any serious thought to the investigation of the claims of another religion.'[21] It has been shown in chapter 2 how his subsequent visit to Calcutta changed his attitude, and we know that he wrote a chapter on Christianity for his first *Satyarth Prakash* in 1874, though this was not included in the publication.[22] So far this manuscript has not become available, but we may presume that by that stage Dayananda would have read the Bible more carefully. He wrote in his introduction to the thirteenth chapter on Christianity of the second edition, 'Many translations have been made of this book by eminent padres of that faith. I have consulted among these translations in Hindi and Sanskrit.'[23]

By that time a number of such translations had become available. Carey's full translation of the Bible into both Hindi and Sanskrit had been completely published by 1819. Dr Wenger revised Carey's Sanskrit translation of the Old Testament, and published it in 1876. There were more Hindi translations on the market: one by Bowley of the Church Missionary Society, and another by Parsons, Holcomb and Owen, published in 1868. The texts presented by Dayananda in his second *Satyarth Prakash* are in a rather Sanskritic Hindi. They are probably taken from one of the above editions, but so far we have not been able to identify it.[24]

One wonders if the Theosophists did in any way influence Dayananda's view of Christianity. In February 1878 Colonel Olcott wrote a letter to Dayananda from the United States wherein he stated that, 'Finding in Christianity nothing that satisfied their reason or intuition . . . they turned to the East for light.'[25] This statement delighted Dayananda, who was at that time in the Punjab, but the actual meeting with Colonel Olcott and Madame Blavatsky did not take place until May 1879 at Saharanpur, whence they proceeded to Meerut to spend five days together. They probably did exchange views on Christianity, but this does not appear to have been an important topic of conversation. Soon afterwards organizational quarrels arose, followed by challenges by Dayananda of the Theosophists' belief in one God, which eventually led in 1882 to the Swami's public denunciation of the Theosophists in Bombay. There is no clear evidence that they influenced the Swami's conception of Christianity except by reinforcing his firm belief in its falsity.[26]

Dayananda interpreted the doctrine of those who informed him correctly when he stated that Christians considered the Bible 'as the root cause of their faith'.[27] Within that context he was right when he wrote at the very beginning of his chapter on Christianity that the crucial question to be asked about the validity of Christianity was the following: 'Is their Bible the work of God, or is it not?'.[28] At various times he himself laid down the criteria by which it could be decided whether a particular scripture was indeed God's work. His criteria are fundamentally internal ones; it is the very contents of the work that should reveal and prove its authorship. A work of divine origin will firstly describe the nature of God, His creation, and the human spirit in the proper way, without error. Secondly, it should not contain any statement that contradicts reason and scientific knowledge, or that offends moral standards. Thirdly, it should not be narrowly limited, but it should comprehensively treat the basic principles of all branches of human knowledge. Finally, it should be universal and not manifest any bias; this meant that the work should not be caught up in the web of history, limited to a particular place, time, or people, nor should it be written in a particular regional language. Dayananda held that all these criteria were perfectly fulfilled in the Vedas.[29]

The Swami's criticism of the Bible is totally intent on demonstrating that that work continuously offends those criteria, and that consequently, 'the Bible was not written by God'. The latter expression runs like a constant refrain through his chapter on Christianity. To reinforce that refutation he also asserted that it was a book 'written by men', even by men 'without any wisdom', in fact by nothing more than 'barbarian' hill-dwellers.[30] His specific criticism mostly concentrated on showing that the God presented in the Bible was totally devoid of the essential qualities of the divine nature. He was not omnipresent as he kept moving from place to place, and seemed to live on a mountain.[31] Far from being omniscient, his knowledge appeared to be extremely limited and often crude, and he in fact was often presented as committing errors. Instead of exhibiting the quality of mercy, he proved himself a very cruel tyrant.[32] In many ways he was subject to the same weaknesses as man: suffering, remorse, anger and envy. He even appeared to commit grievous sins by performing acts involving injustice, deceit, lies, and even idol-worship. To call him a worker of miracles was absurd and against the laws of nature. In fact, he was a man with a body: 'he was a cunning forest-dweller, who took residence on top of a mountain and gave himself the title of God'.[33]

This type of criticism constituted a deliberate frontal attack on one of the principal missionary contentions that the Bible presented a consistent system of truth and morality. Their other important argument for the divine origin of the Bible was the fact of the many miracles. Reverend Nobel reiterated this clearly in the Chandapur disputation: 'Christ has called himself God, and has performed a number of miracles. Therefore there can be no doubt whatsoever about his divinity.'[34] Dayananda often referred to the miracles related in both the Old and New Testaments, and simply dismissed them without further considerations as 'impossible' things that contradicted the very nature of reality and offended reason.[35] In fact, he declared that they were as absurd and even worse that the many nonsensical stories that abound in the Puranas.[36] Anything that was presented as miraculous was immediately and simply rejected as an utter impossibility. The resurrection of Christ was to the Christians the supreme miracle and the greatest proof of his divinity. The following is Dayananda's commentary upon the resurrection account in Matthew, chapter 28:

> This too cannot be believed because it is against the laws of nature and against reason. First there are messengers with God, then they are sent hither and thither and they came down from heaven. Have they not made God similar to a Tahsildar or a Collector? Did Christ rise from death and go to heaven with the same body [he possessed before death]? Since the woman grasped his legs when greeting him, one presumes it must have been that same body. Why then did it not decompose in those three days? And to declare himself all-powerful by his own words, that was just a boast. It was impossible that he met his disciples and spoke to them. If these things had been true, why then wouldn't anybody nowadays rise from the dead? And why would they not also go to heaven with the same body?[37]

Dayananda's method of biblical interpretation cannot be described otherwise than very crude and superficial in its simplistic literalness. As such it stands in contrast with the 'rules of interpretation' which he suggested to the reader in his introduction to his own *Satyarth Prakash.* The reader is told that he will only be able to understand the text properly if he keeps certain guidelines in mind. He should remain aware of the intention of the author and of the larger context of a particular passage. He should respect the meaning the author intends to convey, and always give preference to that meaning which lends rationality to the text.[38] These are excellent rules for fair interpretation, but Dayananda does not seem to have followed them in his interpretation of the Bible. However, in all fairness it is necessary to add that he did not stick to these rules either in his interpretation of Hindu books such as the Puranas.

Another important consideration in judging Dayananda's commentary is the fact that at that time many missionaries treated the Hindu scriptures with the same superficial literalness as he treated the Bible. The latter is not surprising since the dominant attitude of those missionaries towards Hinduism was one of complete condemnation: Hinduism was seen as part of the corrupt world of 'heathenism', it was 'a false religion, the work of the prince of this world, not of God'.[39] Works such as J. Mitchell's *Letters to Indian Youth* criticized the Hindu scriptures in the same manner as Dayananda criticized the Bible. He wrote that they were full of internal contradictions and contained gross scientific errors. Their teachings offended the tenets of rational religion, and they promoted viciously immoral institutions; they were full of absurd miracles and did not have a universal message, as they were only directed towards Hindus.[40] In an important way Dayananda forced the missionaries to focus their criticism on the Vedas; his own criticism of the 'immoralities' and 'absurdities' of the Puranas and of the sinfulness of some Hindu social and ritual customs was as strident as theirs. His basic argument was that this form of corrupt Hinduism was a deviation from the primeval perfection of the Vedic *dharma*.

Dayananda's criticism of the Bible was given a special impetus by his realization that it was to a major extent their acceptance of the Bible as one of several divine revelations that prevented modern Hindus such as the Brahmos from accepting the exclusive nature of Vedic revelation. He had met that attitude first in Calcutta in his contact with Keshub Chandra Sen and his followers.[41] This attitude was also present among the social reformers of Bombay, where texts of the Bible were often read in Prarthana Samaj meetings.[42] A Punjabi Brahmo referred to the same in the Punjab when he wrote that the Aryas turned against the Brahmos because 'they consider that the Brahmo Samaj has denationalized itself by giving an attentive ear to the "Voice of Judea" ', and he called it 'vain to suppose that our forefathers monopolized God's truth'.[43] In order to turn such people toward the Vedas, they needed to realize that the Bible was not divinely inspired.

Dayananda's criticism of the Bible was definitely similar in approach to his criticism of Puranic literature. A further question may be asked: does Dayananda's method of Vedic interpretation differ from the former? In order to compare his interpretation of a Vedic text with that of a biblical text it is useful to juxtapose his treatment of the beginning of Genesis with that of a well-known cosmogonic hymn of the *Rigveda*, namely X. 129, sometimes referred to as the 'Hymn of creation'. Both texts deal with the creation of the world and both are cast in what may be broadly called mythical terms, which even exhibit some similarities. The opening verses of Genesis proclaim: 'In the beginning God created heaven and earth. And the earth was without form and void, and darkness hung over the deep; and the spirit of God moved over the waters.'[44] Dayananda criticized this passage along the following lines. How could God create heaven before space was created, since nothing can exist without space. Since God is perfect, His work cannot possibly be 'without form' (*bedaul*). If God is all-pervading, He could not be said to move over the waters. If His spirit (*atma*) was moving over the waters, then His body must have been somewhere else, and a part of his spirit must have been moving over the waters.[45] This interpretation makes no effort at understanding the text. In fact it makes full use of the Hindu terms that may obscure the intent of the original: *akash* is both heaven and space; *atma* is taken as something that is of necessity embodied; and *bedaul* is taken to suggest misshappenness and ugliness. Admittedly, those were probably the very terms found in the Hindu translation available to Dayananda, but he exploited to the utmost the possible misunderstanding they might convey. The third stanza of the Vedic Hymn of Creation translates as follows:

> Darkness there was: at first concealed in darkness, this All was indiscriminated chaos.
> All that existed then was void and formless: by the great power of warmth was born that unit.[46]

The raw data of this stanza could easily have been subjected to the same cavalier treatment the Genesis verses received. In fact, this stanza does not refer at all to a personal God. This is how Dayananda interpreted it:

> The whole world, before creation, was enveloped in darkness, like the darkness of night it was not possible to know it. This whole world was in the form of *akash* (subtle matter) and it was insignificant in the face of the infinite Lord, it was limited and overshadowed. Thereafter the Lord by his power made it from a material cause into an effect.[47]

Dayananda's approach to a Vedic text was obviously enormously different from his approach to the Bible or to any other text. In the case of Vedic texts, he used his grammatical and lexicological skills to extract particular meanings or to refute interpretations of others. This is only a consequence of his strict and undisputable presuppositions about the Vedas: they contained literally the eternal wisdom of God, and, therefore, their every statement was universal truth; they were the repositories of the principles of all human sciences; they proclaimed a pure monotheism and could not possibly contain anything that offended reason or morality. Since any form of myth was, in the Swami's mind, completely irrational, all Vedic sentences needed to be ruthlessly demythologized. Any form of myth in the Bible or the Puranas was a patent sign and proof of their irrationality; any kind of mythical reference in the Vedas, on the contrary, had to be reinterpreted so that it formed a rational statement. An interesting example of the latter procedure is to be found in Dayananda's interpretation of the famous *Purusha Sukta* (*Rigveda* X. 90). The twelfth stanza reads *asya brahmano mukham asit*, which literally translates, 'of that [*Purusha*] the brahmin was the mouth'. *Purusha*, the cosmic giant, was to Dayananda a name for God. Now, God cannot have a mouth. Therefore, writes the Swami, we have to insert a word in the text in order to make it 'rational': *asya* [*shristau*] *brahmano mukham asit.* This allows for the following translation: 'In the creation by God, he who is similar to the mouth, i.e. is foremost, is the brahmin.'[48]

It is quite clear that Dayananda's approach to the Bible was very different from his approach to the Vedas. Later in the nineteenth century some Aryas, educated in English, read arguments against Christianity of the eighteenth century European Enlightenment and of nineteenth century critical historical scholarship, and these readings influenced their criticism of the Bible.[49] However, it was the Swami's legacy of biblical criticism that kept dominating the writings of the Aryas. Webster noted that the Aryas consistently used the following criteria for the evaluation of religion. These criteria were at the very heart of the Swami's own criticism, and illustrate his continuing influence:

> (1) A religion or scripture or revelation must date from the beginning of creation (tradition assigned an earlier date to the Vedas than to the Bible); (2) it must deal with general principles or laws and not with particular groups or personalities (thereby disqualifying all 'historical' religions); (3) it must contain no inconsistencies; and (4) it must conform to nature and reason (an attack on miracles). In each of these cases the Vedas were acclaimed and the Bible found wanting.[50]

Questions dealing with the nature of God's relations to the cosmos and the manner of creation considerably exercised Dayananda's mind.

Between 1875, the publication of the first edition of his *Satyarth Prakash*, and 1883, the drafting of the second edition, he made substantial changes to his own conceptions.[51] Missionaries also tended to bring this question forward because they thought that the Hindu system was rather vulnerable in that area and could not offer anything comparable to the Christian doctrine of *creatio ex nihilo*, creation from nothingness. In fact, this idea seems to have communicated itself to some Brahmo thinkers. Debendranath Tagore's *Brahmo Dharma*, which was read to the Swami during his stay in Calcutta, has little to say about creation, but what it says is significant:

> Before creation no other object besides the Supreme God existed. So He did not create [the universe] with the help of other materials like an artisan. He thought over the act of creation and having pondered over it created all this existing universe. We can fashion something with earth or stone or iron, but that cannot be called creation. Creation is the production of something at one's desire without the help of any other thing. So we have not the power of creating anything. The power of creation belongs only to the One Supreme God. He alone has made this wonderful machinery of the universe by creating all these conscious and unconscious beings by his own innate power and intelligence.[52]

Dayananda's first *Satyarth Prakash* was clearly influenced by such statements, which later on he categorically rejected.[53] In fact, in his second *Satyarth Prakash* the Swami listed among his objections to the Brahmos the following: 'You believe that the world was created without a material cause, and you also believe in the creation of the soul, just like Christians, Muslims and others.'[54] The very fact that he believed that the Brahmos had adopted that creation doctrine from Christianity made it for him an important Christian doctrine that needed to be refuted.

There was a prolonged discussion of the creation question at the famous Chandapur disputation. One of the questions in the agenda to be discussed by the panel of Aryas, Muslims and Christians was: 'From what material, how long ago, and for what purpose did God create the world?' The Reverend Scott made quite clear what he thought of these questions: 'In my opinion these questions are useless, and it is futile to try answering them.' But since he was expected to provide an answer for the Christian side, he proceeded:

> Though we do not know from what material God created the world, we are able to know that he has brought this world from non-existence into existence;

for at the beginning there existed nothing else besides God. He enacted the deed of creation by his very command. Although we are not able to know how long ago he created the world, we do know that the world did have a beginning.[55]

Scott's statement was measured and prudent, accepting the limitation of human knowledge, and he made it clear that he considered the details of the questions to be of relatively minor importance. Dayananda's approach was very different. He propounded at length and with complete confidence the full details of his newly developed doctrine of the three eternal realities, God, cosmos and souls, and of its concomitant creation theory. To him these were crucial questions which a religion had to be able to give extensive answers to. Moreover, he felt that it was also his duty to demonstrate that the Christian doctrine was unacceptable.

His way of proving the latter was by insisting that the very concept of 'creating something *out of* nothing' was absurd. The very expression entailed a logical impossibility of the type called *vadato vyaghat*, which includes expressions such as 'the son of a barren woman'.[56] This logical flaw corresponds to what in scholastic terms would be called *contradictio in terminis*. The missionaries for their part attacked the Swami's theory in what they considered to be its weakest point, namely the recognition by the Swami of the 'eternal nature of the world as *prakriti*, as material cause'. To them this involved putting the world on terms of equality with God. The approach to the problem was on both sides purely logical, formal and scholastic, and exhibited the typical barrenness and futility of such discussions. No doubt the terminological language barrier between the two cultural traditions prevented either side from gaining a real insight into the position of the other.

Questions of salvation or redemption were much closer to the missionaries' hearts than those of creation, and they were repeatedly discussed with the Swami. As we have seen, Dayananda considered the following as the essential ingredients of the Christian doctrine of salvation. All mankind from Adam onwards has been engulfed by sin; this sinfulness cannot be removed by any kind of human effort, only Christ's atonement can remove man's sins; faith in Christ is the only way to redemption. The three most important elements of that doctrine will be successively treated: sin and the atonement for sin; Christ as incarnation and as redeemer; faith in Christ as man's only door to heaven.

This question is in Christianity closely connected with the account of Adam's fall at the beginning of Genesis. Dayananda understood that connection, and it was clearly summarized by the Reverend Scott at the Chandapur discussion: 'God created Adam without sin, but Satan led him astray and made him sin. Hence, all his descendants are also subject to sin.'[57] Dayananda criticized this doctrine:

If Adam, created sinless by God, was led astray by Satan, . . . then God cannot be called omnipotent. . . . Adam alone committed sin, and yet his whole descendency became sinful, that is totally impossible and cannot be true. He who sins receives the consequent suffering, no-one else can receive it. . . . If Satan led everybody astray, who then led him astray? . . . If it was someone else, there was none but God himself to do it. . . . If Satan caused such disorder in the kingdom of God, why did God not punish, or destroy, or jail him? It is clear from that that God lacked power.[58]

The essential point of Dayananda's argument is expressed in the middle of the paragraph just quoted: 'He who commits a sin, he alone and no-one else can suffer its consequences.' In fact, one of Dayananda's most consistent and pervasive doctrines is that each deed, good and bad, must find its consequences in the perpetrator of that deed: the law of *karma* is totally inexorable and does not brook the slightest exception. This principle of the absolute commensurateness of reward and punishment with the individual act was an obsession with the Swami. That principle was one of the main reasons why he came to reject the endlessness of the state of *moksha*. This was a very deliberate negation of the whole of the Hindu traditional doctrine of the infinite duration of *moksha*, and he was aware of that. He argued: 'Since every one of a man's deeds, and equally their totality, always remains of necessity finite, its reward must also remain finite lest an injustice be done; therefore *moksha* cannot possibly be of endless duration.'[59]

Dayananda relentlessly criticized the ideas of 'forgiveness of sins', and 'atonement for sins' which pervade the Bible. A propos of *Leviticus* chapter IV, he wrote, 'Look at this atonement for sins: it is achieved by committing the sin of the slaughter of useful animals, and that on God's command!'[60] And *Leviticus* chapter V, drew similar sarcasm: 'A Christian commits a sin, then he kills an animal and enjoys its meat, and so he gets rid of his sin!'[61] His comment on Matthew IX, 'Thy sins be forgiven', clearly stated his own concept of the forgiveness of sins:

A sin committed by one person cannot affect another one. . . . He who perpetrates the deed suffers the consequences. . . . *Dharma*, right action, alone is the cause of happy results, not Christ or anybody else. Those who follow *dharma* do not need Christ or such. Neither do the sinners, because nobody's sin can ever be forgiven.[62]

Dayananda highlights three places in the New Testament where the doctrine of reward according to one's deeds is mentioned.

And then he shall reward every man according to his deeds (Matthew XVI: 27). And their works do follow them (Apocalypse XIV: 13). And behold I come quickly; and my reward is with me to give every man according as his work shall be (Apocalypse XXII: 12).

In each case he points out what he regards as a contradiction in the Christian doctrine. If the reward is indeed according to the actions, 'then the doctrine of the forgiveness is futile'. The following is his most extensive statement on this matter:

The God of the Christians says that their deeds will remain with them, namely that each will be rewarded or punished according to his deeds. And yet the Christians say that Christ will take their sins upon himself and that they will be forgiven. The wise should consider whether God's word is true or that of the Christians. In this same issue they cannot both be right; one of them must most certainly be wrong. It makes no difference to me whether the God of the Christians is untruthful or the Christians.[63]

The question of the forgiveness of sins was so important to Dayananda that it became a special topic of discussion at the Bareilly disputation with the Reverend Scott in 1897. Scott presented a very persuasive and humane argument attempting to demonstrate that the forgiveness of sins can be proved in three ways: by reason, by scripture, and by the profound personal experience of many people. He insisted on the divine quality of mercy as a pivot for his argument. All his points met the same response from the Swami: forgiveness and punishment are mutually contradictory; justice loses its rationality if sometimes it punishes and at other times it omits the punishment. In final instance, he declared that justice is the same as mercy: 'to say that sometimes God punishes, and sometimes He forgives, that is a lie, just like saying that sometimes the fire is hot, and at other times it also gets cold'.[64] There was no way in which Scott's arguments could penetrate that formidable, monolithic concept of total justice as Dayananda conceived it. Dejectedly, Scott declared that if one believed the Swami's doctrine, then one may as well banish the words forgiveness and mercy from the world as futile and harmful.[65]

The second important element of the Christian doctrine of redemption Dayananda was familiar with was the faith in the mission of Christ, the Son of God become man in order to redeem mankind from its sins. The second day of the Bareilly disputation was directed to the question 'whether God incarnates himself in a body?'. The Reverend Scott again stressed that one should approach such questions with some humility because men do not know everything about God, and about his qualities such as omnipotence and omnipresence. He attempted to remove some possible misunderstandings by offering some clarification of the idea of divine incarnation: this meant that God revealed Himself in a body, not that God himself changed into an embodied being. He demonstrated that there was nothing irrational or absurd in such a conception. Since the soul of man was in many ways similar to God, there was no reason why God could not inhabit a body in the way the soul of man does. Scott accepted that this 'inhabitation' was in many ways a mystery, but added that the connection of our own body with our soul was equally mysterious. He stressed that naturally God always remained omnipotent, and that he revealed himself in a special way in a particular body which was not inhabited by a human soul. The reason for God's incarnation was his love for mankind; he wanted to save mankind from sin and to put before men a perfect teacher, a perfect ideal, whom they could follow on the road to perfection.[66]

Dayananda's critique was cast in the same unchanging mould. He argued that the idea of incarnation could not be reconciled with God's essential quality of omnipresence, and had, therefore, to be rejected:

> Since God is all-pervading, it is absolutely impossible to say that He assumes a body, or may assume a body or may leave a body. If He is all-pervading, wherefrom did he come in order to assume a body? From above or below, from outside or from sideways? From whichever direction you may declare He came, the conclusion is that such a God is no more all-pervading.[67]

The concept of incarnation was, according to the Swami, similarly incompatible with the divine quality of omnipotence:

> If you say that God assumed a body in order to elevate mankind, . . . then I ask whether that omnipotent God is unable to elevate mankind . . . by his innate power? If you say yes, He is able to do so—then incarnation becomes futile. If you say no, He is not able to do that, then your God is no longer omnipotent.[68]

However, much Scott tried to bring more subtlety and flexibility into the discussion, Dayananda was not to be moved from his simplistic approach which kept putting forward alternatives that were both to be rejected. This is an arid form of scholastic debating technique which is used for scoring points off an opponent, not for clarifying issues. Here follows a final example of the genre:

Was Christ a *jiva* [human spirit] or was he God? If you say that he was a *jiva*, then all men have become forgivers of sins like God, since all men are also *jivas*. If on the other hand you say that Christ is God, then he cannot become himself the supporting witness to his own divinity. If you say that in Christ there were both human and divine natures, then I ask you what were their respective works? Were those two united or were they separate? If you say that they were separate, then there is no relation of mutual penetration. If you confirm that they were united, what then is the difference between Christ and the other *jivas*?[69]

In the process or providing the proof for the incarnation of Christ, Scott appealed to the words of scripture. His reference to the first lines of the Gospel of St John were criticized by Dayananda:

And the text of the Gospel you quoted, namely 'the word became incarnate', that saying is altogether false. A word is nothing but a quality, and as such it can never be transformed into a substance. The Gospel in which such falsehood is written can never be called truthful, neither could it be described as perfect.[70]

Scott tried to explain what the term 'the Word' was supposed to mean in this particular context, but he did not enlighten the Swami, because some years later he commented on the same text of St John's Gospel in the following words:

In the beginning the Word could not exist without the speaker. Therefore, to say that the Word was with God is a futile expression. The Word also can never 'become' God: since the Word was with God from the beginning, one cannot say which of the two existed before the other. Creation cannot come about by means of the Word unless there was a material cause [out of which it could be fashioned]. And the Creator was able to create the world without the Word by simply remaining silent.[71]

From the report of the Bareilly disputation it is quite clear that Dayananda was not prepared to give the Christian doctrine of incarnation a sympathetic hearing. He had made up his mind long before that the Christian idea of incarnation was a mere variant of the Hindu idea of *avatar*. He criticized and condemned the latter as vehemently as he rejected the former, and for the same reason. This reason is not the logical inconsistency which Dayananda finds as much in the concept of *avatar* as in that of incarnation, but lies much deeper. Dayananda was convinced that the myths of Krishna and of Christ were constructed in order to offer men short-cuts to salvation. Since there could be no such short-cuts, the myths were nothing but deceptions.

A final key concept in the Christian view of redemption as Dayananda understood it was that faith in Christ was the only means of securing heaven. In the Chandapur disputation the Reverend Scott clearly stated the doctrine:

> Men cannot by their own strength attain salvation or be delivered from their sins. Therefore salvation is impossible without faith in Christ the Messiah. I too have found salvation and was freed from any evil deeds when I professed faith in Christ. Salvation is impossible for those who act contrary to Christ's teaching. Therefore all should accept faith in Christ the Saviour. By that faith salvation becomes possible, not by any other means.[72]

Dayananda had heard this doctrine earlier and had criticized it. In early 1872 before his visit to Calcutta, Reverend Lalbehari De is reported to have told him, 'Look how excellent Christianity is: the Lord Christ has removed the sins of all by taking them upon himself.' The Reverend De must have also spoken about the specific effect of faith in Christ, as the Swami's reaction clearly indicates:

> Atonement for sins is impossible without undergoing their consequence. No doubt Christ was a great human being. But it is not true to say that he took the sins of all men upon himself and thus cancelled them. That would mean encouragement and support for sins. The conviction that all sins will be removed by professing faith in Christ will result in people committing even more sins.[73]

The Reverend J.J. Lucas in a meeting two years later told the Swami why his conviction was reasonable: 'Man is able to attain salvation by believing in Christ because he was the son of God and the Saviour of mankind, and that is why God sent him. This is proven by the fact that Christ brought many dead back to life.' Dayananda retorted that such reasoning would equally prove that Shukracharya was also sent by God because the *Mahabharata* relates that he brought many dead back to life.[74]

The Swami's fundamental objection to the Christian doctrine that salvation came through faith in Christ, was that salvation can only be achieved by works of *dharma*. The Christians' conviction that only faith in Christ would save them was to him of the same kind as all the short-cuts to salvation offered by Hindu sects, such as pilgrimages, idol-worship, or the repetition of the name of Rama. Dayananda's second objection was that such a doctrine tended to encourage people in their sins because it was easy to get rid of them.[75] Thirdly, he did not accept that Christ was more than a human being; belief in his divinity was itself a lie and could not possibly help man to salvation. Finally, Dayananda completely rejected any claim in the 'power' of faith. He quoted the following text of St John's Gospel, 'Verily, verily I say unto you, he that believeth in me, the works that I do shall he do also; and greater works than these shall he do because I go back to my father' (John XIV. 12). Dayananda's commentary was not without sarcasm:

> Look, if Christians have complete faith in Christ, why then are they not able to quicken the dead and perform other miracles? And if with the power of their faith they cannot perform miracles, then one must conclude for certain that Christ did not perform miracles either, because it was he who said that they would do miracles. Even today not a single Christian can perform a miracle. He who still believes that Christ was someone who raised the dead and who worked miracles, his inner vision must completely have failed.[76]

Dayananda's knowledge of Christianity was limited to one particular school. He obtained it from a group of Protestant missionaries whose conception of Christian doctrine was certainly the dominant one at that time among north Indian Christians. The Swami grasped the bare basics of their beliefs about the fall of man, the mission of Christ, and redemption through atonement and faith. He was, however, never in a position to penetrate any distance into the complexities and subtleties of Christian theological discussion about issues such as the relation of faith and works, the humanity and divinity of Christ, vicarious atonement and grace. There were some obvious barriers to this. The Swami did not read English, and his communication with missionaries was often done through interpreters. Although some of his missionary contacts were well versed in Christian theology, and also in Hindi and Sanskrit, the terminological barriers must have been frustrating on both sides. Moreover, one should not forget that the Swami never really felt any great urge to learn more about Christianity: what he knew of it was so damning in his eyes that further study would have been considered a waste of time.

Dayananda's understanding of the Bible, accessible to him in Sanskrit and Hindi translations, suffered the same serious difficulties relating to terminology. However, in matters of scriptural interpretation there existed a much more formidable obstacle to sympathetic understanding. Dayananda had a fixed idea of the qualities that must of necessity grace the word of God. He was convinced that it could by definition not have any 'historical' connection. This principle was used to discredit Hindu texts such as the Brahmanas, the epics, and the Puranas; on the other hand it forced him to interpret into non-existence any historical or geographic names, in fact anything that had the suggestion of history, in the Vedas. Since the Bible as the history of the fall of man, of the wanderings of the chosen people, and of the advent of the Messiah, is inextricably woven into the warp and woof of the history of mankind, a great deal of it was easily susceptible to the taint of 'historicism'.

There was another fundamental reason why Dayananda found it extremely difficult to empathize with biblical texts. His intellectual make-up was extremely rationalistic, and his mind did not respond to the powerfully expressive and meaningful medium of myth and symbol. He found it impossible to attribute any value to the rich mythology of the Hindu tradition, and carefully demythologized hymns of the Vedas dealing with ancient myths such as those of Indra and Vrithra and of the cosmic Purusha. It is no wonder that the cosmogonic mythology of Genesis became a prime target for his criticism, as did the Apocalypse of St John the Apostle.

A final major obstacle to Dayananda's deeper understanding of Christian doctrine was his concept of ***karma*** and retribution. To him the principle was absolute that every deed must find its proper individual retribution, and, therefore, forgiveness of sins or vicarious atonement were considered as fundamentally contradictory with the justice of God. He vehemently rejected the many ways in which the Hindu ***bhakti*** tradition proclaimed that ***moksha*** could be achieved by total surrender to Krishna and by the power of his ***prasada*** or grace. Dayananda's concept of Christianity was that of a particular school wherein 'works' were of little importance, and such a doctrine was an easy target for his insistence on absolute justice. However, Christianity in all its forms, even in those schools where 'works' are much more important, is essentially a religion of grace, wherein the role of Christ is absolutely essential in the plan of redemption. To Dayananda that role of redeemer, mediator between man and God was absolutely unacceptable. That is why he rejected the *avatar*-hood of Krishna as vehemently as the incarnation of Christ. But, whereas there is within the wide world of Hinduism ample space for a Hinduism without Krishna, Christianity without Christ is inconceivable. Dayananda's conception of Christianity could not be called 'false', but it was superficial, and remained so because he had neither the interest nor the intellectual resources to penetrate it more deeply. The quality of his understanding was hampered from the start by some of his fundamental presuppositions. His *a priori* concept of what scripture must be like and his mental blind spot for mythical expression made it practically impossible for him to positively respond to biblical texts. His concept of absolute justice made it difficult for him to appreciate any doctrine of forgiveness of sin, mercy, atonement, grace, and redemption. His monolithic monotheism made any acceptance of incarnation a total impossibility. During the period of his life most missionaries had similar difficulties in understanding Hinduism, in view of their own concept of scripture and their theological presuppositions. No wonder that was not a period of mutual understanding but rather of Hindu-Christian misunderstanding and often fruitless controversy.

NOTES

[This chapter was first published as 'Dayananda Sarasvati's interpretation of Christianity', in A. Sharma (ed.), *Neo-Hindu Views of Christianity*, Leiden, 1988, pp. 120-42.]

1. Lekhram, *Maharshi Dayananda Sarasvati ka Jivan Charitra*, transl. into Hindi from the original Urdu by Kaviraj Raghunandansingh 'Nirmal', ed. by Pandit Harischandra Vidyalankar, Delhi, 1972.
2. Ghasiram, *Maharshi Dayananda Sarasvati ka Jivan-Charit*, 2 vols., Ajmer, 1957.
3. These have been collected and published in one volume: *Dayananda-Shastrarth-Samgraha*, B. Bharatiya (ed.), Sonepat, 1969.
4. Our references to the *Satyarth Prakash*, 2nd edn., are to the excellent edition by Y. Mimamshak, Sonepat, 1971. All translations are mine.
5. Rev. John Robson, *Hinduism and its Relations to Christianity*, new edition, Edinburgh, 1893; Ghasiram, vol. I, p. 125.
6. Cf. T.J. Scott, *Missionary Life Among the Villages in India*, Cincinnati, 1876, pp. 162-8.
7. Ghasiram, vol. II, p. 190.

8. Scott, p. 166.
9. Ibid.
10. Cf. Ghasiram, vol. I, pp. 166, 244; vol. II, pp. 2, 11.
11. *Satyarth Prakash*, p. 579.
12. Ibid., p. 585.
13. G.A. Oddie, *Social Protest in India*, Delhi, 1979, p. 10. Cf. also Eric J. Sharpe, *Not to Destroy But to Fulfil*, Gleerup, 1965, p. 25.
14. J.C.B. Webster, *The Christian Community and Change in Nineteenth Century North India*, Delhi, 1976, p. 5.
15. Ibid., p. 8.
16. Oddie, p. 10.
17. Webster, pp. 30-5.
18. B. Bharatiya, p. 155.
19. Webster, p. 34.
20. Scott, p. 168.
21. Dr Rudolf Hoernle wrote about his meeting with the Swami in the *Christian Intelligencer* of March 1870; the article was reproduced in full in Lajpat Rai, *A History of the Arya Samaj*, revd. edn. by Shri Ram Sharma, Mumbai, 1967, pp. 28-38.
22. The first *Satyarth Prakash* published in Varanasi in 1875 did not contain the chapter on Christianity. According to Y. Mimamshak (ed.), *Rishi Dayananda Sarasvati ke Patra aur Vijnapan*, 2nd edn., Amritsar, 1955, pp. 20-4, the chapter was written, but not published because of the great rush of getting the book out. The manuscript is held by the descendants of the patron of the publication, Raja Jaikishendas, and the Paropkarini Sabha of Ajmer possesses a photocopy.
23. *Satyarth Prakash*, p. 719.
24. For references, cf. Jordens, *Dayananda Sarasvati*, p. 267 and footnotes. Cf. also P.A. Parapullil, S.J., *Swami Dayananda Sarasvati's Understanding and Assessment of Christianity*, Rome, 1970, pp. 54-5.
25. Letter reproduced in Har Bilas Sarda, *Life of Dayananda Sarasvati, World Teacher*, 2nd edn., Ajmer, 1968, pp. 522-3.
26. For an analysis of Dayananda's relations with the Theosophist leaders, cf. J.T.F. Jordens, *Dayananda Sarasvati*, Delhi, pp. 209-13.
27. *Satyarth Prakash*, p. 719.
28. Ibid., p. 721.
29. For expositions of these criteria cf. *Satyarth Prakash*, 1st edn., 1875, pp. 242-6, *Satyarth Prakash*, 2nd edn., p. 297, B. Bharatiya, p. 137, *Rigvedadibhashyabhumika*, in Y. Mimamshak (ed.), Amritsar, 1967, pp. 39-40, 102-3.
30. *Satyarth Prakash*, pp. 732, 733, 735, 745, 767.
31. Ibid., pp. 723, 757, 779.
32. Ibid., pp. 735, 736, 739, 753.

33. Ibid., p. 760; also pp. 739, 757, 760, 784.
34. B. Bharatiya, pp. 80-1.
35. *Satyarth Prakash*, pp. 724, 729, 734, 754, 775, 791.
36. Ibid., pp. 770, 772, 798, 802.
37. Ibid., p. 791.
38. Ibid., p. 9.
39. E. Sharpe, p. 26.
40. J.M. Mitchell, *Letters to Indian Youth*, 3rd edn., Mumbai, 1857, *passim*.
41. Cf. Jordens, *Dayananda Sarasvati*, p. 83.
42. Oddie, p. 4.
43. *The Arya Samaj and a Refutation of its Tenets*, by A Punjabi Brahmo of the New Dispensation, Lahore, 1883, pp. 4 and 9.
44. This translation of the first two verses of Genesis attempts to reproduce as closely as possible the Hindi version Dayananda quoted.
45. *Satyarth Prakash*, pp. 721-3.
46. Translation of R.C. Zaehner in *Hindu Scriptures*, London; for another similar rendering, cf. W. Doniger O'Flaherty, *The Rig Veda*, Harmondsworth, 1981.
47. *Satyarth Prakash*, p. 305.
48. Ibid., pp. 127-8.
49. Webster, pp. 111ff.
50. Ibid., p. 112.
51. These changes are clearly explained above in ch. 4.
52. Debendranath Tagore, *Brahmo Dharma of Maharshi Debendranath Tagore*, translated into English by Hem Chandra Sarkar, Calcutta, 1928, p. 11.
53. Cf. Jordens, *Dayananda Sarasvati*, pp. 79-81.
54. *Satyarth Prakash*, p. 579.
55. B. Bharatiya, p. 82.
56. Ibid., p. 84.
57. Ibid., p. 96.
58. Ibid., pp. 98-9.
59. For the development of this argument, cf. Jordens, *Dayananda Sarasvati*, pp. 255-8.
60. *Satyarth Prakash*, p. 759.
61. Ibid., p. 761.
62. Ibid., p. 774.
63. Ibid., p. 807.
64. B. Bharatiya, p. 167.
65. Ibid., p. 169.
66. Ibid., pp. 142, 144-5.
67. Ibid., p. 150.
68. Ibid.

69. Ibid., p. 137.
70. Ibid., p. 167.
71. *Satyarth Prakash*, p. 793.
72. B. Bharatiya, pp. 96-7.
73. Ghasiram, vol. I, p. 244.
74. Ghasiram, vol. II, p. 2.
75. B. Bharatiya, p. 99.
76. *Satyarth Prakash*, p. 795.

PART III
Comparative

CHAPTER 8

Gandhi and Dayananda: Their Kathiawari Background

BOTH MAHATMA GANDHI and Swami Dayananda Sarasvati were born in Kathiawar, and spent most of the formative years of their youth in that area: Dayananda lived there for the first twenty-one years of his life, and Gandhi for nineteen years. This chapter assesses in what way their Kathiawari background influenced their growth, and to give some indication of how that initial Kathiawari influence bore fruit in their later years.

Even a superficial look at the two figures, both truly great in the history of modern India, reveals some intriguing similarities and contrasts. Some of these, naturally, are primarily the result of their respective temperament and life-experience. But some must have their roots in the background of their youth.

Whereas Dayananda was a *sannyasi* of the highest Hindu order of the Dandis, Gandhi was a householder, who became obsessed with asceticism and *brahmacharya*. Both started life with disappointments: Gandhi, initially an unsuccessful lawyer, became the great leader of his people, and Dayananda founded a powerful Samaj after a long and frustrating search for the perfect yogic guru. Both became enthusiastic promoters of cow-protection, and with this so fundamentally Hindu approach they both contributed to the intensification of the rift between Hindus and Muslims. About the Mahatma people ask the question: was he a politician or a saint, or was he both? Dayananda, the Luther of India, was himself averse to and ignorant of politics. But his Samaj and his followers have played an important part in Indian politics. That influence is far from dead even today; but one wonders in how far Gandhism still is an important factor.

Both men were extreme and stubborn individualists, adaptable yet extremely determined, and both put the ideas of 'truth' and 'action' at the very centre of their world-view, albeit in very different ways. How, then, can their respective Kathiawari background help a little to better understand their personalities and careers?

Gandhi belonged to a Modh bania family and through his father to the sect of the Vallabhacharyas. Although many sites in Kathiawar, like Dwarka, were associated in legend and literature with the Krishna cycle, Vaishnavism as a major religious force was a relatively recent phenomenon there. It was only in the sixteenth century that the real upsurge of Vaishnavism started in Gujarat with the great *bhakti* poet Narasimha Mehta; and the subsequent success of the Vallabhacharya sect established a tremendous hold particularly over the merchant community of the area. The cult of the sect is centred on Krishna, in particular on the aspect of the youthful lover. The principal gurus of the sect, called Maharajas, direct descendants of the founder Vallabha, were married and demanded from the faithful a complete dedication, '*tan*, *man*, *dhan se*', with their body, mind, and wealth. The famous Maharaj Libel case in Bombay in 1861 had exposed the immoralities committed in their temples, but things went on practically unchanged afterwards.[1] Gandhi himself recalled in his autobiography that the report of immorality in some temples made him lose all interest in the ritual aspect of religion.[2]

Kathiawar had been for many centuries 'a centre of trade between ports on the shores of the Arabian Sea, the Persian Gulf and the Red Sea, and the hinterland of north and central India'.[3] This had led to a clear domination of society by the commercial classes, a factor that makes Kathiawar society very different from, e.g. Maharashtra, where the brahmin elite dominates. This fact of commerce dominating society, and the leading role not of Brahmanical but of merchant classes, encouraged an unusual freedom and variety in social and religious matters. Among the majority of people the Vaishnava-Jain influence was predominant, and the accent was not on orthodoxy, but rather on variety and fluidity in matters of faith and ritual, and a ready acceptance of new sectarian movements. That was the general social climate in which Mohandas grew up.

Whereas the Vaishnavas as an overall group encompassed well over half of the population of Kathiawar, the Shaivites scarcely constituted one-tenth of the total population. Moreover, they were practically all brahmins, with just a few kshatriyas.[4] The great majority of the Shaivites belonged to the sect of the Smartas, a small group to the Lingayat sect. In fact, the Smartas do not, strictly speaking, form a sect; they are rather, as Renou expressed it, the collection of those brahmins who represent orthodoxy with regard to the sects.[5] They are noted for their strong attachment to the doctrine of Shankara, and consider the successor of Shankara, the Shankaracharya of Shringeri Math as their spiritual head. Their main guide in religious matters are the ancient Dharmashastras. Whereas the ritual of the Vaishnavites was mostly Puranic with, especially in the younger sects, a great dose of the vernacular, the Smartas' ritual was Vedic and Sanskritic.

The history of the Shaivites of Kathiawar goes back to the earliest dynasties which were either Buddhist or Shaivite. The most striking symbol of the antiquity of Shaivism in Kathiawar is Somnath, with its temple ruins. This temple existed and was famous at least since the second century AD, and in the subsequent centuries it exerted a great influence not only on Saurashtra but, from the tenth century onward, its influence on south India has been described by a historian as a veritable 'spiritual conquest'.[6] It was also from Saurashtra that hailed the saint Lakulisha, founder of the sect of the Pashupatas, one of the most influential Shaivite sects.[7] The founder himself quickly attained divinization, and his influence spread all over India. The great philosopher Madhvacharya recognized his system as one of the sixteen major philosophical systems in his famous *Sarvadarshanasamgraha*, and the Pashupata movement became later associated with the great resurgence of Shaivism in the seventh century, which spread all over the continent.[8]

This great Shaivite past was still very much visible in the time of Dayananda in the glorious architectural remains of Somnath, and in the innumerable Shiva temples dotted all over the countryside. Many of these were very old, and they easily outnumbered the temples of all other sects together.[9] In Kathiawar the memories of Maratha domination were still very fresh at that time, and one of its main influences had been a greater propaganda of Shaivism. One important figure in this was Vittalrao Devji who built several Shaivite temples.[10]

All these factors together must have created in the Kathiawari Shaivite a very special self-image: the Shaivites constituted a practically purely brahmin elite, closely linked with the most ancient roots of Hinduism through Sanskrit and the Vedic rites, and grown out of a glorious historical past. The presence in the peninsula of a small number of 'fallen' brahmins must have strengthened this feeling. Those were brahmins who had forsaken their Shaivism, and thus had fallen to an inferior status: the Bhojaks, a section of the Shrimali brahmins who had adopted Jainism, the Guglis, the Abotis, the Kandolias, and the Rajgors, priests to Rajputs and Oswal Jains, who had been severed from the Audichya brahmins of Dayananda's family's caste.[11] This consciousness of being part of an elite representing the pure ancient religion of yore must have had a decisive influence on Dayananda in his youth. Two historical facts seem to indicate that in Morvi, Dayananda's home state, this consciousness may have been even stronger than in other states. According to the 1872 census, the concentration of brahmins was significantly higher in the Morvi state than elsewhere in Kathiawar. Moreover, Tankara itself was during Dayananda's youth under one Seth Gopal Medel Narayana of Baroda, who was famous for his vigorous advocacy of Shaivism in the area.[12]

The *Gazetteer of the Bombay Presidency* in its first part on the Gujarat population, describes a fascinating reformer, Madhavgar of Nadiad whose movement started in 1824, and who went to live in Kathiawar.[13] He was a strict Shankarite Vedantin, but his cardinal ideas are fascinating because practically everyone of them later became an integral part of Dayananda's programme. He condemned idol-worship, fasts, and *shraddh*, the Hindu death rites. He did not believe in *avatars* or in pollution by touch. He also did not acknowledge guru-ship in any form and his own movement had no actual seat, no authoritative guru. The parallelism with Dayananda's doctrines is so striking that one wonders if young Mulji ever met one of those teachers in yellow robes, frugally living, carrying the Shaivite rosary of Rudraksha seeds.

These respective self-images of Vaishnavites and Shaivites in Kathiawar were strengthened in the cases of Gandhi and Dayananda by their home environment and education. The freer, more relaxed Vaishnavite attitude to sectarian differences was reinforced in the Gandhi home by the fact that his mother belonged to a different sect from his father, that of the Pranamis. These were noted for their broadminded attitude towards Islamic ideas and for their close contacts with Muslims. The main object of their worship was the Book of Faith compiled by one of the founders. Their gurus observed celibacy and gave readings and conducted *kirtans* in their idol-less temple.[14] Thus, the mother's religious observance was markedly different from that of the father's sect, and Mohandas shared in both. His schooling too reinforced this open communication with people of other religions and sects. Both at Porbandar and Rajkot he attended the local elementary and high school, mixing with everybody; in fact, his best school-day friend was a Muslim. This home environment helps to explain Gandhi's attitude of tolerance towards religious pluralism, a tolerance that often exacerbated the orthodox Hindus, but from which Gandhi never wavered an inch. To him no single religion, not Christianity, not Islam, not Hinduism, had the right to claim exclusive truth for its holy books and its theology, or exclusive religious efficacy for its rites and practices.[15]

In Dayananda's family, orthodox Shaivism dominated completely, and his father insisted on proper observance of the rituals.[16] At that time schools were practically non-existent in Kathiawar, but Dayananda received from an early age a traditional private Sanskrit education. He learnt verses of the *Yajurveda* by heart from the age of five, and was taught Sanskrit grammar by pandits. When his father pressured him to get married, Mulji convinced him to let him continue his studies instead, further studies of grammar, systems of philosophy and *dharma*. In fact, he continued these studies up to the age of twenty-two, and then planned to go to Varanasi to pursue them even further. But the irrevocable decision of his father to arrange his marriage made him then run away from home. Thus the home-environment and the early studies of Dayananda strongly fostered that peculiar awareness of the Kathiawari Shaivite in him: the feeling of belonging to an elite with deep roots in the past, through Sanskrit and the Vedic rites, representative of the hoary essence of Hinduism.

As Gandhi said in his autobiography, 'Jainism was strong in Gujarat and its influence was felt everywhere and on all occasions.'[17] According to the 1883 *Bombay Gazetteer* two-thirds of the commercial classes, the dominant ones, were Jains. They were not just concentrated in a few urban centres, but penetrated the whole area. Captain Le Grand Jacob already reported in 1842 that 'The Jains are very numerous, scarcely a village of any size has not two or three or more families.'[18] They also penetrated the whole social fabric:

> They are bankers, merchants, money-lenders, and shop-keepers, and many of their class have within the last few years entered Government and state service. But the bulk are engaged in trade, and are found in every situation of life, from the millionaire banker to the village grocer.[19]

Their temples were to be found all over the peninsula. 'In proportion to their number', noted Reclus' *Universal Geography*, 'the Jains possess more religious edifices than the other Hindu sects'.[20]

Another indication of their importance and vitality in Kathiawar is the fact that the early leaders of modern Jain reform came from there. First there was Vijayasharma Suri (1868-1922), a monk who wrote extensively in Sanskrit, Gujarati, and Hindi, and became editor of important Jain works. The monk Ratnachandra born in 1879 was engaged in similar work.[21] Rajchandra Rajivbhai, the reformer who influenced Gandhi, was born in Morvi, and Virchand Gandhi, the lawyer-reformer who represented Jainism at the World's Parliament of Religions in Chicago in 1893, was the son of Kathiawari Jain banias.[22]

The Gandhi household was not narrowly sectarian, in fact, very often discussions were held with representatives of various faiths, and young Mohandas used to quietly sit in and listen. This accessibility was particularly true in the case of the Jains. It should be remembered that the majority of the caste of the Gandhis, the Modh Banias, were Jains. In fact, the Jain and Vaishnavite Modh Banias belonged to the same caste. These caste bonds were so strong that on the one hand some Jains intermarried with Hindus of their caste, whereas on the other hand they were forbidden even commercial contact with Jains of certain other castes.[23] The Jains had adopted many Hindu ways of thinking, shared in the celebration of their festivals and even in the actual worship of Hindu idols. The officiating priests in Jain temples were mostly brahmins, and the basic constituent parts of their worship were identical with those used in Hindu temples.[24] They observed, like the Hindus, only four of the traditional sacraments, which were performed according to Vedic rites.[25] Von Glasenapp observed that the only real differences were that 'the Jains do not give any meaning to bathing in holy rivers, they cremate their ascetics, they do not offer gifts to the dead, they do not practice widow-burning'. The signal feature of these social and religious differences is that they all are 'relatively small, and, most importantly, they only deal with such matters that do not in any way offend the susceptibility of ritual purity of even the most ritually sensitive Hindu'.[26] In other words, none of them entailed a ritual pollution that may have prevented social intercourse. This closeness in social and ritual customs was so great that it worried the census officials, and that it made von Glasenapp remark that, 'the approximation of the Jains to general Hinduism has ever increased in the last century, so that, if the process continues in the same degree, one has to expect a complete absorption of Jainism into Hinduism'.[27]

It is no wonder, then, that there was a constant calling of Jains and Jain monks in the Gandhi household. After her husband's death, Gandhiji's mother 'relied at times on the advice of a Jain monk. When Gandhi decided to go to London to study law, she withheld her permission until Mohandas had taken three solemn vows suggested by this monk—vows not to touch meat, wine, or women'.[28]

Jainism always remained very special to Gandhi. In fact, he did not accept that Jainism was really distinct from Hinduism. He stated 'I do not regard Jainism as separate from Hinduism' and often reiterated that strongly held opinion.[29] Once he was pointedly asked the question 'What is the difference between the Gita's theism and the Jain doctrine that there is no God.' He answered, 'I have never seen any difference between the Jain doctrine and the general Vedic doctrine. The difference is only one of point of view. The *Gita* is a poem—and imaginary—Jainism on the other hand states the truth logically and unpoetically.'[30]

What was Dayananda's awareness of Jainism during his youth? There is no evidence that he had any direct contact with Jains, but presumably his father did at least have some business relationship with them, because of their prominence in the money business and the fact that his father had himself 'a banking house' and also held the office of tax-collector.[31] Young Mulji on his part must have been aware of some prominent aspects of Jainism. It should be remembered that he was not just an ordinary youth, who may walk through life without noticing what his eyes register. In an area notorious for its lack of education and scholarship at the time, he was a studious young man who stuck to his studies when most youths had long abandoned them, if they ever had any. He had considerable stubborn willpower and a deep and serious interest in religious matters. His family was involved in the important public areas of business and administration. That kind of temperament and background made him into the type of person who would be aware of the important events and situations around him, especially those relating to government and religion.

A first aspect of Jainism he could not have failed to become aware of was one it shared with Shaivism: that it was a community with glorious ancient roots in the history of Kathiawar. Indeed, the glory of the ancient Jain kings rivalled that of the Shaivite rulers. The Jains traced their history back to the third century BC. They claimed that the twenty-second Tirthankara Arishtanemi died in Saurashtra and that the Jain canon was first fixed there too, at a council held at the town of Valabhi. Their prosperity and influence increased down to the thirteenth century AD reaching its peak under the great Kumarapala, and was devastated when the Muslim invaders razed their temples, shrines, and libraries. The architectural glory of ancient Jainism, created, as Mrs Stevenson said, 'in the sunshine of royal favour',[32] shone as much as that of Shaivism. On the hills of the fabulous sites of Girnar and Shatrunjaya, the Jain temples numbered in the thousands. In the field of Sanskrit learning no single Gujarati outshone the great Hemachandra (1088-1172), grammarian, philosopher, politician, and literateur of prodigious output. A modern historian has called him 'the first great literary man who was born in Gujarat, who worked for Gujarat, and created the group consciousness of the Gujaratis'.[33] Important facts like these could not have escaped the notice of an inquisitive youth like Dayananda, and he must have felt that, however different the Jains may be, they did share with the Shaivites that one particular quality of being deeply rooted in the ancient land of Saurashtra, of having close bonds with a sacred and glorious antiquity.

There was another special and prominent feature of the Kathiawar Jain community: the Dhundhiya or Sthanakavasi sect. The same iconoclastic onslaught of the Muslims that on the one hand had driven the Jains into a closer association with the Hindus, had produced on the other hand the opposite effect of causing some Jains to rethink their own position, especially on idolatry. These Dhundhiya Jains, mostly concentrated in Kathiawar,[34] were most probably the first non-idolatrous sectarians the future iconoclast Dayananda ever saw. That he must have been aware of them has been clearly demonstrated by Mrs Stevenson, the Jain specialist who spent many years in Kathiawar at the close of the nineteenth century. In a letter to J.N. Farquhar she wrote:

> Tankara is fourteen miles south of Morvi, and about twenty-three north of Rajkot. In the thirties, the father of the present Thakur Sahib of Morvi was ruling. He was very devoted to a certain Sthanakavasi monk, and the Prime Minister was also a Sthanakavasi, so that the sect was then very powerful and influential in the Morvi state. All monks and nuns travelling from the town of Morvi to Rajkot (another Sthanakavasi stronghold) passed through Tankara, where Amba Sankara and his son lived.[35]

Amba Sankara's son was the future Dayananda, and it is difficult to imagine that an educated, religiously inquisitive youth belonging to the ruling strata of society would not have been aware of the existence and beliefs of the Stanakavasis.

The sect originated with one Lonka Sha (1452) who on reading the Jain scriptures discovered that there was no mention of idol-worship. Thence he tried to restore Jainism to its 'original' purity, a task Dayananda would later undertake for Hinduism.[36] They rejected idol and temple worship and pilgrimages, put great stress on a strict moral life, and exacted a more disciplined life from their monks. Another indication of their vitality in Morvi is the fact that the great modern reform leader Rajchandra Rajivbhai, who would have later considerable influence on Gandhiji, was a Sthanakavasi born in Morvi.[37]

Two lesser Jain practices of Kathiawar are worth mentioning in connection with Dayananda, because they became later on part of his reform programme although the alternative Hindu practice was sanctioned by great antiquity. The Jains did not indulge in *shraddh*, the elaborate periodic rituals for the dead, which particularly in Gujarat often entailed enormous costs.[38] They only approved of ceremonies performed on the day of death and rejected all commemorative rituals.[39] The other custom was that, whereas the Hindu *sannyasis* were not cremated but either buried or exposed to the elements after death, the Jain monks were always cremated like anybody else.[40]

Thus, being natives of Kathiawar, both Gandhi and Dayananda could not escape the presence and influence of Jainism. But on account of their very different societal background, the influence reached them in very different ways. With Mohandas, the influence was a direct influence of Jain ideas and attitudes resulting from his contacts with the Jains. For instance the Jain doctrine of *anekantavada*, or the essential relativity of doctrinal structures, definitely influenced him as Stephen Hay has shown. One can also recognize other Jain influences in Gandhi's relations and correspondence with Rajchandra Rajivbhai, whom he considered to be the only guru he ever had.[41] The influence was more of an indirect nature in the case of Mulji. It was not Jain ideas that impressed themselves on his mind, but rather some salient characteristics of the Jain community and in particular of the Sthanakavasi sect, and these impressions were lasting as his later writings clearly show. For instance, in 1880 the Swami was drawn into a controversy with some Jains which lasted for two years. He asked Krishnadas Sevaklal, the Secretary of The Bombay Arya Samaj, to collect Jain works. Thus he acquired a set of 20 volumes of ancient

Jain works and another 50 volumes of commentaries and contemporary works. These formed the basis of Dayananda's chapter on Jainism in his second *Satyarth Prakash*.[42]

One of the major characteristics of the Vaishnava-Jain ethos of Kathiawar was its insistence of *ahimsa*, non-violence, and the resulting aversion to the slaughter of animals and the practice of strict vegetarianism. Both Gandhi and Dayananda would later in life become in their different ways strong protagonists of non-violence and vegetarianism, and both would, again in quite a different manner, single out cow-protection as the focal aspect of that non-violence. Gandhi professed that to him 'the central fact of Hinduism is Cow-protection'. The cow was not in itself a sacred animal to him but had been 'selected for apotheosis', 'as symbol of the entire sub-human world', and through his protection of *go-mata*, mother-cow, man should realize 'his identity with all that lives'. Cow-protection thus became the central symbolic act of non-violence, the essential ritual, one could say, of the Gandhian religion.[43] When Dayananda, late in life, started his campaign against cow-slaughter with his pamphlet *Gokaruna-nidhi*, 'The Treasure of kindness to Cows', his organization, his nationwide appeal for signatures, and his campaign lacked any symbolic character. Cow-protection was to him justified by purely economic arguments, economic arguments which do not hold economic water, but which are still fervently repeated by his followers.[44]

Gandhi was in his youth completely part and parcel of that Jain-Vaishnava ambience of *ahimsa* and vegetarianism that dominated then, as it still does now, Gujarat in particular. The main impetus for this approach had come from the Jains. They invented the institution of the Pinjarapol, or animal home; they bought up animals at the very slaughterhouses; they went even so far as literally rustling them when they suspected they were to be slaughtered.[45] This tenderness for animal life had been strengthened by the *bhakti* movement, in particular by the cult of Krishna the cowherd so popular in Gujarat, so that it had communicated itself somehow even to the Rajputs and to the Muslim zamindars, as Captain le Grand Jacob already noticed.[46] Notwithstanding young Mohandas' temporary meat-eating jaunt 'to become as strong as the mighty Englishman', as he confessed in his autobiography, he inherited from his background that typically Gujarati abhorrence for the killing of animals, and in particular of the cow.

Dayananda was part of the orthodox Shaivite community who in their traditional rituals at least in principle approved of the killing of animals and the consumption of meat, especially in the form of the *pindas*, the meat-balls consumed at the daily sacrifices and at the rituals of *shraddh*.[47] He did not have that deep psychological aversion that Gandhi felt. In this context it is interesting to note that the Jains of Gujarat suffered persecution from the Shaivite ruler Ajayapala, the successor of the great Jain patron Kumarapala. One cannot but wonder if that Shaivite animosity had not been at least partly caused by Kumarapala's drastic edict against all animal killing even ritualistic slaughter, so important to the Shaivites.[48] In fact, it took Dayananda a long time to get to the position of declaring all animal slaughter prohibited. Even as late as 1875, in his first *Satyarth Prakash*, he still admitted the rightfulness of ritual killing. Towards the end of his life Dayananda opted for the Gujarati type of absolute non-violence and vegetarianism, but his prohibition never had that sentimental, symbolic aura one finds in the Gandhian approach.

There is yet another way in which Kathiawar distinguished itself from many other parts of India: it was *par excellence* the land of *sadhus*, *sannyasis*, monks, and saints. The ascetic tradition there also had a special flavour. Stephen Hay contrasts it with the Bengali approach when speaking of the vision of Hinduism as a function of its reinterpretation in modern times: 'the Bengali vision dominated by the joyful equanimity of the Upanishads; the Kathiawari image infused with the unconquerable willpower of Jain monasticism'.[49] The census of 1872 shows that although Kathiawar had only about 24 per cent of the total population of Gujarat, it supported 43 per cent of the number of ascetics listed.[50] The countryside was dotted with the innumerable memorial monuments and stones to saints of all religions and sects, often converted into shrines. Asceticism, particularly in its most radical form of Jain asceticism, was constantly and everywhere present in Kathiawar and could not fail to exert considerable influence on those with religious aspirations.

Gandhiji came to asceticism proper by a circuitous road. Two factors stand out: the traumatic experience of his child marriage and the deep religious conversion that shook him in South Africa. When he came to asceticism, his approach definitely had Jain overtones. The basis of his asceticism was the assumption of a radical dualism of spirit and matter, and he saw in asceticism the method by which the spirit could be cleansed from the infiltration of impure matter. This is nothing else but the Jain *karma* theory, which considers the *jiva* as spiritual entity soiled by the infiltration of *karma*, the dust of evil and ignorance. Moreover, the very idea of pursuing an ascetic life while yet continuing to live as a householder, is also a characteristic Jain approach. Jainism has always provided for the layman a set of vows ascending in strictness, by which he can gradually make his life approximate closer and closer to the life of the monk, without leaving his household environment. Thirdly, Gandhi's asceticism had a radical harshness characteristic of the rigours of Jain monasticism.[51]

Dayananda, on the other hand, arrived at asceticism in the most direct way by running away from home and a looming wedding to become a *sannyasi.* His Shaivite Smarta background directed him straight to the Shankaracharya order of the Dashanami Dandis, into which he got initiated very early by putting great pressure on some monks of the order. Once he was initiated, many roads remained open to him, as he was his own master. He could have chosen a quiet, orderly, comfortable, scholarly life in one of the monasteries—and in fact he was explicitly offered this chance with an abbotship in the future.[52] But he chose differently: he became the rugged, self-disciplined, frugal, naked *sannyasi* who braved the harsh, cold land of Kumaon, roamed the stark Vindhya range, and astounded the people of the Doab with his unflinching endurance of hunger and cold. That 'unconquerable will-power of Jain asceticism' as Stephen Hay called it, had also shaped his concept of the true seeker of *moksha*, and in that way both the 'naked fakir' and the naked *sannaysi* betrayed their common Kathiawari background. Even in his last will Dayananda showed that the memory of the land of saints was still strongly with him. He stipulated that his body not be buried (as was the custom with *sannyasis*), but that it be cremated and that his ashes be scattered. Dayananda was afraid that a place of burial would gradually become a place of worship, a type of worship he abhorred. He had seen too many such shrines during his youth in Kathiawar.[53]

Howard Spodek has shown in detail how the political methodology of Gandhi had its roots in the peculiar conditions of Kathiawar.[54] It should be remembered that Gandhi came from a family that had served as prime ministers for several Rajput rulers, and that in Rajkot the peculiar dualism of the Indian and British Raj were singularly evident. Kathiawar also had a special tradition of passive resistance, of which Gandhiji must have been aware. Dayananda's father, although involved in tax-collecting and, therefore, also to a certain extent in administration, was not as far as we know involved in higher politics. And Dayananda himself never had great interest in, or knowledge of political matters. Perhaps his early experiences of Kathiawar, a lawless land into which the British had forced some order, partly influenced his favourable judgement of the advantages of British rule in his first *Satyarth Prakash*.[55] As for political theory, no more need to be said than that he was a slavish and rather naive commentator of the *Laws of Manu*.[56] Another observation may be put forward—during the last years of his life, Dayananda made a deliberate foray into Rajputana, with the express aim of converting the Rajas to his Vedic religion and opening an extra front for the attack on corrupt Hinduism. One could not possibly imagine a Bengali or a Punjabi reformer taking such a step. But for a Kathiawari it is not so surprising in view of the continuing rule in the area during the nineteenth century of scores of *rajas*, important ones and petty ones.

Both Gandhi and Dayananda were deeply influenced by Kathiawar, the land that nurtured them in the first lustrum of their lives. First there was for them a general common Kathiawar, land of Jainism, of intense cow-protection, centre of asceticism, land of innumerable small kingdoms—which influenced both the Mahatma and the Swami. But secondly, there was for each of them a different homeland within that homeland. The Gandhi caste and sect background, intensely Kathiawarian, comprised sentimental Vaishnavism, small-state political involvement, erosion of the borders between Hindus and Jains, and belief in vaishya power.

The Shaivite brahmin caste background of Dayananda was intensely different, displaying a brahmin pride hanging on to Vedic sacrifices and Sanskrit lore, a Shaiva faith accentuating the numinous aspect of God, an aloofness that anchored itself in the greatness of Shaiva antiquity and a conviction of brahmin supremacy. Both the Swami and the Mahatma carried that double heritage through life, and both moulded it to greatness.

NOTES

1. Cf. Karsondas, Mulji (publ. anon.), *History of the Sect of Maharajas or Vallabhacharyas in Western India*, London, 1905; *Report of the Maharaj Libel Case*, Mumbai, 1961.
2. M.K. Gandhi, *An Autobiography, or The Story of My Experiments with Truth*, tr. from Gujarati by Mahadev Desai, Ahmedabad, 2nd edn., 1940, p. 16.

3. S.N. Hay, *Asian Ideas of East and West, Tagore and his Critics in Japan, China, and India*, Cambridge, MA, 1970, p. 276.
4. *Gazetteer of the Bombay Presidency*, vol. 9, Part 1, *Gujarat Population*, Mumbai, 1891, pp. 530, 541.
5. L. Renou and J. Filliozat, *L'Inde Classique*, vol. 1, Paris, 1947, p. 623.
6. B.A. Saletore, *Main currents in the Ancient History of Gujarat*, Vadodara, 1960, pp. 45-7.
7. H. von Glasenapp, *Der Jainismus*, Hildersheim, 1964, p. 443.
8. K.M. Munshi, *Gujarat and its Literature*, Mumbai, 1935, p. xxl.
9. *Gazetteer of the Bombay Presidency*, vol. 8, *Kathiawar*, Mumbai, 1884, pp. 355-692.
10. Ghasiram, *Maharshi Dayananda Saraswati ka Jivan-Charit*, vol. I, Ajmer, 1957, p. 47.
11. *Bombay Gazetteer*, *Gujarat Population*, pp. 8, 9, 14, 17.
12. Ghasiram, p. 47.
13. *Bombay Gazetteer*, *Gujarat Population*, p. 546.
14. Pyarelal, *Mahatma Gandhi*, vol. 1, *The Early Phase*, Ahmedabad, 1965, pp. 212-14.
15. For a detailed study of these ideas of Gandhi cf. J.T.F. Jordens, 'Gandhi and Religious Pluralism', in H. Coward, *Modern Indian attitudes to Religious Pluralism*, New York, 1987, pp. 3-17.
16. For the details of Dayananda's youth cf. Dayananda's two autobiographical fragments: Lecture 15 of his Pune lectures, *Poona Pravachana arthat Upadesh-Manjari*, Yudhisthir Mimamshak (ed.), Delhi, 1969, and the autobiography in *The Theosophist*, vol. 1, pp. 9-13, 1879.
17. *Autobiography*, pp. 33-4.
18. *Selections from the Records of the Bombay Government*, no. 37, New Series, Mumbai, 1856, p. 291.
19. *Bombay Gazetteer*, *Kathiawar*, p. 148.
20. E. Reclus, *The Universal Geography*, A.H. Keane (ed.), vol. III, *India and Indochina*, London, n.d., p. 167.
21. von Glasenapp, pp. 74-5.
22. S.N. Hay, 'Jain Influences on Gandhi's early Thought', in S.N. Ray, *Gandhi, India and the World*, Melbourne, 1970, pp. 31-2.
23. von Glasenapp, p. 325.
24. *Bombay Gazetteer*, *Gujarat Population*, pp. 111-13.
25. V.A. Sangave, *Jaina Community, a Social Survey*: Mumbai, 1959, p. 267.
26. von Glasenapp, p. 443.
27. Ibid., p. 444.
28. S.N. Hay, p. 30.
29. M.K. Gandhi, *Collected Works*, vol. XXV, p. 167; also XIII, p. 220; XXXIV, p. 24; XXXV, p. 167; XL, pp. 104, 117.

30. Ibid., vol. IL, p. 327.
31. Cf. *The Theosophist*, vol. I, p. 10, October 1879.
32. Mrs Sinclair Stevenson, *The Heart of Jainism*, London, 1915, p. 17.
33. K.M. Munshi, p. 22.
34. *Bombay Gazetteer*, *Gujarat Population*, pp. 106, 148.
35. J. N. Farquhar, *Modern Religious Movements in India*, rpt., Delhi, 1967, p. 104.
36. von Glasenapp, p. 69.
37. J.N. Farquhar, p. 327.
38. *Bombay Gazetteer*, *Gujarat Population*, pp. xxvi, 50, 102.
39. A.K. Forbes, *Ras Mala*, London, 1878, p. 644.
40. Cf. von Glasenapp, Stevenson, and *Bombay Gazetteer*, *Gujarat Population*.
41. Cf. S.N. Hay, 'Jain influences on Gandhi's early Thought', and J.T.F. Jordens, 'Gandhi and Religious Pluralism'.
42. Cf. J.T.F. Jordens, *Dayananda Sarasvati*, *His Life and Ideas* , Delhi, 1978, pp. 190-3, 265-6.
43. Cf. J.T.F. Jordens, 'Gandhi's Religion and the Hindu Heritage', in S.N. Ray, *Gandhi*, *India and the World*, Melbourne, 1970, pp. 39-56.
44. Cf. J.T.F. Jordens, *Dayananda Sarasvati*, pp. 219-23.
45. Cf. *Bombay Gazetteer*, *Gujarat Population*, pp. 46, 116; *Selections*, p. 29.
46. Cf. von Glasenapp, p. 335; *Selections*, p. 29.
47. Cf. P.V. Kane, *History of Dharmashastra*, vol. II, Part 2, Pune, 1941, pp. 776-83; D.R. Shastri, *Original Development of the Rituals of Ancestor Worship in India*, Calcutta, 1963, pp. 161-3.
48. R.C. Majumdar (ed.), *The History and Culture of the Indian People*, vol. V, *The Struggle for Empire*, 2nd edn., Mumbai, 1966, p. 78.
49. S.N. Hay, *Asian Ideas*, p. 287.
50. *Bombay Gazetteer*, *Gujarat Population*, p. 530.
51. J.T.F. Jordens, 'Gandhi's Religion and the Hindu Heritage', pp. 51-2; R. Williams, *Jaina Yoga*, London, 1963.
52. Cf. J.T.F. Jordens, *Dayananda Sarasvati*, p. 27.
53. Ibid., pp. 215, 242.
54. H. Spodek, 'On the origins of Gandhi's Political Methodology: the heritage of Kathiawad and Gujarat', *The Journal of Asian Studies*, vol. 30, 1971, pp. 361-72.
55. Cf. J.T.F. Jordens, *Dayananda Sarasvati*, p.124.
56. Ibid., pp. 122, 125.

CHAPTER 9

Two Giants Look at the Cosmic Man

HOWEVER MUCH one may agree or disagree with the theories and approach of either or both Ambedkar and Dayananda, one has to acknowledge that each was in his own inimitable way a towering personality in the history of social reform in India in modern times. In their respective times they stood out from amongst their contemporaries and powerfully influenced the making of social history. The idea of bringing them together in confrontation of the same problem was suggested by what Ambedkar himself wrote in his Preface to *Who Were the Shudras?* apropos of his own interpretation of the Purusha-Sukta:

> The book treads heavily on the toes of the Arya Samajists . . . these conclusions are bound to act like atomic bombs on the dogmas of the Arya Samajists. I am not sorry for this clash with Arya Samajists. . . . I am convinced that the Hindu society will not accept the necessity of reforming itself unless and until this Arya Samajist ideology is completely destroyed. The book does render this service, if no other.[1]

Both reformers were in revolt against the orthodox caste ideology and structure, which for centuries had been justified by the pandits as an essential part of the divine order of things through reference to the famous Purusha-Sukta, Hymn to the Cosmic Man, of the Vedas. A comparison of the respective approaches of Ambedkar and Dayananda to social reform may, therefore, find an ideal start in the comparison of their comments on this hymn, by asking the following questions. What kind of status and authority do they give this text, and how do they interpret it; do they think its very composition tells us something about the social history of ancient India; what do they say about its normative value?

First, a few general remarks seem appropriate about the Purusha-Sukta itself. It is a cosmogonic hymn that is found with some variations in *Rigveda* X.90, *Yajurveda* XXXI.11 and *Atharvaveda* XIX.6. It ascribes the genesis and process of cosmic evolution to sacrificial power by mythically presenting the cosmogony as resulting from the sacrifice of the cosmic *purusha*. This sacrificial act of the gods makes all existence evolve out of this *purusha*. In verse 12 is to be found the only Rigvedic reference to the four orders of society, the four varnas or classes: 'The brahmin was his mouth, the kshatriya was made of his arms, the vaishya was made of his thighs, and the shudra sprang from his feet.' Thus, the four varnas are said to be produced from this primeval sacrifice, just like the gods, the animals, the four quarters, the sky, the earth, the Vedas, and the seasons. The hymn has many obscurities of detail, but leaving these aside, its essential message seems to be quite clear: that the creative power was a sacrificial power, that the division of society into four classes is an integral part of cosmogony itself, and that the definite hierarchy in society with the brahmin at the top and the shudra at the bottom of the scale is, therefore, divinely ordained. This last is clearly suggested by the mention of the mouth, arms, thighs, and feet of the *purusha* as the parts from which the classes were produced.

The Dharmasutras have much more to say about this hierarchy. Let us limit ourselves to Manu. Manu's Dharmashastra comes at the end of a long development between late Vedic times and the turn of the era. Its position is particularly important because it became and remained the highest authority on *dharma* through the centuries. First of all, Manu accepts the account of the origin of the classes as given in the Purusha-Sukta: 'For the sake of the prosperity of the whole world, the Lord caused the brahmin, the kshatriya, the vaishya, and the shudra, to proceed respectively from his mouth, his arms, his thighs and his feet' (I.31). But Manu goes much further in the explicitation of the varna theory. Belonging to a varna is the result of birth: *karma* accumulated in a previous life has produced in the individual to be born certain qualities, a particular mixture of the three *gunas*, *sattva*, *rajas*, and *tamas*, which assigns him at birth to his rightful varna (XII.9, 40). The hierarchy from mouth to feet, from high to low, from brahmin to shudra, is constantly reaffirmed, (e.g. I.92; VIII.270, 413). In fact, the whole legal structure of the *Laws of Manu* is a continuous affirmation of high and low, of privilege and disability in the juridical, social, occupational, and religious spheres. The two middle varnas, kshatriyas and vaishyas, are not as much in focus as are the high-born and privileged brahmins and the low-born and deprived shudras.

Ambedkar and Dayananda take different points of view at the very start of their commentary on the Purusha-Sukta: they regard the *Rigveda* itself in a very different light. To Dayananda the *Rigveda*, as integral part of the Samhitas, the four Vedas, is divine revelation, and contains nothing but revealed truth. The sacred text in the sacred language reveals not only the divine teaching and the ideal social programme, it also reflects the historical time when, at the beginning of creation, this truth and this order did in fact reign supreme in Aryavarta. Therefore, as he repeatedly sets out to prove in his works, the text itself is above all possible suspicion. A correct interpretation will reveal its meaning, and that meaning once established, must be of universal and eternal validity. The problem posed by the Purusha-Sukta can, therefore, in Dayananda's mind, constitute merely a problem of right interpretation.

Ambedkar, on the other hand, says that he is

> guided by the best tradition of the historian who treats all literature as vulgar—I am using the word in its original sense of belonging to the people—to be examined and tested by accepted rules of evidence without recognizing any distinction between the sacred and the profane and with the sole object of finding the truth. If in following this tradition I am found wanting in respect and reverence for the sacred literature of the Hindus, my duty as a scholar must serve as my excuse.[2]

What Ambedkar wants to investigate as a historian is the origin of the shudras and the causes of their degeneration. In doing this he deals with Vedic material as historical material. In fact, Ambedkar denies the 'sacredness, of the texts; the brahmins hold them sacred, he says, for two reasons only: because they are the production of their forefathers and because they support and perpetuate their privileges.[3] He refers to the social philosophy of the Purusha-Sukta as 'an idea which came to birth when the mind of man was primitive and was without the rich endowment of varied thought available in modern times'.[4] Therefore, to him the text is not only not sacred, it is, moreover, sociologically speaking, primitive and crude.

Dayananda accepts the *Purusha-Sukta* as being a cosmogonic hymn, and he treats it in his *Introduction to the Commentary on the Rigveda*, etc., under the heading 'On Cosmogony'. For him the word *purusha* means the one God, and he explains the cosmogonic teaching of the hymn as follows. God is the all-pervading spirit, the indwelling ruler, creator of the diversified universe, and also its absorber. He is the creator of the Veda and he far exceeds cosmic reality. The universe is built up from the basic twenty-one constituent elements of Samkhya cosmology, and it has seven concentric circles. In other words, Dayananda's interpretation of this often obscure text has a double effect. On the one hand, it yields the essential dogmas of Dayananda's theology on God's relationship to the cosmos, as they are detailed in chapter 8 of his *Satyarth Prakash*. On the other hand, his interpretation completely evaporates two aspects of the hymn that belong to its very essence: the fact that the hymn is a myth, and that it stresses the cosmic power of sacrifice. In view of the fact that Dayananda considered all mythology and sacrificial theology irrational and even immoral, this is not surprising.

Ambedkar too acknowledges that what we have here 'is a cosmogony', which is not unique, however, but similar to those found in other civilizations like the Egyptian and the Semitic ones.[5] He recognizes it as a 'myth', but for him a myth only means a theory of the origin of the universe conceived in the form of a 'legend',[6] an innocent piece of a poet's 'idle imagination'.[7] As such it has no real value any more, except 'to amuse children'; it satisfies the curiosity of scholars and has only a purely academic interest. In fact, 'Nobody relies on them. No Hindu ever remembers them.'[8] This judgement naturally cuts short all interest Ambedkar sees in the Purusha-Sukta as cosmogony. As such it has nothing significant to tell, but, as we will see, it does have considerable interest for the clues it gives us for the solution of the historical problem of the origin of the shudras in the stanza that deals with the varna system.

Now we consider the crucial stanza 12:

Brahmano asya mukham asid
Bahu rajanya kritah
Uru tadasya yad vaishyah
Padbhyam shudro ajayata

(The brahmin was the mouth thereof
The arms were made into kshatriyas
What were his thighs became the vaishyas
From his feet the shudras originated.)

How does Dayananda interpret it? He refers to it primarily in his *Introduction to the Commentary on the Vedas*, in his *Commentary on the Yajurveda* when commenting on 31.11, and in his fourth chapter of the *Satyarth Prakash*, where he considers the varnas. Of these the *Introduction* is the earlier text in our possession,[9] and there Dayananda explains the stanza:

The brahmin is said to be produced from the mouth of the *Purusha*, that means from such foremost qualities like knowledge, etc., such acts like truthful speech and teaching etc., ... The shudra, whose special mark is the quality of service on account of his dependence, should be known as produced from the feet (the lowest of the limbs), that is from qualities of the lowest category like dullness of intellect.[10]

Here Dayananda clearly affirms a qualitative hierarchy from the brahmin down to the shudra. This hierarchy is explained by the expression that the varnas are produced from different 'parts' of the *purusha*, which parts are explained as referring to superior, or medium, or inferior 'qualities'. The interpretation goes no further, but it refers to the chapter on *Varnashrama*, where as it were a rider is added: 'That man deserves to be a brahmin, who is endowed with the highest qualities like knowledge, etc., and who is engaged in the worship of God and in the study of the Veda.'[11] This interpretation leaves questions unanswered (after all it is only an Introduction), and can easily give rise to the type of objection that is raised by the 'objector' in the fourth chapter of the *Satyarth Prakash*:[12] 'Just as the mouth can never become an arm . . . or *vice versa*, in the same way a brahmin can never become a kshatriya or *vice versa*.' In his answer Dayananda further qualifies his interpretation of the stanza. He tells the objector that he has translated wrongly 'Of him the brahman is the mouth', because thus he connects *asya* with *mukham*. *Asya* clearly refers grammatically to *purusha*, of 'the formless spirit', but to ascribe bodily organs to him is patently contradictory. Dayananda also mentions other absurdities that would follow if one said that the brahmin was created from the mouth of the *purusha*. Therefore, since contradiction is *a priori* impossible in the *Rigveda*, *asya* cannot be connected with *mukham*. It should be connected with a word not expressed but supplied from the context, namely *shrishthau* (locative singular case of *shrishthi*) *asya shrishthau mukham asit*. Then the verse translates: 'In His creation, he who is (like) the mouth (the best and most prominent) is a brahmin.' This is also exactly the interpretation given in the *Commentary on the Yajurveda*.

We can notice here a shift in interpretation between the *Introduction* and the writing of the second edition of the *Satyarth Prakash*[13] and of the *Commentary on the Yajurveda*. The shift seems not to be in the meaning of the text,[14] but it rather consists of a tightening of text-interpretation. The *Introduction* still connected *asya* with *mukham*, but went on to insist that the latter really means 'foremost qualities'. Later on the link between *asya* and *mukham* is definitely broken: the verse now speaks no more of 'the mouth of the *purusha*'. Thus, one could say, this stanza of the hymn has become completely 'demythologized', and is brought into utter agreement with the basic theological principles of Dayananda. Basically, what has been solved is not a question in Dayananda's mind as to the nature of varna, but a question of grammatical Vedic text interpretation.

What then, are the basic ideas on varna that Dayananda sees expressed in the hymn? Varna implies a hierarchy of quality, but this is not determined by birth: the quality of man should determine his varna. It is also implied that this order of society as described in the Purusha-Sukta was in fact the order existing in Vedic times, and that it is the normative ideal order for all times.

Ambedkar deals with the stanza in question in a totally different manner. His first reaction is to notice how different these verses are from the rest of the hymn. 'Prima facie, he says, these verses do no more than explain how the four classes . . . arose from the body of the Creator.'[15] But, in fact, they do more. Amidst cosmogonic imagination we find here 'a divine injunction prescribing a particular form of the constitution of society'.[16] This stanza cannot be dismissed as mere cosmogonic speculation, it contains 'a mandatory injunction from the Creator to the effect that society must be constituted on the basis of four classes'.[17] Ambedkar spends no time on text criticism: in fact, he did not see his ignorance of Sanskrit as a bar to his historical research.[18] He affirms:

> Such a construction of the verses may not be warranted by their language. But there is no doubt that according to tradition this is how the verses are construed, and it would indeed be difficult to say that this traditional construction is not in consonance with the intention of the author of the Sukta.[19]

That is all Ambedkar has to say about the text itself. This injunction, he continues, then became the rigid mould of Aryan society, never questioned (except by the Buddha), defended by the brahmins and their Dharmasutras, and was finally invested by Manu 'with a degree of divinity which it did not have before',[20] when Manu stated, 'The Veda is the only and ultimate sanction of *Dharma*' (II. 6).

Ambedkar's critique of the Purusha-Sukta then proceeds to use the historical method. His first line of argument is that the Sukta departs from the general Rigvedic context in very significant ways. The *Rigveda* contains other cosmogonies, which not only evolve differently, but which moreover do not speak of the four varnas but of the creation of men, and of Manu as the progenitor of the human race. Whereas the *Rigveda* does refer to a division of labour, nowhere but in this Sukta is this division converted into rigid occupational categories. The *Rigveda* also speaks of an Indo-Aryan nation grown out of the assimilation of the five tribes, something again overlooked by the Sukta.[21]

One can see where the line of argumentation is heading for, and the final conclusion is reached in the latter part of the book. After having argued that there were originally only three varnas (the shudras were at first kshatriyas) in the *Rigveda* and in the Brahmanas, Ambedkar comes back to the Purusha-Sukta. The mention of four varnas in the Sukta is incongruous and leads to an absurd position. The only way out of this absurd incongruity is to declare the Purusha-Sukta a late interpolation. This Ambedkar then sets out to prove by 'the canons of historical criticism'.[22] Language comparison is taken to prove later composition: Colebrooke,[23] Max Mueller and Weber are quoted to establish this point. Other arguments put forward to argue the late composition of the text are: its absence from some editions, its placement in miscellaneous and supplementary portions of the Vedas, and the freedom taken with the text itself by the different editions. These arguments conclusively prove, says Ambedkar, that the Purusha-Sukta is, in fact, a late interpolation.[24]

Ambedkar goes one step further. He notes the 'difference in form' between stanzas 11-12 and the rest of the Sukta, and suggests that these verses on varna were an even later addition. His final conclusion is 'that the Sukta is an addition to the *Rigveda* made at a later stage and is, therefore, no argument that there were four varnas from the very beginning of the Aryan society'.[25]

Having thus closely considered the different ways in which Dayananda and Ambedkar deal with the Purusha hymn we can now compare more closely their respective frameworks of thought and methods of argumentation. The question we ask is not about the objective validity of their various arguments, but about their comprehensive framework of thought and method of reasoning as they are exemplified in their treatment of the Sukta.

Dayananda's reasoning revolves within a very definite framework, the essentials of which are his basic dogmas that the Vedas contain not only infallible revealed truth about God, but also the blueprint of the ideal society, a blueprint which, moreover, is the actual description of that ideal society as it existed in the Vedic Golden Age. This conception of the Vedas makes it absurd and impossible for Dayananda to approach and study the Vedas in a comparative and historical way. What indeed can be gained from comparing revealed divine truth predating history itself with the feeble human intellectual efforts of other cultures or of post-Vedic times, except a confirmation of the divinity of the former? And how can historical research tell us more about the ideal structure of society than the God-given blueprint of the Vedas does?

The only way in which Dayananda can discuss a Vedic text and still remain within this frame of reference, is by asking one very important question: what exactly is the meaning of this particular text? To answer this question only two methods are legitimate and available. First, there are the tools of grammar and linguistics, a science perfected by the sage Panini. Second, there is logical reasoning. God's word is by definition eminently reasonable and cannot contain contradictions and absurdities. Therefore, any interpretation that involves such contradiction must needs be wrong. We have seen how, in dealing with the Purusha-Sukta, these are the only tools in fact used by Dayananda. *Asya* cannot be connected with *mukham* because it would imply a contradiction, which is impossible. *Asit* is said to refer to all times, past, present and future, according to the grammatical rule enunciated in Panini's *Ashtadhyayi* 3,4,6. These two arguments are the ones that justify the translation, 'In the creation of God, he who is (the best and most prominent like) the mouth, is a brahmin.'

Ambedkar's frame of reference concerning the Vedas is utterly different. To him the Vedas are only a 'vulgar' historical text. As such they do not reveal sacred truths, but they furnish, in the midst of a lot of primitive myth and legend, a certain number of data that have historical interest: they tell us something about the composition of society in Vedic times. This society was the result of a particular historical evolution and its structure has nothing sacred or ideal about it. The text itself was composed by ordinary mortals, and, therefore, its very composition was motivated by human desires.

This framework dictates the way Ambedkar will analyse and study the text itself. Since the text is but a human composition and not a word-for-word divine utterance, its meaning need not be agonizingly established: the general consensus of the translations of scholars is sufficient to yield its essential meaning. Once this meaning is established and the particular social data are clarified, the historian goes to work. He compares these data with the other data on the same topic found in the same work, he compares them with those found in later works, and with those found in other cultures of a similar antiquity. We saw how this comparison led Ambedkar to the conclusion that the Purusha-Sukta was an interpolation and did not reflect the conditions of Vedic times.

There is a second method by which Ambedkar scrutinizes the text: from the theoretical sociological angle. Whereas Ambedkar's historical approach is somehow parallel to the linguistic approach by Dayananda (in that both are more of a 'technical' nature) this sociological approach is rather parallel to Dayananda's use of logical reasoning (in that both are of a 'theoretical' nature). The basic objection of Ambedkar to the Sukta in this context is that it elevates the real to the status of ideal, that it makes a real order of society into a static norm. This view, he says, is 'opposed to all morality. No society with a social conscience has ever accepted it'.[26] This is so because, in his view, social ethics are an essentially dynamic force, changing with the very process of history in the continuous interaction of individuals and classes. Therefore, he concludes, the very composition of the Sukta was not a function of social ethics, but it was inspired by an ulterior class motive: the wilful degradation of the shudras.

This last point reveals a difference between Dayananda and Ambedkar at a very deep level in their fundamental conception of social ethics and of the ideal society. To Dayananda, both are basically static, as they are enshrined in the Vedas and in the Vedic times. To Ambedkar, both are dynamic concepts, being progressively discovered in the march of history itself. This does not imply, naturally, that Dayananda was a static conservative. Only the frame of reference is a static one, because revealed by God. In his times he was an ardent reformer, because that ideal society of yore had degenerated and needed to be rebuilt from the very ruins of Hinduism. However, in this dynamic task of rebuilding, man is not groping in the dark; he possesses the divine blueprint of the Golden Age of the future in that of the Golden Age of the past.[27]

A few similarities only are to be found in Ambedkar's and Dayananda's treatment of the Sukta, but they are significant. Both emphatically reject the assignment to social status by the accident of birth, as upheld by traditional orthodoxy. Both accept, be it in very different ways, the morality and necessity of social mobility for the individual. Both also accuse the brahmins of having ossified and perpetuated a system of varna-by-birth for selfish reasons: to perpetuate their own privileges and to deprive others of many basic rights. In these three important points the two reformers radically oppose the traditional doctrines and structures of orthodoxy. And orthodoxy was very aware of it. Ambedkar, being an untouchable, was beyond the strictures of orthodoxy, but Dayananda, the brahmin, was not, and in 1881 a Council of orthodox pundits declared that in five points of doctrine Dayananda offended orthodoxy. One of these points was his denial of the full authority of the brahmins.[28]

We have noted in Ambedkar and Dayananda a very close relation between their fundamental frame of reference regarding the Veda and Vedic times on the one hand, and their methods of criticism of Vedic material on the other. We would now like to suggest that in both personalities there is a deeper source of both these factors and their close relationship. That source is their basic passion for social reform. Both were in different ways great masters of their disciplines: Ambedkar's historical and sociological competence were vast, and Dayananda's linguistic and theological powers were admirable indeed. Yet, their works cannot be taken to be primarily scholarly works. To view and criticize them as such would be an academic exercise of little value. Their writings are works in which these considerable powers of analysis and reason are put to work by an overriding, all-absorbing passion for social reform. Their writings, to be properly understood, must be connected with their activity as reformers. In fact, their writings are essentially an integral part of that very activity.

The author of *Who were the Shudras?* was the untouchable who became the great leader of his brothers in their fight for social justice; the author of the *Satyarth Prakash* was the brahmin who, disgusted with the decadence of Hinduism, wanted to restore it to its ancient glory. Their respective interpretations of the *Purusha-Sukta* find their ultimate justification in those facts. Dayananda's interpretation of the Sukta was basically concerned with one thing: to interpret it in such a way that orthodoxy could no longer claim it as a divine proof of brahmin privileges, as an argument for caste by birth, as a barrier against social mobility. Ambedkar wanted to show that in early Vedic times, there were no shudras, they were in fact kshatriyas, and, therefore, the Sukta which mentions shudras had to be proven to be a later fabrication. This is not to accuse them of intellectual dishonesty. It is only to stress that both these men harnessed their considerable intellectual powers of analysis and reason not just in the service of 'academic' interest, but for the much more worthwhile cause of building a better society.

One cannot but admire these two giants of thought and action as they look at the Cosmic Man: they appear as men of one piece, integrated personalities, in whom the passion for social reform guided both their intellectual and their organizational genius at every moment of their struggle.

NOTES

[This chapter was first published as: 'Two Giants look at the Cosmic Man: Dayananda and Ambedkar interpret the *Purusha-Sukta*', *Journal of the Oriental Institute of Baroda*, vol. 33, Vadodara, 1983, pp. 1-10.]

1. B.R. Ambedkar, *Who were the Shudras? How they came to be the Fourth Varna in the Indo-Aryan Society*, Mumbai, 1946, pp. xvi-xvii. Hereinafter quoted as *Shudras.*
2. *Shudras*, p. xix.
3. Ibid., p. xx.
4. Ibid., p. 6.
5. Ibid, p. 3.
6. Ibid., p. 23.
7. Ibid., p. 4.
8. Ibid., p. 3.
9. It definitely predates the *Yajurbhashya* and the second edition of the *Satyarth Prakash* with which we are dealing here.
10. *Rigvedadibhashyabhumika*, Ajmer, 1980, p. 133.
11. Ibid., p. 257.
12. *Satyarth Prakash*, Ajmer, 1966, p. 81
13. The first edition of the *Satyarth Prakash* also refers to the Purusha-Sukta, but it does not go into detail about its interpretation. Cf. *Satyarth Prakash*, Varanasi, 1875, p. 96.
14. This is evident from what we called the 'rider' in the section of the *Bhumika* on *varnashrama*.
15. *Shudras*, p. 3.
16. Ibid., p. 4.
17. Ibid.
18. Ibid., p. xiv.
19. Ibid., p. 4.

20. Ibid., p. 6.
21. Ibid., pp. 11-12
22. Ibid., p. 147.
23. Ibid., pp. 148-9.
24. Ibid., pp. 149-51.
25. Ibid., p. 153.
26. Ibid., p. 15.
27. For a detailed analysis of these ideas, cf. J.T.F. Jordens, *Dayananda Sarasvati, His Life and Ideas*, Delhi, *passim*.
28. For details of this meeting, see Jordens, *Dayananda Sarasvati*, ch. 3.

CHAPTER 10

Dayananda and Karsondas Mulji: Their Condemnations of the Vallabhacharyas

IN THE LATTER half of the nineteenth century, two prominent personalities—Karsondas Mulji and Dayananda Sarasvati—caused considerable upheaval among the Vallabhacharyas of Mumbai by their concerted onslaught on the sect. This chapter analyses the source, nature, strengths, and weaknesses of the attacks of these two reformers. Although Karsondas's polemic war occurred in the early 1860s (culminating in the notorious Maharaj Libel Case in which a leading guru of the sect sued him for libel)[1] and Dayananda's controversy belongs to the mid-1870s, by which time Karsondas had died, it is important to note that there was a definite historical link between their campaigns.

In November 1869, the famous Varanasi disputation took place between Dayananda and a galaxy of orthodox pundits on the question whether idol-worship was sanctioned by the Vedas.[2] This event, widely advertised, attended by a large distinguished audience, and extensively reported in the press, made the Swami into a public figure. Two Mumbai visitors were present on that occasion and called on the Swami afterwards. One of them was Dharmsi, brother of Lakhmidas Khimji and a close associate of Karsondas Mulji who was a major witness for the defence in the Maharaj Libel case; and the other was Jaikishendas Jivanram, an enthusiastic *advaitin* follower of Shankara's theology. Both were very much opposed to the Vallabhacharyas, and impressed by the ideas and public performance of Dayananda, whom they urged to come to Mumbai. No doubt they told the Swami of the fight by

Karsondas Mulji (who was still alive at this time) and of his triumph in the Maharaj Libel Case.[3]

Two aspects of Dayananda's approach impressed the Mumbai visitors most: firstly, his total and vehement opposition to all forms of idolatry and to all aspects of Puranic sectarianism as corruptions of the ancient *dharma*; and secondly, his conviction that 'pure Hinduism' was to be found in the Vedas. In fact, these two themes had played a major part in the case for the defence in the Maharaj Libel Case. But on that occasion the defence, whose witnesses were mostly members of the trading castes and ignorant of Sanskrit, had to rely on a foreigner, the British indologist Dr John Wilson, for expert testimony on ancient texts and history.[4] In Dayananda, the reformers found a famous pandit hailing from their own area, who could plead their cause with authority because his knowledge of Sanskrit and ancient Vedic texts was such that it enabled him to tackle and confound a panel of Varanasi pandits.

The idea that 'authentic' Hinduism was to be found in the Vedas had remained a concern of Karsondas after the completion of the court hearing. Shortly before his death, he published a small pamphlet in Gujarati entitled *Ved Dharma*. The contents of this tract are most revealing: Karsondas

> was in favour of calling the Hindu religion by the title of *Arya Dharma* and said that the genuine kernel of the *Arya Dharma* was to be found in the Vedas. In this book he dealt with the language of the Vedas, and the reason why people were left in ignorance of the Vedas, and said that whatever was written in the *Puranas* was not written in the Vedas. . . . Karsondas in this brochure says that in the Vedas was to be found the nucleus of a pure religion.[5]

His collaborators continued this study after his death by establishing for that purpose a Veda Sabha, in which Lakhmidas Khimji, Mulji Thakarshi, and Sevaklal Karsondas were involved.[6] Two Bhatia friends, Sundardas Dharmsi and Liladhar Hari, members of the Vallabhacharya sect who had become disenchanted with its current state, had also been moving on their own accord in the same direction. They had founded their own society for the study of early Hinduism, the Vedokt Shravan Sabha, and started a monthly called *Hridayachakshu*. In 1870 they became friends of Sevaklal Karsondas.[7] It is not surprising that this group of people, on hearing about Dayananda and his Varanasi disputation from their friends who attended it, were keen that the Swami should come to Mumbai. When they finally heard from him that he was wending his way towards western India, they translated a synopsis of the Varanasi disputation into Gujarati and published it in the *Arya Mitra* a month before the Swami's arrival in Mumbai.[8]

The historical connection between Karsondas Mulji's endeavours and those of Dayananda subsequently become strikingly clear when we look at the people who supported the Swami's visit to Mumbai. These included Lakhmidas Khimji, Thakarshi Narayanji, and Mathuradas Lowji who had been major witnesses for the defence in the Maharaj Libel Case,[9] and Pranjivandas Vadhaji and Chhabildas Lallubhai who had been amongst the few outspoken supporters of Karsondas Mulji.[10] Thakarshi Narayanji became foundation Vice-President of the Arya Samaj, and Sevaklal Karsondas foundation Treasurer. The two Bhatia friends, Liladhar Hari and Sundardas Dharmsi, were foundation members and regular committee members of the Arya Samaj for 20 years.[11] The foundation President, Girdharilal Dayaldas Kothari, was a close associate of Lakhmidas Khimji; and Pranjivandas Vadhaji, another foundation member, was a personal friend of Karsondas Mulji. Chhabildas Lallubhai supported the Swami in every way and, though he himself did not become a member of the Arya Samaj, his son Ramdas, at that time a student at Elphinstone College, was also a foundation member.[12] There remains no doubt that among the people who promoted Dayananda's visit and who urged him to found the Arya Samaj, the major part was played by a group of friends who had openly supported Karsondas Mulji and had endeavoured to keep his ideas and his cause alive. In this connection it is interesting to note that the word 'Arya' featured both in the writings of Karsondas and in the name of the reformers' journal years before Dayananda arrived in Mumbai and founded his Arya Samaj. Thus there was a clear historical link between Dayananda's attack on the Vallabhacharyas and that of Karsondas Mulji.

The ideas and attitudes of participants in religious controversies are often deeply rooted in some personal experience which must be taken into account for the full understanding of their ideas. In different ways, this was the case with both Karsondas and Dayananda. Karsondas was born into the Kapole Baniya caste and into a Vallabhacharya family. In his childhood he was formally initiated into the sect, receiving the sacred *mantra* and the *kanthi*, a necklace made of *tulsi*, and on Sundays he regularly visited with his family the temple of Maharaj Jivanji. At fifteen he started to take note of, and reflect on, some of the customs he witnessed in the sect: he saw the Maharaja pressing the toes of some female devotee who then followed him into his private quarters;

he saw the guru throwing coloured powder over women's breasts during the Holi festival; he saw people devoutly drinking the water wrung out from the Maharaja's loincloth after his bath, or ecstatically chewing the leavings of his food or his betelnut. Within a year he stopped going to the temple.[13] In that same year he had married and had entered an unnamed English school.[14] It seems warranted to suppose that his personal aversion to the customs of the sect was partly caused by his early contact with modern European-inspired ideas of reform. He then started studying at Elphinstone College, but was banished from his aunt's home when she discovered an essay he had written in favour of widow remarriage. Condemned by his father too as a rebel, he decided to make his own way and live separately.[15] Thus, Karsondas's experience as an adolescent of certain sectarian practices, strengthened by his early contact with ideas of reform was decisive both in turning him away from the sect adhered to by his family and in establishing for himself greater freedom outside family pressures

Dayananda's encounter with the Vallabhacharya sect happened in Mahura at a very crucial stage of his personal development. At the age of twenty-one, he had run away from home to avoid an impending marriage. He had taken *sannyasa* and for fifteen years had roamed around north India studying Vedanta and Yoga in his individualistic search for the achievement of personal perfection. But the Swami was not by nature a mystic or an introvert: it seems that his search was frustrating and that the doors of perception remained closed to him. At the end of 1860, he arrived at Mathura where he spent three years as the prize pupil of the great grammarian, Swami Virjananda Sarasvati. During that period the lone searcher for perfection underwent a radical transformation. He passionately embraced the new ideal that would inspire his remaining years: the reform of corrupt contemporary Hinduism by a return to the pristine purity of ancient times. No doubt, the influence of his guru played an important part in this redirection, but Mathura's role was equally vital.[16]

In Mathura Dayananda was, for the first time in his life, in constant, immediate contact with the pulsating, chaotic life of a most sacred Hindu pilgrimage place. He lived in a cell on the ground floor of the Lakshminarayana temple on the principal *ghat* of Mathura, Vishrant Ghat. His guru lived on the arterial road leading from the Holi Gate to Vishrant Ghat. In his cell, at his guru's home, and on the way from one to the other, Dayananda's senses were constantly assailed by the brash, noisy tamasha of the pilgrimage place, the throbbing heart of Vaishnavite Mathura. Dayananda had been brought up in Shaivism, but had gradually moved towards the *advaita* doctrines of Shankara. During his stay in Mathura he turned back from *advaita* to Shaivite monotheism.[17] But in Mathura, Shiva had no rights, as the contemporary visitor Bholanath Chander remarked: 'He has only one temple dedicated to him, and appears to have been permitted to reside much as a foreigner holding a passport—as an interloper.'[18]

Not only Mathura, but also the whole Braj-mandala, the 500 square miles and more of its environs, were considered holy because this was the birthplace of Krishna.[19] This is exclusive Krishna territory replete with temples, hills, lakes and groves, all commemorating the antics of the child Krishna and the amours of his youth. 'For nine months of the year festival follows upon festival in rapid succession, and the ghats and temples are daily thronged with new troups of way-worn pilgrims.' Naturally, Mathura is also one of the major centres of the Vallabhacharya cult.[20] It is extremely important that at this crucial time of the gestation and birth of the reformer in Dayananda, the excesses of popular Hinduism suffocating him were purely Vaishnavite, and exclusively Krishnaite. It is no wonder that when he reflected on the corruption of contemporary sectarian Hinduism, the Vaishnavites and specifically the Vallabhacharyas, were usually the first sects that came to his mind.[21]

Both reformers wrote extensively about the Vallabhacharyas, and it is to those writings that we now turn to assess the thrust, validity, and shortcomings of their critique. Karsondas's criticism is to be found in his newspaper articles, in his deposition as defendant in the Maharaj Libel Case, and in the large volume he published anonymously, entitled *History of the Sect of Maharajas, or Vallabhacharyas in Western India.* Dayananda wrote an early critique of the *Bhagavata Purana* in pamphlet form entitled *Bhagavata-Khandanam*, and some pages of criticism of the sect in the first edition of his *Satyarth Prakash*, published in 1875.[22] During his visit to Mumbai he wrote a full, 80 page pamphlet about the sect entitled *Vedaviruddhmatkhandana*.[23] In the second edition of the *Satyarth Prakash*, which he wrote in the year of his death 1883, he thoroughly revised and extended the criticism contained in the first edition.[24]

Both reformers repeatedly and vehemently denounced the sexual malpractices of the Maharajas and of some of their followers. With Karsondas, this aspect of the affair was nearly obsessional. This is no wonder, because there are clear indications that he had become strongly affected by the acute puritanism of his era that influenced many Indian reformers. He recommended as properly decent attire for Indian ladies, 'heavy silk saris, stockings and slippers or shoes',[25] and he strongly disapproved of the dhoti for men because 'several parts of the bodies remain naked and sometimes decency is not preserved'. In the same vein, he disapproved of eating with hands and fingers as 'not befitting normal civilised times'.[26]

As to Dayananda, he took *sannyas* at the age of twenty-one: up to then he had successfully resisted his parents' efforts to arrange his marriage, but he finally had to run away from home because the pressure became too intense. But his refusal to marry had nothing to do with prudishness. In fact, during the long years of preaching before his visit to Calcutta, he was known as the naked *sannyasi* who never wore more than a loincloth, summer and winter, day and night. It was on the advice of his Calcutta Brahmo friends, in particular of Keshub Chandra Sen, that he started wearing city clothes in public.[27] Another indication of the absence in him of puritanical attitudes is his strange and daring doctrine of *niyoga*. He proclaimed that this was a Vedic institution sanctioning temporary unions between widows and widowers for a wide variety of reasons, including even simple sexual need.[28] The Arya Samaj never condemned the doctrine, but the Aryas, aware of its radical and impractical nature, and often under scathing attack about it, never attempted to implement it. To Dayananda, the only sexual unions sanctioned by Vedic *dharma* was that of man and wife, and that of the *niyoga* partners.[29] His indignation about, and condemnation of, the sexual abuses prevalent among the Vallabhacharyas were on purely moral grounds, just as were his denunciation of Tantric sexual practices. The myth of the amours of Krishna was abhorrent to him because it defiled the character of Krishna whom he considered to have been the brave and moral hero of *Mahabharata* times, and no more than that.

One of the principal recurrent themes in the criticism of the Vallabhacharyas by both reformers is that the sectarian creed is of recent origin and not in conformity with the ancient doctrines of Hinduism. Nearly half the article by Karsondas which became the document accused of libel in the Maharaj case was devoted to that argument. Its essential form is very simple. The Shastras declare that in the *kaliyuga* false religions will arise. The *kaliyuga* has now been current for 5,000 years. The Vallabhacharya sect is less than 400 years old. Therefore, that sect is heretical, in company with all other recent ones such as the Daduists, the Ramsnehis, the Ramanandas and the Sahajanandis.[30] In his lengthy history of the sect, Karsondas does not go beyond this simplistic argument. To him, mere enumeration of the abuses rampant in the sect was ample proof that his argument about heresy was right. The transcript of his statements under cross examination in the Libel Case indicates that his argument was not very well thought through:

> I said there are about a hundred sects in India, but I don't think the old religion is represented by any one sect at present. Some of the sects follow the old religion more or less. The Vallabhacharya sect professes to follow the old religion, but I am not certain whether it does. It differs widely in its doctrines from those of the old religion, and conceives itself to be far superior to all other sects.[31]

Even more revealingly he stated: 'I do not believe in the modern stories in books which are written after the Veda, which I have not read.'[32] Karsondas appears to have been poorly informed about Hinduism, its history and doctrines, and it seems that his criticism was primarily founded on his abhorrence of abuses. In his history of the sect, he wrote that he would present 'a succinct view of Hinduism in its primitive condition'. In fact, all he did was to quote Max Mueller's words, 'The key-note of all religion, natural as well as revealed, is present in the hymns of the Veda. There is the belief in God, the perception of the difference between good and evil, the conviction that God hates sin, and loves the righteous.'[33] He also agreed with that scholar that the *Rigveda* was the most ancient part of the Vedas, professing a basic monotheism, and characterized by its 'poetical and mystical' approach.[34] It is in this context that Karsondas, for the first time, adopted Max Mueller's name for the ancient Hindus: 'the Aryans'.[35] Karsondas was no doubt aware of his own lack of scholarship, and he did wish to study more, but never got far in this endeavour, badly prepared as he was for it and overwhelmed by the demands of his career.

For Dayananda, the argument of the corruption of Vedic religion in later times and the reinstatement of that religion, became the passionate focus of his whole reforming endeavour. After leaving his guru Virjananda in 1863, it took him six years of intensive study of Hindu texts to reach the conclusion that only the Samhitas, the *Rig*, *Yajur*, *Sama* and *Atharvaveda* contained authentic, revealed, *dharma*.[36] It is significant that his first publication was a criticism of the *Bhagavata Purana*, the text *par excellence* of Krishnaism. In his subsequent publications, he consistently criticized the doctrines and practices of Puranic Hinduism, but no single sect drew the lengthy denunciations reserved for the Vallabhacharyas.

Karsondas's criticism of the Vallabhacharyas was fully developed in his volume on the history of the sect. The first two chapters deal with early Vedic literature and the rise of the sects. Chapters 3 to 7 specifically treat the Vallabhacharya Sect: its origins, scriptures, doctrines, and worship. The last four chapters describe the 'profligacy' of and oppression by the Maharajas, and opposition to them, from the Chhapan Bhogan dispute[37] to the Maharaj Libel case. The middle chapters are meant to constitute criticism of the doctrines from a rational or theological point of view, but they are in fact largely descriptive and contain extremely little critical analysis of any kind. Karsondas criticized the excessive importance given by the sect to the position of guru, 'direct mediator', avatar of Krishna 'superior to Hari in his power of salvation'. He considered such emphasis pernicious because it drew attention away from knowledge of the true God.[38] He also disapproved of the way in which the sublime ideal of early Hinduism, 'reunion with Brahma, absorption into Brahma', had been 'debased into a sexual and carnal coition with the most sensuous of the manifestations or 'avatars' of God'.[39]

The above is about all to be found in the way of criticisms of ideas. Karsondas was not a theological thinker but primarily an enthusiastic popular moralist. He did not manage to stay for more than a couple of sentences at a time on the discussion of ideas, and then tended immediately to veer off into a denunciation of immorality. In fact, he seems to have had but little interest in religious ideas as such. His main biographer states that 'There is no adequate material before us to come to a right decision about Karsondas's religious views.'[40] Another biographer has even suggested he may have been an atheist.[41] From the evidence it appears that the theology of Karsondas did not reach beyond a rationalistic belief in God as the maker of the universe, coupled with a strong conviction of the importance of morality, in other words, a vague deism.

Dayananda's criticism of the Vallabhacharya sect spans the last twenty years of his life. Before analysing its thrust and recurring motifs, we will sketch the historical development of the main lines of his attack. His *Bhagavata-Khandanam*, published in 1864, is a minute pamphlet in Sanskrit, which sets out to prove the single point that the *Bhagavata Purana* was not written by the sage Vyasa, and could not be considered as authoritative. His first proof was historical: in the text it is claimed that it was recited by Shuka to Parikshit; but since Shuka had died before the war of the Bharatas, that is an historical impossibility. Secondly, the text contained grammatical errors and logical contradictions, and also slander of the Vedas, of Shiva, of Krishna, and of Brahma, according to Dayananda. Therefore, such writing could not possibly have been composed by the sage Vyasa, it totally lacked authoritative status.[42]

In his first *Satyarth Prakash*, written before his visit to Mumbai, Dayananda included a few pages on the sect.[43] Here he concentrated on the immoral aspects of the lives of the founders and of their successors, the Maharajas. It is a detailed catalogue of instances of sensuality and greed, all of which are also to be found in the Maharaj Libel case proceedings. Naturally Dayananda, who had lived for three years in Mathura, a centre of the cult,[44] must have come to know about the sect; but still one wonders if Karsondas's friends whom he met in Varanasi did not give him the Gujarati edition of the proceedings of the case. The first edition of the *Satyarth Prakash* does not venture into a theological discussion of the beliefs of the sect.

When Dayananda arrived in Mumbai on 20 October 1874, the battlelines between him and the Vallabhacharyas were immediately drawn up. This is not surprising, as his hosts were the foremost critics of the sect, the inheritors of the legacy of Karsondas. The press announcement of the Swami's arrival, containing an invitation to the discussion of religious topics, and the Swami's very first lectures against the Vallabhacharyas, were received by them as a direct challenge. The twenty-four questions sent to the Swami to ascertain his doctrinal positions probably came from them. Answers to these were written, and were published by Dayananda's collaborator Swami Purnananda.[45] These were the first moves in a confrontation that did not abate till the Swami left Mumbai. Public lectures were disrupted, or rebutted in counter-lectures, there were rumours of an assassination plot by the sectarian leaders, and challenges to a public disputation were thrown about. In fact, there were three such disputations in which the Vallabhacharyas put up against the Swami, the pandits Icchashankar Sukul, Kamalanayanacharya, and Ramlal. These pandits did not fare well on those occasions, and especially the second one, held in the Framji Cowasji Hall, discredited the sect as it ended in the abject retreat of Pandit Kamalanayanacharya.[46]

During his stay in Mumbai the Swami produced his pamphlet against the sect entitled *Vedaviruddhmatkhandanam*, 'Criticism of a belief contrary to the Vedas.' It is written in a didactic question-and-answer form, and deals with all important aspects of the sect in sixty-two items. The Swami's Sanskrit text was accompanied by a Gujarati translation prepared by Shyamji Krishnavarma. Although the pamphlet mentioned incidentally the immoral practices of the sect, essentially it concentrated on doctrinal issues. The Swami took pains in its preparation to consult some of the major sectarian works. He quoted from the *Anubhashya*, Vallabha's famous commentary on the *Brahmasutra*, and also from a small but extremely important text also by him, the *Siddhantarahasya*. He referred to Vitthala's *Vidvanmandana*, and had consulted contemporary works such as the *Shuddhadvaita Martanda* of Giridhara, Pandit Gattulal's *Satsiddhantamartanda* and the vernacular work *Rasabhavana*.[47] He would have had no difficulty in getting hold of these works through his Mumbai friends, especially Sevaklal Karsondas, who later on provided the Swami with an impressive number of books on Jainism.[48]

In 1883, the year of his death, Dayananda rewrote his *Satyarth Prakash*, and fundamentally altered the section on the Vallabhacharyas. He retained the catalogue of immoralities of the sectarian leaders, but added a significant section of theological criticism.[49] Most of the latter is closely parallel to the contents of his pamphlet, some of which have however been omitted. This did not constitute a change in his ideas; the reason is simply that some topics dealt with in the pamphlet, such as the idea of God, and idolatrous and superstitious practices, had been fully treated elsewhere in the *Satyarth Prakash*.

Dayananda's criticism includes a more general denunciation of widespread Puranic practices, such as the investiture of the idol and its worship, temple rites, and a variety of 'superstitions', which are not of special importance here. His specific criticism of the sect's doctrines is basically of two kinds, historical and theological. His fundamental historical argument runs as follows. The founders and leaders of the sect, through both their writings and their actions, proved to be despisers of the Vedas. Therefore, they were in fact *nastikas*, a term used to refer to those such as Buddhists, Jains, or Charvaka materialists[50] whose disbelief in the Vedas puts them outside the boundaries of Hinduism. The biographies of the founders were indicted for two reasons: they referred to actions in breach of *dharma* (especially the successive adoption of first *sannyasa* and then marriage), and they recounted impossible miracles. The evidence of the sensuality, greed and ignorance of the Maharajas was equally damaging. In short, the biographies of these leaders were replete with untruths, and their actions clearly proved their opposition to the Vedas and Vedic *dharma*. Dayananda clinched the argument that they did not profess the true Vedic *dharma* by quoting Vallabha's dictum, 'Laukik and Vaidik dharm are not right, only Vaisnavism is natural (*sahaj*), and transcends all others.'[51]

The Swami's theological arguments against the Vallabhacharya doctrines are most clearly expressed in his pamphlet. For clarity's sake they are arranged here under three headings: the concept of God, *moksha* and the way to achieve it, and the idea of the guru. It is immediately obvious that these topics are in no way peripheral, but go right to the heart of the matter.

As for the concept of the divinity, Dayananda approached this from different angles. First, he attacked the Puranic view of Vishnu as the four-armed husband of Lakshmi, resident of the *Vaikuntha* (heavens), and endowed with a glorious body. This view was to be rejected simply because God is by definition simple, incorporeal, indestructible, and all-pervading.[52] Along the same lines it was argued that the concept of avatar (incarnation), was absurd: God cannot be born because this would negate his essential qualities of omnipotence, omnipresence, eternity and immateriality.[53] Finally the Swami denounced the Puranic tradition of calling the Lord *mayavin*, the one who possesses the wondrous power of *maya*. This cannot be because, according to Dayananda, the concept of *maya* had intrinsic implications of deceit and trickery, which could never be imparted to the Lord.[54] The conception of Krishna as '*Parabrahma* himself residing in *Goloka*' was patently false. Krishna was no other than the great hero of *Mahabharata* times, a human being who was born and died five thousand years ago. That statement was considered by Dayananda sufficient to completely discredit the Vallabhacharya doctrine that the absolute is in the final instance Bhagavat Parabrahman Shri Krishna.[55]

The pamphlet ended with a criticism of the philosophical facet of Vallabhacharya theology called *shuddhadvaita*, pure non-dualism.[56] Non-dualism, argued Dayananda, posits the identity of the universe as both cause and effect. In Vallabhacharya terms that means that 'the One Absolute Brahman has manifested himself in order to enjoy the play of duality, similar to the love between man and woman'.[57]

Dayananda reduced the complex metaphysics of the Vallabha system to the following basic propositions: all reality is ultimately one, but it has modified itself into a duality, thus manifesting the universe. Then he declared these propositions to be against reason. On the one hand, the Absolute cannot become the universe because it is by definition all-perfect and all-wise, and in becoming the world it would acquire all the imperfections evident in the world. On the other hand, if the universe, that is matter and spirits, is indeed identical with the Absolute, then it should manifest all the perfections of that Absolute, which it patently does not. Dayananda then proceeded to show that Vallabha had misinterpreted the great Upanishadic aphorisms such as '*sarvam khalv idam brahma*' and '*ayam atma brahma*', by forcing onto them a non-dualist meaning. According to Dayananda these aphorisms did not express a relationship between *brahman*, the Absolute, and the world, but were only statements about the nature of *brahman*-in-itself.[58]

The second central topic of Dayananda's criticism concerns *moksha* and the path that leads to it. He stated that the four degrees of *moksha* propounded by the Vaishnavites were in fact meaningless. *Salokya*, sharing the same world with God, *samipya*, being in close proximity to Him, *sanujya*, being like a younger brother to him, and *sayujya*, being united with Him—all these were descriptions of states which belonged naturally to all creatures by virtue of the simple fact that God is the all-pervading presence in the universe and the innermost dweller in all His creation and His creatures. To describe *moksha* in those terms was, therefore, futile. If, Dayananda continued, you say that *moksha* means living in the *Goloka* (paradise), then you are wrong again; since this paradise with its cows and meadows, and groves and palaces, keeps its inhabitants dependent on matter and on other creatures, and since such dependence necessarily involves discomfort, sickness, and pain, such heaven could not possibly deserve the name of *moksha*'.[59]

Dayananda realized that the central doctrine of the Vallabhacharyas about the way to the achievement of *moksha* was contained in the *Siddhantarahasya*, which Vallabha claimed had been revealed to him by Lord Krishna in person. He quoted this text in full in his pamphlet. According to this doctrine, the *dosas*, or impurities of body and soul which prevent the blissful union of man with Krishna, can only be removed by an act of total self-dedication, by which all activities and possessions of the devotee are offered to Krishna before they are enjoyed. Through this ceremony of dedication, called *Brahmasambandha*, all impurities are removed and the devotee becomes as pure as Krishna himself: thus he enters the *pustimarga*, the way of divine favour, along which the grace of Krishna draws the devotee to the highest beatitude of *mokṣha*.[60]

First Dayananda criticized more peripheral aspects, such as, if Krishna had been dead for 5,000 years, how could he have spoken to Vallabha? He asserted that offering 'everything' to God was a meaningless expression, because 'everything' included misery and evil. He also remarked that offering one's wife to another was a great sin. Here it is apposite to note that in the vernacular translation of the *Siddhantarahasya*, the Sanskrit term '*swami*', referring in the original to Krishna, was translated as '*Gosain*', so that the offering of everything was clearly interpreted as meaning offering everything before enjoyment of it to the Maharaj.[61]

Dayananda then moved on to state his theological objections to the removal of the impurities by the act of *samarpan* (offering). Impurity was to him a very concrete entity, the necessary fruit of the deed, *karmaphala*. The fruit of any action, according to Dayananda, is inexorably tied to the individual agent and cannot be transferred to another; the only way in which it can be deleted is by that particular agent experiencing (suffering or enjoying) that particular fruit. This universal moral law of the inexorable necessity of the fruit of all action to be experienced by the agent himself is the cornerstone of Dayananda's moral theology. He, therefore, asked the Vallabhacharyas: 'Where do the impurities go?' From there he continued: 'If you say, they are annihilated, that is impossible; if you say that they are transferred to someone else, that too is impossible; if you say that they are transferred to Krishna, that is absurd for he would then have to undergo the punishments to sorrow and even the torments of hell.'[62]

The third essential Vallabhacharya doctrine criticized by Dayananda was the central position accorded to the guru in the sect. In fact, he started his pamphlet with discussion of this. The guru is absolutely necessary to the Vallabhacharyas: he is the one who administers the initiation and receives the vital *samarpan* which provides entry into the *Pustimarga*. Vallabha was entitled to do so because he was not just a human being, but the reincarnation of Lord Krishna himself. This divine connection was transmitted by him through his descendants: the males of the line of Vitthalnath, Vallabha's second son, are the Gosains who remain the only gurus of the sect, human representatives of Krishna himself, qualified to accept the crucial *samarpan*.[63]

To Dayananda, the idea of the guru with its implications of infallible, divine knowledge and of special powers of intercession, was always anathema. He taught that in the final instance, there is only one guru in the full sense of the word, God himself. On the lower human level a guru cannot be more than a wise man, steeped in the Vedas, who transmits the imperfect knowledge he has acquired.[64] The Swami persistently warned his sometimes too enthusiastic followers never to regard him as a guru, but always to test his teachings with the twin touchstones of reason and of Vedic lore, and to accept or reject them accordingly.[65] His clear instructions in his will that his body should be cremated, and not buried as was the custom for *sannyasis*, were primarily prompted by the fear that a grave over his remains might elicit the kind of veneration and implied divinization so rampant in Hinduism.[66] He told the Vallabhacharyas that it was absurd to consider Vallabha a guru, since he had long been dead. As for calling anyone else in the sect a guru, that too was unacceptable. They were all idol-worshippers, opponents of *varnashrama dharma*, and used non-Vedic, fabricated *mantras*. Therefore, they were despisers of the Vedas, *nastikas*, and as such disqualified from any teaching of true religion. The only persons who, according to the Vedas, could perform the human guru function, were firstly the devout father for his son, and secondly, wise men steeped in Vedic lore and living according to its precepts.[67]

Such were the criticisms levelled by the two great antagonists at the Vallabhacharyas. Their campaigns had a strong impact on the Mumbai scene, and brought discredit to the sect. This was primarily brought about by the expose of the greedy and licentious behaviour of the Maharajas. The latters' defence relied heavily on unlawful pressure on their followers[68] and was singularly lacking in depth: they were unable to produce a single scholar to defend effectively the origins of their sect and the character and validity of their interpretation of Hinduism.[69]

What were the strengths and weaknesses of their opponents' attacks? Karsondas Mulji addressed himself primarily to the malpractices and his writings were characterized by the hard-hitting skill of the journalist and the obsession of the puritan, which made them quite effective in rousing public indignation. His excursions into the history of

Hinduism were unashamedly derived from the writings of Western scholars, and he acknowledged his complete ignorance of the Vedas. The ideological base of his minimal theological criticism was a very vague deistic belief in monotheism, in association with morality.

Dayananda was not obsessional about the malpractices, though he strongly condemned them from the point of view of morality in the same way as he criticized other sects of Hinduism and aspects of Christianity and Islam. To him questions of history and dogma were much more important, because the proof that the sect's beliefs were contrary to what he considered as being the basic tenets of Vedic religion, was to him the final, conclusive condemnation. It has been shown how he disposed of central Vallabhacharya concepts such as a heavenly Krishna-Bhagavan, avatar, *shuddhadvaita*, *moksha*, and *dosha*, by the application of his own two basic dogmatic tenets: the nature of God as eternal, non-corporeal, omnipotent, omniscient and omnipresent; and the inexorable law of *karma* and its retribution governing man's ascent to *moksha*. His process of criticism was much more probing and sophisticated than that of Karsondas, yet it was simplistic in its own way by failing seriously to consider the great complexity and subtlety of the Vallabhacharya doctrines. Dayananda's rather blunt objections would elicit from theologians thoroughly versed in the Vallabha system, a wide range of intricate and pertinent rejoinders. To imply that they did not believe in the omnipotence, etc., of Bhagavan Krishna, or were not conversant with the difficulty of reconciling the doctrine of *karma* with that of *prasada* (grace), would seem to them ludicrous and proof of ignorance, because the theologians of the sect had thoroughly considered these topics.[70]

However, both antagonists' criticisms display a much more fundamental flaw: neither of them ever came to grips with the central concept of *bhakti* which, after all, is the very essence of the Vallabhacharya faith. In Hinduism the *bhakti-marga*, the way of devotion, is not just a method of giving vent to superficial emotionalism. At its highest level it entails an engagement of the will, illumined by the intelligence, and an attempt to reach the level of renunciation necessary for the attainment of *moksha* through a positive attitude of loving dedication to the Lord. This essence of *bhakti* has a long history in Hinduism, starting with the *Bhagavad Gita*, and developing in rich treasures of hymnal literature and profound theological treatises. Karsondas never touched on this aspect of *bhakti*, and Dayananda only referred to it once, in his very early *Bhagavata-*

Khandanam, where he stated, 'Scripture says "*Moksha* cannot be achieved without knowledge". Therefore, the statement that "*bhakti* is the giver of *moksha*" is in contradiction with the Vedas.'[71]

It follows from the very essence of *bhakti*, with its accent on will, emotion, and personal dedication, that this approach to the divinity will make extensive use of myths and symbols, as is clearly evident in the great *bhakti* literature, from popular hymns to theological treatises. The Lord and his manifestations become the focus of religious concentration and fervour, fostering the luxuriant growth of myths and symbols. These cannot be shrugged off as mere childish fantasies; they constitute a profound and valid medium by which the human intelligence attempts to penetrate and clarify what it experiences as the mysteries of the divine. It is only fair to state that both Dayananda and Karsondas were narrow rationalists who simply could not comprehend that language. Karsondas vaguely acknowledged that the *Bhagavata Purana* was 'allegorical', but that is as far as he went.[72] Dayananda consistently treated myths and symbols in a narrow literal way, denying them the serious consideration they deserved. That, too, was the way he treated the texts of Christianity, Islam, as well as those of Puranic Hinduism.[73] It is also a characteristic of his commentary on the Vedas: all the mythological stories and allusions are systematically reduced to straightforward statements of a physical or moral nature.

No doubt both Dayananda and Karsondas were effective critics of the Vallabhacharya sect in as far as they exposed its current abuses and roused public indignation which gradually forced the sect to make certain reforms. However, one doubts if they succeeded in diverting many adherents from the way of *bhakti*. In the final instance, neither was a fair, informed, or effective critic of the great *bhakti* tradition as presented by the foremost theologians of the Vallabhacharya sect.

NOTES

[This chapter was originally published as: 'Modern Critics of the Vallabhacharyas: were they Critics of *Bhakti*?', in G.M. Bailey and I. Kesarcodi-Waston (eds.), *Bhakti Studies*, New Delhi, 1991, pp. 309-28.]

1. For reports on this case, cf. *Reports of the Maharaj Libel Case and of the Bhattia Conspiracy Case Connected with it*, *Bombay Gazette*, Mumbai, 1862; a lot of material is also included in *History of the Sect of*

the Maharajas, or Vallabhacharyas, in Western India, published anonymously by Karsondas Mulji, London, 1865, ch. XI and Appendix.

2. For detailed description on that debate, cf. Lekhram, *Maharshi Dayananda Sarasvati Ka Jivan Charitra*, transl. from the original Urdu by Kaviraj Raghunandansingh 'Nirmal', ed. by Pandit Harischandra Vidyalankar, Delhi, 1972, pp. 142-200, 613-18; and B. Bharatiya (ed.), *Dayananda-Shastrarth-Samgraha*, Sonepat, 1969.
3. Ghasiram, *Maharshi Dayananda Saraswati ka Jivan-Charit*, vol. I, Ajmer, 1957, p. 322.
4. Cf. *Report, passim.*
5. B.N. Motiwala, *Karsondas Mulji; A Biographical Study*, Mumbai, 1935, p. 319.
6. Cf. C. Dobbin, *Urban Leadership in Western India*, Delhi, 1972, p. 254; Ghasiram, I, p. 322.
7. Damodar Sundardas, *Mumbai Aryasamajano Itihas*, Mumbai, 1933, pp. 2-4.
8. Lekhram, p. 259.
9. *Report*, pp. 133-8, 142-6, 150.
10. Motiwala, pp. 43, 194; Dobbin, pp. 255-6.
11. Damodar Sundardas, *passim.*
12. Ibid., p. 35.
13. *Report*, pp. 120-1.
14. Motiwala, p. 17.
15. Ibid., pp. 18-19.
16. For a close analysis of Dayananda's transformation in Mathura cf. J.T.F Jordens, *Dayananda Sarasvati, His Life and Ideas*, Delhi, 1978, pp. 32-8.
17. For details cf. ibid., pp. 41-3.
18. Bholanath Chunder, *The Travels of a Hindoo*, vol. 2, London 1869, p. 29.
19. For a description of this area, cf. F.S. Growse, *Mathura, a District Memoir*, 2nd edn., Allahabad, 1880, pp. 66-7; D.L. Drake-Brockman, *Muttra: a Gazetteer*, being vol. VII of the *District Gazetteers of the United Provinces of Agra and Oudh*, Allahabad, 1911, pp. 94ff.
20. Growse, p. 48.
21. The first pamphlet he wrote was a criticism of the *Bhagavata Purana*, *Bhagavata-Khandanam*, Agra, 1864; rediscovered and published by Y. Mimamshak, Sonepat, 1971.
22. *Satyarth Prakash*, Allahabad, 1875. This volume is extremely rare, but a microfilm is available at the Australian National University Library, Canberra.
23. First published in Mumbai, 1875. Available in the edition published by Govindram Hasanand, Delhi, n.d.
24. Published by the Vedic Yantralay, Allahabad, in 1884. Numerous

editions are available. The best critical edition is the one edited by Y. Mimamshak, Sonepat, 1971, to which we refer in this chapter.

25. Motiwala, p. 238.
26. Ibid., p. 227. Other indications of puritanism may be found on page 241. Karsondas was married three times. He lost his first and second wives very quickly, but the third one bore him four sons and a daughter. She was very disturbed about her husband's social radicalism, was in constant apprehension of caste-retaliation, and hostile to his involvement in social reform causes. Cf. Motiwala, pp. 22, 201, 273, 370.
28. For a full discussion of the doctrine and references to primary sources, cf. Jordens, pp. 117-19, 146-7, 262-3.
29. For Dayananda's concept of marriage cf. his *Sanskaravidhi*, 2nd edn., Allahabad, 1884. The best edition now available is that prepared by Y. Mimamshak, Sonepat, 1971. The relevant section is that pertaining to the wedding rites.
30. This article was written in Gujarati, entitled 'The Primitive religion of the Hindu and the present heterodox opinions', and published in the *Satya Prakash* on 21 November 1860. A full English translation is available in *Report*, pp. 1-3, and *History*, pp. 172-5.
31. *Report*, p. 121.
32. Ibid., p. 122.
33. *History*, p. 1.
34. Ibid., p. 4.
35. Ibid., pp. 10-11.
36. For a detailed description of this evolution, cf. Jordens, chs. II and III, *passim*.
37. This refers to a controversy started in 1855, when the Maharajas disputed the right of brahmins to partake in the foodstuffs (fifty-six kinds, from where the name *chhapan-bhoga* offering) which had been offered to Shiva. For details, cf. *History*, pp. 153-7.
38. *History*, pp. 81-5.
39. Ibid., pp. 125-6.
40. Ibid., p. 73.
41. Ibid., p. 251.
42. *Bhagavata-Khandanam*, pp. 3, 6-9.
43. Cf. pp. 337-42.
44. The township of Gokul, 8 km from Mathura was in fact the headquarters of the sect, 'throughout the year crowded with pilgrims, of whom the majority come from Gujarat and Bombay'. Growse, pp. 382ff.
45. For full text, cf. Lekhram, pp. 260-2. They contain a detailed statement of what kinds of religious texts the Swami considered authoritative.
46. For details of these debates and references to the sources, cf. Jordens, pp. 147-9.

47. For these works, cf. S.N. Dasgupta, *A History of Indian Philosophy*, vol. IV, Cambridge, 1961, ch. 31; Karl H. Potter, *Bibliography of Indian Philosophers*, Delhi, 1970, *passim*; M.I. Marfatia, *The Philosophy of Vallabhacharya*, Delhi, 1967, pp. 91-314.
48. Cf. letter of Sevaklal Karsondas to Dayananda in Munshiram Jigyasu (ed.), *Rishi Dayananda ka Patravyavahar*, vol. I, Gurukul Kangri, 1910, pp. 253-64.
49. *Satyarth Prakash*, ed. by Y. Mimamshak, pp. 552-63.
50. *Vedaviruddhmatkhandana*, pp. 15, 74.
51. Ibid., p. 73.
52. Ibid., pp. 16, 46.
53. Ibid., pp. 40-4.
54. Ibid., p. 47. For detailed analysis of the criticism by Vallabha of Shankara's concept of *maya*, and of Vallabha's own concept, cf. R. Barz, *The Bhakti Sect of Vallabhacharya*, Faridabad, 1976, pp. 64ff., 78; Dasgupta, vol. IV, pp. 358-70; J.G. Shah, *Shri Vallabhacharya: His Philosophy and Religion*, Nadiad, 1969, pp. 104-25; Marfatia, pp. 56-66.
55. *Vedaviruddhmatkhandana*, p. 64; for the concept of Bhagavan Krishna, cf. Shah, pp. 69-84; Marfatia, pp. 33-43.
56. A description of the doctrines of *shuddhadvaita* can be found in Dasgupta, pp. 320-32; Marfatia, pp. 33-43.
57. *Vedaviruddhmatkhandana*, p. 80.
58. Ibid., pp. 76-84.
59. Ibid., pp. 51-2.
60. For a clear expose of these doctrines, cf. Barz, pp. 80-93; Marfatia, pp. 70-90; Shah, pp. 149-229.
61. *Vedaviruddhmatkhandana*, pp. 54-5. It is noteworthy that Karsondas interpreted the passage in the same way: *History*, pp. 81ff. This was strongly condemned as a false interpretation by those sympathizing with the sect, e.g. Bhai Manilal C. Parekh, *Shri Vallabhacharya: Life, Teachings and Movement* (*A Religion of Grace*), Rajkot, 1943, pp. 359-60.
62. *Vedaviruddhmatkhandana*, pp. 67-8. For an analysis of Dayananda's concept of *karma* and its relationship to *moksha*, cf. Jordens, pp. 108-9, 255-8, 281-2.
63. Cf. Barz, pp. 37-9. It is interesting that a modern apologist such as Parekh seems to sidestep this issue completely in his work; cf. Parekh, pp. 366-8.
64. *Satyarth Prakash*, 2nd edn., pp. 32, 53.
65. Cf. the important statement of the Swami made at the time of the foundation of the Arya Samaj in Mumbai, Damodar Sundardas, pp. 8-9, translated in Jordens, p. 145. Further references, ibid., p. 203.

66. Full text of the will in *Rishi Dayananda Sarasvati ke Patra aur Vijnapan*, Y. Mimamshak (ed.), Amritsar, 1958, pp. 386-9.
67. *Vedaviruddhmatkhandana*, pp. 7-14.
68. Cf. the Bhattia Conspiracy case in *Report*, pp. 30-58.
69. Parekh comments on this, pp. 367-9.
70. Cf. the expose of the various aspects of the system in Dasgupta, Barz, Shah and Marfatia, *passim.*
71. *Bhagavata-Khandanam*, p. 16.
72. *History*, p. 49.
73. For example, cf. Jordens, pp. 266-9, 271-2.

PART IV

Arya Samaj

CHAPTER 11

The *Shuddhi* of the Arya Samaj

THE CONCEPT OF *shuddhi*, literally the state of being pure, is a very central and ancient one in the Hindu tradition. From the earliest times, it referred to the state of purity necessary for the performance of *dharma*. As *dharma* has both a ritual and a social dimension, *shuddhi* refers to the quality necessary to perform religious rites and to participate in social intercourse. Of the many causes of pollution and the loss of *shuddhi*, the main ones are: birth and death which cause pollution, and so does the touch of polluting materials or the contact with impure persons.[1] By extension the term *shuddhi* signifies the rite by which pollution is removed: the many purification rituals after birth and death or after contact with polluting materials or persons can all be subsumed under it. *Shuddhi* as a rite, therefore, restores to the Hindu that ritual purity which is necessary for the performance of Hindu rites, and for the social interaction with his caste-fellows.

In the nineteenth century *shuddhi* first appeared in the context of crossing the *kala pani*, the black waters. The high-caste Hindu, especially the brahmin, would necessarily have come into close contact with many elements of pollution if he left India for overseas. Orthodoxy, therefore, required him to undergo on his return a purification ceremony before he was again acceptable as a full member of his caste.

The second use of the term was for the reinstatement of a 'lapsed' Hindu. An interesting case which occurred in Mumbai in the early 1850s shows the reluctance of orthodoxy for this process. A brahmin boy, Shripat Sheshadri Paralikar, aged twelve, was attending a Christian mission school, where his elder brother, who had become a Christian, was a teacher. With great difficulty the father succeeded in obtaining custody of his son, only to find out that two months' stay in the home of a non-Hindu had polluted Shripat: he was declared an outcaste by the brahmins. The reformer Balshastri Jambhekar came to his help. He succeeded in getting the agreement of learned pundits from Nasik and Pune, and even from the Shankaracharya of Karvir Math, that Shripat should be readmitted to the Hindu fold after purification rites in both Mumbai and Varanasi. Nevertheless, the Mumbai Hindus boycotted Shripat, his family, and his supporters. In fact, Balshastri himself had later to undergo the humiliating ordeal of a penance before the Pune brahmins would accept him back into his caste brotherhood. This case was widely publicised in India. Calcutta brahmins held a special meeting and decided by overwhelming majority that readmission was possible; but they determined that the proper expiation would have to consist of the gift of a hundred cows to the brahmins.[2]

This reluctance of the brahmins towards *shuddhi* showed how ignorant they were of their ancient law-books. The *Atharvaveda* and the Brahmanas refer to the rite of *vratyastoma*, devised to readmit anyone fallen outside the pale of orthodox Aryan society, making him capable of studying the Veda and eligible for social intercourse with the Aryans.[3] Later law-books, e.g. the *Devalasmriti*, very probably written after the early Arab raids into India, give at length special provisions for the readmission into Hinduism of people forcibly converted, or enslaved by the 'Mlechcchas'.[4] It is interesting to note here that it was not until the 1920s that the *Devalasmriti* and until the 1930s that the *vratyastoma* arguments were re-discovered by both orthodox and Arya Samajists for proving the lawfulness of *shuddhi*.[5]

Swami Dayananda Sarasvati, the founder of the Arya Samaj, was the first reformer to seriously turn his attention to *shuddhi* as reconversion. The question first arose during his first and only visit to the Punjab in 1877, towards the end of his life. In Jalandhar, six months after his arrival in the Punjab, he performed the *shuddhi* of a Hindu who had become a Christian.[6] Kharak Singh, who was born a Sikh, then became a Hindu, and consequently was baptized by Reverend Robert Clark of Amritsar, became an Arya on meeting the Swami.[7] Later on, in Dehradun, in 1879, the Swami reconverted a born Muslim giving him the new name of Alakdhari.[8] These are the only *shuddhis* recorded in Dayananda's life. Two important points need to be noted. For Dayananda *shuddhi* was never a major issue, and he never prescribed any particular rite, but he clearly proclaimed the principle that reconversion was the right procedure, a principle the Arya Samaj would later fully put into practice. Secondly, the area where the problem first emerged was the Punjab.

The heartland of the Punjab, the submontaine and central districts, which Dayananda visited and where the Arya Samaj would mainly flourish, was divided among three communities: the Hindu minority (36.65 per cent), the Sikhs (12.08 per cent) with their powerful base thanks to the long Sikh rule, and the Muslims who dominated in numbers (50.12 per cent).[9] These three communities constituted the most important units of society.

The introduction of British administration brought profound changes to the Punjab. Hundreds of new jobs were created both inside and outside the government services. At first they were filled by English-educated Indians mostly from Bengal. Educational facilities soon multiplied and a host of new professional and economic opportunities arose. The people who eagerly grasped these opportunities were the Hindu merchant classes, primarily the Khatris, traditionally literate and progressive. They were followed by the Sikhs, whereas the Muslims lagged far behind. The Punjab government's policy of religious impartiality which lasted till the late 1880s favoured this process.[10]

British administration brought another new element into the Punjab: the Christian missionaries. The American Presbyterian Mission was first in the field in 1834; within a year they had a High School and a printing press. The Church Missionary Society followed in 1854, and in 1855 the Church of Scotland. Missionary propaganda spread quickly and forcefully through the agencies of preaching, education, publication, orphanages, zenana missions and even mission colonies. Two factors tended to boost the impact. When the missionaries noticed the many opportunities in the Punjab, they invited Indian Christians, particularly Bengalis, to come and take up positions, thus laying the foundation of a compact community of educated Indian Christians.[11] Moreover, over two-thirds of the First Punjab Commission were Evangelicals,[12] who strongly believed in the mission of Christianity and tended to support the missions, thus presenting a united front of the Raj and the Church. When one takes into account the fact that missionary activity was a totally new experience to the Punjabis, it is no wonder that, when they saw the quick and efficient ramification of the various missionary institutions, the close affiliation between government and missionaries and the tally of Christian converts (about 4,000 by 1881),[13] the fear of a 'Christian threat' was engendered in their minds.

Dayananda's stand on *shuddhi* was taken in the context of this threat. Whereas in the first days of his visit some voices were raised accusing him of being a crypto-Christian in the pay of the British, his vehement denunciation of Christianity soon dispelled any doubt on that score. This was the first time the Punjabi Hindus felt that their defence was changed into attack. The missionaries realized the impact of the Swami: all the leading missionaries of the Punjab made a point of visiting him. And when the few reconversions occurred, strengthened by the prevention of the imminent conversion of many others, they realized that the Hindus had found a new voice and a new aggressive self-assurance.

The history of the *shuddhi* movement of the Arya Samaj after the death of Dayananda in 1883 falls into two main periods: from 1883 to 1900, and from 1900 to 1925. From the year 1884 onwards numerous references to *shuddhi* ceremonies are scattered in the pages of the Punjab Arya Samaj journals. These reconversions are all of individuals from either Christianity or Islam: 39 *shuddhi* are reported in 1884, 55 in 1885. They included some persons not born as Hindus.[14] This increase in individual *shuddhi* is definitely connected with the considerable success of the missionaries during the 1880s: between 1881 and 1891 the number of Christian converts rose from 4,000 to 19,000.[15] The editor of the *Arya Patrika* put it as follows:

> Up to this time the Hindu community has been the storehouse on which other religions used to feed themselves, but the Hindus also have been forced by circumstances to feel that if they will take no steps to recover their lost brethren, they one day, one by one, will be engulfed wholly by other religions.[16]

These early beginnings of *shuddhi* brought great difficulties to the Aryas. Although they were members of a body with a programme of radical reform, nevertheless their whole social and most of their ritual life still remained part of their caste *biradari*. Participation in *shuddhi* created the danger of their own excommunication, which, in fact, occurred in a few cases. It was the Amritsar Arya Samaj that devised a means by which orthodoxy could be appeased. They secured the full collaboration of the most orthodox pandit Tulsi Ram: the *shuddhi* ceremony was approved by him and the converts were sent with a 'purification letter' of the pandit to Hardwar, where a final dip in the

Ganges completed their purification. For this reason Amritsar became the centre of individual *shuddhis*, performed in such a way that orthodoxy approved.[17]

Dayananda might well have been horrified by this superstitious dip in the Ganges, and some Aryas soon started to protest against it. But it took ten years before the protest movement won out. In 1893 the ceremony was changed to a purely Vedic formula. The elements of the rite were the shaving of the head, *havan*, explanation of the *Gayatri*, investiture with the holy thread where applicable, explanation of the Samaj duties, and finally distribution of sherbet by the converts to all present.[18] After ten years the Aryas felt they were in a sufficiently strong position to forego orthodox requirements without courting the danger of excommunication.

During this period the Arya Samaj was often closely associated with the Sikhs in the work of *shuddhi*. The Sikh community was in earnest search of its identity, and a number felt that they had a lot in common with the Aryas in a common heritage and shared goals, and in the common threat of Islam and Christianity. Yet at the same time that some Sikhs and some Aryas were collaborating, other Aryas were increasingly criticizing Sikhism, a criticism that grew shrill with Pandits Guru Datta and Lekh Ram in the late 1880s, leading later to a complete break. But even while the controversy grew, Aryas and Sikhs kept collaborating in the matter of *shuddhi* as both were interested in stemming the tide of conversions that was eating away their communities. A Shuddhi Sabha was formed, mainly controlled by Sikhs but with the help of Aryas of the 'College Party'. The radical Sikhs then introduced a 'pork test' for the converts: the consumption of pork was the symbol of return to Hinduism or Sikhism. The Aryas of the vegetarian 'Mahatma Party' dissociated themselves from this degenerate action, and continued their own form of individual *shuddhi*.[19]

During the later 1880s some Aryas were beginning to be concerned about the success of the missionaries among the outcastes, clearly demonstrated in the census reports. Two events occurred in the nineties which would lead to a radical transformation of the *shuddhi* movement from 1900 onwards.

On 31 March 1896 the Shuddhi Sabha converted five people at once, on 5 April a group of six, and in August the Lahore branch converted a group of over two hundred Sikhs. This event had two important new elements. First, the fact that a large homogeneous group was purified at once; second, these people were not Muslims or Christians, they were simply Sikhs who had become outcastes years before because the patriarch of the family had taken in a Muslim woman. In other words, this *shuddhi* was not strictly a re-conversion but the admittance of an outcaste group to full caste privileges.[20]

The second event was one in which Lajpat Rai played a leading role. The famine of 1896 had left in its wake a great number of orphans, many of whom were taken care of by Christian missionaries. The Samaj saw the danger of losing so many children from the Hindu fold, and mounted their own rescue operation: four new orphanages were founded in the Punjab, and by the end of 1897 nearly 1,000 orphans had been resettled.[21] This movement was revived in 1899, when the Samaj sent its members to Bombay, Kathiawar and the Central Provinces: more than 1,700 orphans were brought back to the Punjab, as local arrangements proved impossible.[22] This remarkable operation put the Arya Samaj on the map as an organization that could rival the Christians in philanthropic work. Although it did not entail any *shuddhi* activity, it did influence its development in some ways. It helped the Samaj to think in large numbers and to realize that they were now strong enough to cope with them. Since a lot of the orphans came from the lowest strata of society, the outcastes, it drew the Samaj's attention to their lot. The publicity showed to the orthodox that the work of the Samaj was doubtlessly for the good of Hinduism as a whole, and the Orphan Relief Movement got throughout the full cooperation of the orthodox, of reformist groups like the Brahmos, and even of the Jains.[23]

In June 1900, the Lahore Arya Samaj performed the *shuddhi* of a small group of Rahtias, Sikh untouchables of the level of the Chamars. It snowballed in no time. Another group of Rahtias was admitted in Lahore, and then Jalandhar and Rupa followed within a couple of months. Within a year the movement spread to the Ods, and to the Meghs in 1903. In the short span of three years a movement sprang up that involved many thousands of outcastes.[24] This movement set the definite seal of approval on the extension of the concept of *shuddhi*: it was now a question of groups, of whole castes, achieving their upgrading from untouchable to touchable status. Though they were Hindus before, their rights were very restricted, and they were a source of pollution to caste Hindus. *Shuddhi* gave them the right to the full performance of *dharma*: access to all Vedic rites and the right to mix socially with the caste Hindus. The ceremony clearly demonstrated their new status. They were taught the sacred *Gayatri* and given the sacred thread to wear. They distributed sherbet or sweetmeats to the caste Hindus and were given access to the wells from which they had been banned. And finally, they were enrolled in the Arya Samaj with the right to participate in its community services.

What were the circumstances and motives that led to this new approach? The initial move was made by the untouchables themselves. The first group of Rahtias had, before being accepted by the Lahore branch, tried unsuccessfully for a whole year to get admitted by the Jalandhar Arya Samaj.[25] The famines that ravaged north India at the end of the nineteenth century had most harshly stricken that most vulnerable section of society, the untouchables. They were desperately looking for some improvement in their condition, and India was becoming more acutely aware of the great problem in the lowest strata: the Brahmo and Prarthana Samajes started relief work in the late 1890s. But again it had been the Christian missionaries who were primarily and actively concerned, and this led to mass conversions. The census reports put the increase of Christians into bold evidence. The *Arya Messenger* wrote: 'While the people of India increased in 1891-1901 at the rate of $1^1/_2$ %, the native Christians increased at the rate of over 30%.' [26]

The successful movement soon spread outside the Punjab. The Sheikhs of Larkhana in Sind, a low-caste half-Hindu half-Muslim group, were purified by the Sukkar Arya Samaj. A similar group, the Subrai Labanas of Ludhiana, and another, the Maiwaris of Ajmer, soon followed suit.[27] With the arrival on the scene of a leader, Chaudhry Ram Bhaj Dutt, the movement changed into higher gear, becoming a veritable campaign. Aryas went out into the villages and convinced the outcastes and the local orthodox of the advantages of *shuddhi*. An All-India Shuddhi Sabha was established, and the movement spread systematically out into Kashmir and the United Provinces. By 1910 there had been between 60,000 to 70,000 *shuddhi* in the Punjab alone,[28] and between 1911 and 1921 the number of Aryas in Kashmir rose from 1,047 to 23,116, and in the United Provinces the number reached 205,000 in 1921.[29] This was a truly massive achievement by a small group of Aryas over a period of twenty years.

Before considering the religious, social, and political implications of the *shuddhi* movement, a very important event of the early 1920s must be recalled. The Khilafat Movement of 1921 had an unexpected result in the Moplah rebellion. The Moplahs were a group of about one million Muslims, poor, uneducated, and endued with a brand of fanaticism that had led to no less than thirty-five minor outbreaks during British rule. They lived in Malabar in the midst of some two million Hindus. In this violent outbreak of 1921, the Moplahs threw the British out of the area and proclaimed *swaraj*. Their fanaticism turned on the Hindus with massacres, forcible conversions, desecration of temples, rape, pillage, and arson. It took the Raj about four months, up to the end of 1921, to restore peace, during which time up to 10,000 Moplahs were killed. In the flush of the Khilafat movement these Moplahs were declared 'martyrs', but as the news of the atrocities committed by the Moplahs on the Hindus percolated into India, their image became somewhat tarnished. The political leaders, nevertheless, kept cautiously clear from outright denunciation, and supported a call for funds to take care of the orphans of the Moplah martyrs.[30]

The Hindus who had been forcibly converted, on the other hand, found themselves excommunicated. The question of reconversion was raised, and the Arya Samaj was asked to send a representative to Malabar. At first orthodoxy was very reluctant, but the Arya leaders had long experience in convincing the orthodox of the acceptability and necessity of *shuddhi*. The Arya Samaj first took care of the physical well-being of the stricken: 45,000 Rupees were spent in eight months in the daily distribution of food. The Aryas finally prevailed on the Raja of Calicut to call a meeting with Nambudiri pandits. In conjunction with them a schedule of *shuddhi* rites was drawn up that would satisfy orthodoxy. No doubt the timely rediscovery of the *Devalasmriti* helped to appease the orthodox. As a result practically all the forcibly converted, a figure that may have reached 2,500, were administered *shuddhi* and restored to their old caste privileges. This achievement, publicized to the full, enhanced the stature of the Arya Samaj in the eyes of the orthodox and of the whole of Hindu India. The significant new direction it gave to the *shuddhi* movement will be discussed later.[31]

The effect of *shuddhi* on the convert's religious life depended on his previous status. If he was an individual reinstated into his former caste, it simply meant that he regained whatever religious rights he formerly enjoyed. For the large groups of untouchables it had a two-fold effect. First of all it gave them access to the Vedas and the Vedic rites, symbolized by the sacred thread. Secondly, practically all became members of the Arya Samaj, and, thus, eligible to participate in its religious activities. Mostly it was this second privilege that made the first effective in reality, because they would have experienced great difficulty in finding an orthodox brahmin prepared to open the doors for them. For the third category, individual converts born Christian or Muslim their only access to religious rites was through their membership of the Arya Samaj.

In the reports extant there is a noticeable absence of any form of religious instruction of the convert. *Shuddhi* was not a rite that presupposed an inner religious conversion reinforced by instruction to foster a new interior life. It was a rite of access, for which only a clear decision was necessary. In this *shuddhi* is a typically Hindu procedure. Hinduism itself constitutes the immense availability of religious structures and practices. A change in the individual's religious life is not a question primarily of inner conversion, but rather the acquisition of the right of entry into the manifold sects, panths, orders, and *sabhas*, and the right of access to the very heart of orthodoxy, the Vedas and the Vedic rites. In general it would be true to say that for the new converts their new right to that deepest treasure of Hinduism became actual only for those who joined the Arya Samaj. Outside its ambit it was practically impossible to activate that right.

What happened to the convert in relation to the existing caste system? In the case of individual converts who had been born Hindus, they simply were received back into their old caste.[32] Those, however, who had been born Christians or Muslims, had no caste to go back to and their problem was acute. As members of the Arya Samaj, they could share its life. But the other members of the Samaj were still totally dependent on their caste for social intercourse and marriage.[33] Therefore, they generally refused any social intercourse with those converts outside the Samaj functions, out of fear of their own *biradari*.[34] The Samaj became acutely aware of this problem, and during the 1880s and 1890s voices were constantly raised protesting that the Samaj was not living up to the social ideals of Dayananda. Some proposed that Muslim converts be organized into separate groups, but that was an impossible solution. A group of radicals then established within the Samaj a new organization, the Arya Bhratri Sabha. Their programme was a radical one indeed: the new converts should be totally integrated with the Aryas, and the Arya Samaj should in effect become a new caste, a new *biradari*. The majority of Aryas were totally opposed to this idea, and rightly argued that such a transformation would be diametrically opposed to Dayananda's reform programme. The result was that, although the voices of the radicals kept resounding through the Arya journals, their efforts remained ineffectual. Nevertheless, these were the people who later stood solidly behind the group conversions, and thus effectively steered the Samaj into a new direction.[35] As for the individual converts from Christianity and Islam, they remained doomed to a social life in limbo except for their regular contacts with Aryas in the Samaj functions.

The raising of the ex-untouchables to a higher status presented a much greater social problem. Orthodoxy was adamantly hostile at first. In fact, even the 1901 annual meeting of the Social Conference was not able to endorse the radical step of the purification of untouchables.[36] At first the Rahtias were prevented by the orthodox from using the village wells.[37] The Sanathan Dharm Sabha was the spearhead of orthodox resistance to the Arya Samaj, and it used preachers, newspapers, and tracts in its campaign, accusing the Samaj, among many other endictments, 'that its efforts to improve the Hindus were lessening their strength and weakening their feelings of nationality and national sympathy'.[38] This had an ironical twist, because it was precisely the growth of Hindu nationalism that would later make orthodoxy relent. As the trickle of converted untouchables became a flood, orthodoxy first withdrew into grudging and resigned acceptance: it was realized that the Arya Samaj was in fact performing a necessary function for the sake of Hindu unity by stemming the tide of conversion to Christianity. The Aryas were no more excommunicated and the orthodox accepted the new social rights of the converts: they accepted them as touchable, non-polluting, but avoided social contact, leaving them to their own *biradaris.*[39] These ex-untouchables were mostly accepted as members of the Arya Samaj, but they were excluded from the caste circle of the Aryas except in a few rare cases.[40] The radicals found this an impossible and unworthy situation, and inaugurated in 1922 a new reform body, the Jat Pat Todak Mandal, whose leading figure was Bhai Paramanand. This time the aim was not to form a new caste, but to work for the abolition of the caste system by the promotion of inter-caste dinners and marriages. This would, said their programme 'foster feelings of social equality, fraternity, and liberty among the Hindus and unite them into a coherent nation'.[41] This effort too, however, had only very limited success, as it was not acceptable to most Aryas.[42]

In how far did the *shuddhi* of untouchables lead on to lasting effects of social and economic betterment? Extremely little information is available to attempt to answer that question. In some areas the follow-up was remarkable. The Arya Megh Uddhar Sabha of Sialkot, which looked after some 36,000 converted Meghs, is an outstanding example. Tracts of land were acquired to settle the converts, primary and central schools were established, better housing was provided, wells were dug, and a hospital was erected.[43] In Lahore the practical leadership of Lajpat Rai was behind the effective organization for the uplift of Hindu sweepers and Chamars.[44] But the over-all impression is that in general the follow-up was poor, and that the converts soon found that they had not gained very much in solid reality.

How did the *shuddhi* movement affect communal strife? Between Hindus and Sikhs there was initially some cooperation, because they had a common platform against the Muslims and the Christians in both *shuddhi* and the anti-cow-slaughter agitation. The event that destroyed this shaky union was the conversion of the Rahtias, outcaste Sikhs, who were received by the Aryas into Hinduism. This led to increased tensions, the defection of Sikh leaders from the Samaj, and to a total break-down of Arya-Sikh relations.[45]

No doubt in these years *shuddhi* was a contributing element in the increase of Hindu-Muslim antagonism: most individual converts did come from Islam,[46] and the infamous 'pork test' of the Shuddhi Sabha was a slap in the face of Muslims. However, in those years *shuddhi* was not a major element; the anti-cow-slaughter movement was much more important, as was the systematic anti-Muslim crusade of the Aryas under the leadership of Lekh Ram against the Ahmadiyas.[47] Between 1883 and 1891 no less than fifteen riots erupted in the Punjab over cow-killing.[48]

So we come to a final question: in what way did the *shuddhi* movement affect the political scene? Up to 1899 the Congress was rather ineffective in the Punjab, and the Aryas tended to be inward-looking and non-political. Two factors brought this quickly rising intelligentsia into the Congress, which they dominated from 1900 onwards. The uneasy truce in communal Hindu-Muslim antagonism between 1898 and 1907 freed their minds from communal problems, and the leadership of Lajpat Rai engendered a desire to transform the Congress from a do-nothing organization to a 'vehicle for national regeneration': they joined forces with the extremist faction. The Punjab disturbances of 1907, and the resulting government policy of coercion and conciliation changed the scene. The Lajpat section pulled back, and Punjabi politics came under the dominance of moderates. The disturbances had led to a revival of Hindu-Muslim tensions and the efforts of the government to give greater opportunities to Muslims in employment added fuel to the fire. Punjabi politics once again assumed a primarily communal character. Hindu Sabhas were founded everywhere, and also Shuddhi Sabhas, for the defence of Hinduism. An All-India Shuddhi Sabha was established, primarily directed by Punjabi Aryas. Thus the *shuddhi* movement did definitely influence Punjabi politics after 1908, but it mostly remained only a provincial phenomenon.[49]

In the 1920s *shuddhi* erupted on to the scene of national politics. The aftermath of the First World War brought the Rowlatt Satyagraha, the Khilafat Movement, and the Hindu-Muslim collaboration which lasted till 1922. Two events contributed most directly to the break-up of that coalition: the Moplah rebellion at the end of 1921 and the sudden termination by Gandhi in February 1922 of Non-Cooperation. As Congress politics went into a decline, separate communal consolidation became the main concern of both Hindus and Muslims.

The *shuddhi* of the Hindus forcibly converted during the Moplah rebellion put the Arya Samaj and its work dramatically on the national stage, and it conclusively convinced the orthodox of the importance of *shuddhi*. The most commanding figure of these years was Swami Shraddhanand. He more than anyone else symbolized the new rapprochement between the orthodox and the Aryas, which was particularly evident in his collaboration with Pandit Madan Mohan Malaviya. And it was *shuddhi* that gave the first powerful thrust in the direction of Hindu *sangathan*, of the national consolidation of Hinduism.[50]

The community involved this time were the Malkanas in the western part of the United Provinces. Their religious status was a confused one. They had been deeply influenced by Islam and Muslim culture, even to the point of using Muslim functionaries in some of their ceremonies. They had retained basically many Hindu practices, yet in the census they tended to declare themselves Muslims. Between 1907 and 1910 there had been some tentative attempts at reconversion, but the decisive break-through came in 1922 when the Hindu Rajputs in their Kshatriya Upkarini Sabha passed a resolution in support of receiving the Malkanas, and permitting them to be reunited with the Rajput Hindu brotherhood after purification.[51]

At first nothing concrete was done, but the resolution received wide publicity. The Muslims started to take measures of defense. Then a meeting was held of Aryas, orthodox, and Sikhs, and a new organization was founded, the Bharatiya Hindu Shuddhi Sabha. Shraddhanand was elected president and head of the managing committee with Lala Hans Raj as Vice-President. A huge effort of publicity and fund-raising followed, and orthodox bodies everywhere were enlisted for support. Between April and June, 147 villages were covered resulting in the purification of some 30,000 Malkanas. Notwithstanding some disagreements between Aryas and orthodox, the coalition kept strong and powerful, facing an increasingly organized anti-*shuddhi* campaign of the Muslims. The *shuddhi* movement rose to a rapid peak in 1923, and then tapered off slowly to 1926.[52] *Shuddhi* thus reached its dramatic culmination in the 1920s, creating an unprecedented alliance between Aryas and orthodox, contributing strongly to the growth of Hindu consolidation, the *sangathan*, 'the consolidation of the Hindu community in order to maximize the Hindu potentialities of moral and ritual purity, physical strength, numerical increase, and political power'.[53] Thus it helped to lay a firm foundation of the influence of the Mahasabha and later the RSS (Rashtriya Svayamsevak Sangh).

What general trends have emerged from this survey of the Arya *shuddhi* movement between 1880 and the mid-1920s? The concept originated in the peculiar social set-up of the Punjab where Muslim and Christian aggressiveness made the Hindu minority feel threatened. Starting out as a movement of individual conversions, it transformed itself into a mass-movement rescuing untouchables from Christian conversion. From the Punjab it spilled over into the Gangetic plains. The Moplah rebellion raised the issue of *shuddhi* into a national one, intimately connected with the need to build up Hindu national unity. Now the threat was no more a Christian one, but a Muslim one, and the Malkanas became the focus of national Hindu concern.

It was primarily *shuddhi* that progressively brought about a radical change in the relationship of the Aryas with orthodoxy. The collaboration with an orthodox pundit in Amritsar in the beginning was an isolated phenomenon in a general orthodox opposition. But as the Hindu community grew more and more aware of the onslaught of Christianity, and even more of the gathering organizational strength of the Muslims, and of its own lack of cohesion, their attitude changed. The aftermath of the Khilafat Movement and of the Moplah rebellion led to the close cooperation between Aryas and orthodox for the sake of Hindu *sangathan*. In the realization of this cooperation the *shuddhi* of the Malkanas was decisive.

In the political sphere proper, the early years, when the Punjabi Aryas were absorbed by their own concerns, were unimportant. After the disturbances of 1907, *shuddhi* played its aggravating part in increased communal tensions within the Punjab. And finally, in the 1920s, it became the spearhead of a drive for Hindu solidarity *vis-a-vis* the Muslims, contributing greatly to the antagonism between the two communities that would remain a major element in all later political developments.

NOTES

[This chapter was originally published as: 'Reconversion to Hinduism, the Shuddhi of the Arya Samaj', in G.A. Oddie (ed.), *Religion in South Asia*, New Delhi, 1984, pp. 239-52.]

1. Cf. P.V. Kane, *History of Dharmashastra*, vol. 4, 2nd edn., Pune, 1973, pp. 268-9.
2. Cf. T.V. Parvate, *Mahadev Govind Ranade, a Biography*, Mumbai, 1963, pp. 35-6; Dhananjay Keer, *Mahatma Jotirao Phooley, Father of our social revolution*, Mumbai, 1964, pp. 59, 60.
3. Kane, op. cit., vol. 2, part 1, Pune, 1941, pp. 385-7.
4. Kane, ibid., pp. 285-9.
5. Cf. R. Graham, 'The Arya Samaj as a Reformation in Hinduism with Special Reference to Caste', unpublished Ph.D. dissertation, Yale University, 1942, pp. 511, 560; G. Thursby, 'Aspects of Hindu-Muslim Relations in British India: a study of Arya Samaj activities, Government of India policies, and communal conflict in the period 1923-1928', unpublished Ph.D. dissertation, Duke University, 1972, pp. 40-1.
6. Pandit Lekhram, *Maharshi Dayananda Sarasvati ka Jivan Charitra*, trans. into Hindi by Kaviraj Raghunandansingh, Delhi, 1972, p. 371; Pandit Ghasiram, *Maharshi Dayananda Sarasvati ka Jivan-Charit*, vol. II, Ajmer, 1957, p. 71.
7. Graham, p. 201, fn. 1.
8. Ghasiram, p. 171.
9. K.W. Jones, 'The Arya Samaj in the Punjab: a study of social reform and religious revivalism, 1877-1902', unpublished Ph.D. dissertation, University of California, Berkeley, 1966, pp. 5-6.
10 Cf. N.G. Barrier, 'The Punjab Government and Communal Politics 1870-1908', *Journal of Asian Studies*, vol. 27, 1968, pp. 523-39.
11. Jones, thesis, pp. 13ff; also K.W. Jones, 'The Bengali Elite in Post-

Annexation Punjab: an example of Inter-Regional influence in 19th century India', *The Indian Economic and Social History Review*, vol. 3, 1966, pp. 376-95.

12. Cf. N.G. Barrier, p. 526.
13. K.W. Jones, 'Communalism in the Punjab, the Arya Samaj Contribution', *Journal of Asian Studies*, vol. 28, 1968, p. 42.
14. Graham, p. 456.
15. Jones, p. 42.
16. Graham, p. 458.
17. Ibid., p. 457.
18. Ibid., pp. 463-5.
19. Ibid., p. 466; K.W. Jones, '*Ham Hindu Nahin*: Arya Sikh Relations, 1877-1905', *Journal of Asian Studies*, vol. 32, 1973, pp. 463-4.
20. Jones, thesis, p. 201.
21. Ibid., p. 239.
22. Graham, pp. 413-14.
23. Jones, thesis, pp. 235-42.
24. Graham, pp. 488-92.
25. Ibid., p. 489.
26. Ibid., p. 491.
27. Ibid., p. 492.
28. Ibid., pp. 495-8.
29. Figures quoted in ibid., pp. 417, 432, 442, 444.
30. Cf. R.C. Majumdar, *History of the Freedom Movement in India*, vol. III, Calcutta, 1963, pp. 190-200.
31. Cf. Graham, pp. 508ff; Thursby, pp. 34-42.
32. Graham, p. 457.
33. Ibid., p. 482.
34. Ibid., p. 463.
35. Ibid., pp. 477-85.
36. Jones, thesis, pp. 261-2.
37. Ibid.
38. Ibid., p. 263.
39. Graham, p. 518.
40. Ibid., p. 519.
41. Ibid., p. 538.
42. Ibid., pp. 540, 544.
43. Ibid., p. 521.
44. Lajpat Rai, *A History of the Arya Samaj*, revd. edn. by Shri Ram Sharma (ed.), Mumbai, 1967, p. 126.
45. Cf. Jones, '*Ham Hindu . . .*'.
46. Cf. Jones, n. 13, p. 50.
47. Jones, thesis, pp. 135-6.

48. Barrier, n. 10, p. 528.
49. Cf. Barrier, 'The Arya Samaj and Congress Politics in the Punjab, 1894-1908', *Journal of Asian Studies*, vol. 26, 1967, pp. 363-79.
50. Cf. Thursby, pp. 34-40.
51. Ibid., p. 47.
52. Ibid., pp. 45-6.
53. Ibid., p. 73.

CHAPTER 12

A Fake Autobiography

By now the so-called long lost autobiography of Swami Dayananda Sarasvati entitled *Yogi ka Atmacharitra,* subtitled 'Autobiography of Yogi Dayananda', edited and translated by Dinbandhu and published at Rohtak in 1972, has been exposed as an unhistorical document by several able historians like Shri Ram Sharma and Bhavanilal Bharatiya. This paper adds another blow to that task of demolition.

The *Yogi ka Atmacharitra* tells the story how Dayananda during his Himalayan journey is supposed to have visited the old monastery of Himis. There the Swami, so goes the tale, saw the famous Tibetan version of the Life of Jesus, and the book then proceeds to give a great deal of detail about this document and its contents (pp. 214-21). The editor gives a most interesting footnote on page 220:

> At different times two other persons have seen this book about the life of Jesus at the Himis monastery. About ten years after the death of Dayananda it was seen by Nicholas Notovitch, a Russian, and about 63 years later it was also seen by Swami Abhedananda, principal of the Ramakrishna Vedanta Math. It was seen first of all by Maharshi Dayanand.

The 'second viewer', Nicholas Notovitch, wrote a book about his travels: *The Unknown Life of Christ*, translated from the French by Violet Crispe. Now, if it could be conclusively proved that the story found in the *Yogi ka Atmacharitra* is dependent upon Notovitch's book, then the conclusion is inevitable that the 'autobiography' was not written before the publication of Notovitch's work in 1895, and that it was, therefore, certainly not written by Dayananda. This chapter is concerned with providing that proof.

We are not concerned here with exposing the spuriousness of Notovitch's own work; that task has long been accomplished. The object is to show that the compiler of the *Yogi ka Atmacharitra*, or even of the Bengali fragments, if they do exist, used Notovitch's work in the process, and, therefore, wrote long after Dayananda's death. It is obviously not sufficient to indicate similarities between the two accounts. These would not be direct arguments of plagiarism. If there existed in fact documents about the life of Jesus at Himis, then one would expect the accounts of two witnesses to be similar. A different approach is necessary. A significant detail has to be found by which, unwittingly, the plagiarist himself shows that he is using Notovitch's work.

In the account of the *Yogi ka Atmacharitra* the head of the Himis monastery is related to have told Dayananda the following:

> Jesus had come to India in order to gain the knowledge of religion. In their library there is a lengthy description of this matter in a manuscript volume. This book is a translation into Tibetan. The original book in the Pali language is kept in the Maravur monastery near Masa. In this book there are fourteen sections and 244 double verses (*slokas*) I translated these verses and brought them with me. The summary of them will now be told. (214)

The most remarkable thing is that the translation of 'The Life of Saint Issa' in Notovitch's work (pp.133-98) contains exactly 244 verses divided into fourteen chapters. This is the point where the compiler of the so-called autobiography has made a serious error and shown his hand. Indeed, the arrangement into 244 verses and fourteen chapters has nothing to do with the original manuscript Notovitch claimed to have seen. The arrangement is completely a creation of Notovitch, as is made abundantly clear by his own statements:

> At last, acceding to my earnest entreaties, he ended by bringing me two large bound volumes with leaves yellowed by time, and from them he read to me, in the Thibetan language, the biography of Issa, which I carefully noted in my *carnet de voyage* as my interpreter translated what he said. This curious document is written under the form of isolated verses, which very often lack sequence. (127-8)
>
> The two manuscripts from which the lama of the convent Himis read to me all that had relation to Jesus, from collections of different copies in the Thibetan language, being translations from various rolls belonging to the library of Lassa, and brought from India, Magadha, and Nepal about three hundred years after Christ, to a convent on Mount Marbour, near the town of Lassa, where the Dalai-Lama now resides.
>
> These rolls were written in the Pali language, which certain lamas still study, in order to be able to make translations into the Thibetan dialect.
>
> The references to Issa in the chronicles are not categorical, but mingled

without sequence or order, with other narratives of contemporary events. (205-6)

Notovitch thus makes it quite clear that the original manuscript was rather a hotchpotch of fragments, and he continues on the next two pages to illustrate this, declaring that the manuscript treats successively the death of Jesus, his preaching, the origin of Jesus and his family, the incarnation of Jesus, and finally the history of Israel. He concludes with the following remarks:

> I have dealt with all these fragments concerning the life of Issa in chronological order, and have endeavoured to give them the unity of character which they absolutely lacked. (207)

It is thus abundantly clear that the chronological order of Notovitch's 'Life of Saint Issa' is completely his own arrangement, and that the division into fourteen chapters is also completely his own. How then can one possibly explain the fact that the *Yogi ka Atmacharitra* not only declares that the Himis manuscript contained fourteen chapters and 244 verses, but also, in its summary of this document, closely follows the chronological arrangement of the chapters of Notovitch? Only one explanation is possible: the compiler of the *Yogi ka Atmacharitra* had Notovitch's book right in front of him when he was faking the autobiography. Whoever it was could, therefore, not have composed the text before the year 1895, when the book was published. By that time Swami Dayananda had been dead for twelve years, and the 'autobiography' is, therefore, a later fabrication.

The publication of the *Yogi ka Atmacharitra* was, apart from anything else, a pitiful gesture. The greatness of Dayananda Sarasvati stands clearly revealed in the events and deeds of his life. When solid historical evidence shows him in that light, what need is there for fiction to try to enhance his stature? That type of fiction can only result in the final instance in cheap hero-worship and in the substitution of a great, eminently real and realistic, reformer figure of modern India by a hollow myth.

NOTE

[This chapter was originally published as: '*Yogi ka Atmacharitra:* another nail in the coffin of a fake autobiography', *Paropkari*, Ajmer, vol. 15, no. 1, 1981, pp. 34-47.]

CHAPTER 13

Sectarianism: The Case of the Arya Samaj

DAYANANDA SARASVATI wrote a great deal about the sects of Hinduism. This is not surprising since 'many sects were widespread and powerful' in his homeland of Kathiawar.[1] Large sections of both the first and second editions of his main work, the *Satyarth Prakash*, were devoted to a denunciation of the sects, and, in addition, he wrote special pamphlets about two major sects, the Vallabhacharyas and the Swaminarayanas.[2] Dayananda concentrated his attack on what he saw as the basic evils of sectarianism: the corruptive, idolatrous deviation from the sacred, universal norm of Vedic *dharma*, and the wilful promotion of dividedness and hostility within the Hindu commonwealth. The sects' deviation from the Vedic norm was to his mind most clearly evident in the books venerated by the sectarians. His criticism of the Vallabhacharyas focuses on the *Bhagavata Purana* and on the writings of the founders, and his pamphlet against the Swaminarayanas consists of a detailed analysis of their main scripture, the *Shikshapatri.* He realized that the position of the gurus was central in the organization and persistence of the sects; he ridiculed their claims to infallibility, challenged their modicum of real scholarship, and bitterly exposed what he considered to be their moral frailties. His final accusation was that they had created, promoted, and exacerbated dividedness and hostility among the Hindus and made Aryavarta 'full of darkness'.[3] He contrasted this sorry state with the universality and unity of the Vedic *dharma* in the Vedic Golden Age.

When Dayananda was persuaded by a group of Bombay reformers to participate in the establishment of the Arya Samaj, he was clearly aware of the danger that such a body may well transform itself into yet another sect. A couple of years earlier he had written in his first *Satyarth Prakash* that the Brahmo Samaj was already breaking up into separate sections and was going the way of the sects, leading to error and hostility.[4] In his address to the founding fathers of the Arya Samaj he made his attitude very clear:

> If you are able to achieve something for the good of mankind by a Samaj, then establish a Samaj; I will not stand in your way. But if you do not organize it properly, there will be a lot of trouble in the future. As for me, I will only instruct you in the same way as I teach others, and this much you should keep clearly in mind: my beliefs are not unique, and I am not omniscient. Therefore, if in the future any error of mine should be discovered after rational examination, then set it right. If you do not act that way, then this Samaj too will later on become just a sect. This is the way by which so many sectarian divisions have become prevalent in India: by making the guru's word the touchstone of truth and thus fostering deep-seated prejudices which make people religion-blind, cause quarrels, and destroy all right knowledge. That is the way India arrived at her sorry contemporary state, and that is the way this Samaj too would grow to be just another sect. This is my firm belief: even if there be many different sectarian beliefs prevalent in India; if only they all acknowledge the Vedas, then all those small rivers will re-unite in the ocean of Vedic wisdom, and the unity of *dharma* will come about.[5]

Right through his life the Swami took steps to prevent the Aryas from extolling him to the position of guru. He refused any office or title in the Arya Samaj, and insisted on becoming an ordinary member; his name in fact appears in its proper alphabetical place in the membership list of the Bombay Arya Samaj.[6] He did not allow individuals to make him into their personal guru.[7] He specified in his will that his body be cremated, and not buried as was the Hindu custom for *sannyasis*, for he feared that his tomb would become a place of guru-worship.[8] From the extensive correspondence of Dayananda it is clear that he consistently refused to interfere in Samaj matters or to dictate policy, though sometimes he was pressured to do so.[9] Never did he claim that his opinions or his writings had a quality of infallibility. He often changed his mind on important doctrinal issues, or on the interpretation of a particular Vedic text, and he acknowledged that he had changed his opinions because he had come to a better understanding of the issues. To him there was no final authority except the Vedic revelation.

Dayananda saw an intimate connection between sectarianism and the internal division and hostility that rent Hinduism apart. He was against the barriers set up between Hindu and Hindu by the institutions of caste and sect. He was afraid that hasty radicalism in implementing reforms in the manner of the Brahmos would tend to isolate the Aryas from other Hindus. That is why he shed in the latter part of his public life some of the more radical attitudes he had adopted as a rural *sannyasi* reformer during his early period along the banks of the Ganga. There are occasions when he submitted to food taboos he considered completely invalid, in order not to jeopardize his influence on sections of the Hindu population.[10] He encouraged the Aryas to adopt the same practical attitude.

That is how Dayananda viewed the phenomenon of the sects: he saw it as a system that created false gurus and false scriptures, drowned religion in a mass of superstition, and rent the body of Hinduism into a thousand pieces. In other words the contemporary situation (in which on account of his background he exaggerated the importance of sectarian adherence and impact) was viewed in purely negative terms, and was constantly contrasted with the idealized picture of the Vedic *dharma* as practised in the Golden Age of yore. The latter was to be recreated in the future, but this task would take much time, energy, and collaboration. The Arya Samaj was to play a key role in that reconstruction by a constant and determined exposition of that Vedic *dharma*. Without losing sight of that goal, the Aryas had, however, to cope with the present: they should avoid separating themselves from the living reality of Hinduism by making the necessary social compromises. Once separated from other Hindus, their effectiveness would be reduced to nothing.

How did the Arya Samaj cope with the legacy of the Swami after his death? The Aryas were influenced by three compelling forces. First, there was the ideal of the Vedic *dharma*, the fundamental legacy of the founder, most systematically expounded in his major work, the *Satyarth Prakash*. Secondly, there was what may be called that gravitational force of sectarian formation that asserts itself regularly among reform bodies in the history of Hinduism, and of which Dayananda was well aware. Finally, there was the concrete reality of their involvement with the Hindu socio-ritual system through the connections of caste and kinship. How did these forces affect the Arya Samaj in its development after the Swami's death?

Among the Punjabi Aryas there soon emerged a group who felt more radically committed to the ideal of the Vedic *dharma*. Many of these felt that the Arya leadership, centred on the Dayanand Anglo-Vedic College at Lahore, had too secular an orientation and neglected the radical socio-religious message of the Swami. They eventually precipitated a split in 1874, and their branch was variously called the 'Radicals', the 'Mahatma Party', and the 'Gurukul Party'.[11] Each of these names reveals an aspect of their programme. As 'Radicals' they saw the need for initiatives such as a rigorous imposition of vegetarianism on all Aryas, a serious commitment to preaching the Arya message, and implementation of marriage reform by increasing the marriage age, fostering cross-caste alliances, and promoting widow-remarriage. The title 'Mahatma Party' referred to their tendency to look upon the Swami more as a guru and upon his writings as definitive statements. They became the 'Gurukul Party' because they advocated the idea that Arya children should be isolated in special schools where they would be educated according to the ideals proposed by the founder.

Within this section of the Punjab Arya Samaj there sprung up smaller groups of an even more radical nature. They acknowledged that the Gurukul Party had the right theoretical approach, but objected because the theory was not put into practice; their declared aim was to do just that. Three such attempts at organizing 'practical radicalism' were launched in the last years of the nineteenth century: the Arya Shiromani Sabha, the Arya Bhratri Sabha, and the Arya Dharm Sabha. Their central aim was to implement the socio-ritual ideals of Dayananda; all rituals should be purely Vedic according to the Swami's ritual handbook, the *Sanskarvidhi*, and caste restrictions should be abandoned especially in the matter of marriage endogamy. Implementation of these two vital reforms would of necessity have elicited sanctions on the part of the caste organization, and consequently social ostracism in the crucial sphere of marriage arrangements. It is not surprising, therefore, that none of these attempts at organizing radicalism got any further than talking and planning, and that none of them became a living reality.[12]

These attempts at the concrete realization of the ideal Vedic *dharma* clearly exhibit some important characteristics of sect-formation. First of all they tended to exalt the founder to the position of guru. Pandit Gurudatta, an influential leader of the radicals, was the first to consider more and more Dayananda's writings as having a quality of infallibility.[13] Secondly, there was a tendency toward a rite of initiation: the Shiromani Sabha derived its very name from an initiation ceremony which included a ceremonial shaving of the head. This initiatory ceremony was accentuated by the injunction that only the Vedic rites described in Dayananda's *Sanskarvidhi* should be performed. Thirdly, the radicals envisaged a socio-ritual consolidation of the elect group by restricting marriage alliances. This is evidenced by expressions such as, 'It is time that we cut the orthodox caste connection and form a living connection between Aryas', and 'We are in danger of being swallowed by Hinduism.'[14] The following rules were mooted: Aryas should marry Aryas; marriage alliances should disregard caste restrictions and follow varna classifications; the *shuddhi* ceremony was not necessary for becoming an Arya. The first two of these rules accentuated sect exclusiveness, the last one, openness of the sect by 'conversion'.

These attempts at organizing radicalism foundered on account of two connected reasons. The social life of the Aryas was in fact dominated by caste and kinship connections, of which the crucial axis was the marriage alliance. The Aryas knew from some bitter experiences that the rupture of that connection could bring outcasting, social ostracism, ruin of vital kinship bonds, and a drastic restriction of marriage prospects. Only exceptionally brave and independent persons could face such potential disasters, and there were not enough people of that category around for even a limited experiment. Moreover, the Aryas understood that such action would entail a breakaway from Hindu society, and the overwhelming majority had no intention of facing that consequence. In this respect their reaction was in line with the ideas of the founder himself.[15]

The result of these two basic realities, the vital connection of the Aryas with Hindu society and their wish to remain within the world of Hinduism, was that their attempts at reform were 'slow, piecemeal—moving forward in an uneven rhythm of boldness and timidity, of accommodation and innovation'.[16] Their use of Vedic rites was introduced very gradually, and before the end of the century only the bravest dared to do so. The use increased as the objection of the orthodox relented. The earliest introduction of the *shuddhi* rite created vehement orthodox opposition. The Aryas managed to elicit a less hostile reaction by adopting 'orthodox' rites of *shuddhi*, including penance at Hardwar. Only at a later stage, when the Hindu community, shocked by the evidence of the census figures that the number of Hindus was being eroded by the disproportionate increase of Muslims and Christians, did the *shuddhi* movement become acceptable to the orthodox, and the Aryas turn bolder in their experiments.[17] Widow-remarriage was still a bold step in the 1880s, and, therefore, rather exceptional. The Aryas were convinced that imprudent radicalism had cut some Brahmos off from the tree of Hinduism, and were determined that the Arya Samaj should avoid making a similar mistake. In the first decades of the twentieth century the idea that Hinduism needed to be defended, and, therefore, needed to close ranks, led to increasing collaboration between orthodox and Aryas: this was very notably evident in the involvement of both groups in the activities of the Hindu Mahasabha and in the *shuddhi* movement of the 1920s.[18]

Although this careful gradualism has remained a characteristic of the contemporary Arya Samaj, the observer can even today detect in Arya writings and statements scattered seeds of sectarian tendencies. For instance, the urge to elevate Dayananda to the status of guru manifests itself regularly. The titles given him range from Maharshi, Gurudev, Yogishwar, Trata (saviour), Mahan Sant, to Deva, Devata, and Bhagavan.[19] The most striking example of this tendency is to be found in the voluminous work *Yogi ka Atmacharitra*, published by Dinbandhu Shastri at Rohtak in 1973. The editor claims that he is publishing an autobiography of Dayananda Sarasvati which had been lost. The clear aim of the work was to prove once and for all two propositions: that the Swami was, in fact, the instigator and secret leader of the 1857 Sepoy Mutiny, and that he was the most accomplished Yogi and Guru that ever lived, no less an incarnation of divine truth than the great *rishis* of old. The work is patently a fake and could not have been written by Dayananda. The publication caused quite a stir in Arya circles, and it is important to note that the volume has been denounced as a fake by many Arya scholars and leaders.[20]

The shrine built in memory of the founder at Ajmer, the place of his death, would not have met with the founder's approval. Such a shrine, as Dayananda well knew, constitutes for the more fervent Aryas a constant temptation for exaltation of the founder and the beginnings of a cult of him. However, responsible Arya leaders have consistently resisted such tendencies and the Swami has never become the object of worship, which happened to Ramakrishna in Bengal.

It has been shown that in the early history of the Arya Samaj small groups of radicals contemplated innovations that had a sectarian direction, and some reasons for their failure have been indicated. Attention has also been drawn to the fact that some seeds of sectarianism are ever present in the Arya Samaj. The concluding part of the chapter attempts to argue that there are some fundamental reasons why the Arya Samaj could not really become a sect. Some basic prerequisites for sect-formation are absent in its structure and history. The formulation of what we call 'basic prerequisites of sect formation' arose from two interacting processes: the consideration of the history of the Arya Samaj, and the reflection on the way sects arose in Hinduism. The first was considered in the first part of this chapter. The latter will not be argued in detail; it is the result of reflection on a range of literature dealing with the history of the sects.[21] This led to the isolation of some basic conditions that appeared to play an important part in the emergence of sects. Looking back over the history of the Arya Samaj it appeared that in its case these conditions were not present. If their absence is indeed a major factor preventing sect formation in the Arya Samaj, then our formulation of basic conditions of sect-formation is confirmed by our analysis of the history of that Samaj, and thus contributes to the understanding of the phenomenon of sectarianism in Hinduism.

A fairly general pattern of sect-formation is that after the death of the prime guru, a successor or a group of individuals continue the personal inspiration and charisma of the founder. It is usually these disciples, or successors, who propagandize the new approach, recruit followers, create a continuing tradition, and organize the faithful. The Arya Samaj did not have that kind of tradition. Dayananda, though a *sannyasi* of considerable yogic accomplishments (an aspect exalted and exaggerated by those followers who tend to elevate him to the position of guru), did not primarily appeal during or after his life as a charismatic person communicating an inspiring new approach to religious experience, but rather as a forceful propagator of ideas and convictions. He did not create a body of 'disciples' in the sense of closely attached followers whom he trained in a new path; in fact one could not say that he preached a special method of religious experience. In this respect his approach was very different from other modern religious personalities such as Ramakrishna and Keshub Chandra Sen.

The individual approach of Dayananda, moreover, was such that another general characteristic of most sects was ruled out from the very start: the identifying symbols of sectarian adherence. These include special *tilak* marks, special *mantras*, specific ritual observances, and often a primary sectarian scripture which encapsulates the message and inspiration of the original founders. Repeatedly, Dayananda mocked all kinds of sectarian body symbols and demonstrated the absurdity and futility of their *mantras.* In the ritual sphere he professed a blanket condemnation of all rites except the Vedic ones. These in fact constitute not a sign of distinction within the Hindu fold, but rather the common ancient heritage of all Hindus; they are symbols of universality, not of particularity. The Arya Samaj has no doubt always given a very special place to the *Satyarth Prakash* as the *summa theologica* of the founder. There has been a tendency among some Aryas to look upon it as an infallible document, and its centenary was celebrated with great pomp. However, the *Satyarth Prakash* is not an inspirational work firing the imagination and activating emotions. On the contrary, it is basically a theological exposition of doctrinal, ethical, and historical issues in a dull and factual style. It could never have the appeal of works such as the *Saundaryalahari*, the *Vachanas* of Basava, the hymns of the Alvars, the *Jnaneshvara*, Kabir's *Bijak*, Dadu's *Banis*, or many of the sectarian Puranas.

There is one more characteristic frequently connected with sect formation that is absent in the case of the Arya Samaj: a strong regional base. Most sectarian movements with significant impact had such a base, and continue having it even if some wider dissemination took place. By the time of Dayananda's death, the Arya Samaj was established among some elite groups in Bombay, Rajasthan, Punjab, and the U.P. These regional groups were very different in cultural background and in their approach to the meaning and function of the Samaj. The strongest base of the movement was at that time in the Punjab, where the Samaj had recruited a significant proportion of the Western educated elite. However, the Punjab leadership at that time represented the most 'secular' branch of the Arya Samaj, and as such the least likely to steer the organization into a sectarian direction.

The absence in the Arya Samaj of these important factors, a guru-disciple *parampara*, special symbols (*tilak*, *mantra*, ritual, book), and a strong cultural-regional base, made the development of the organization into a sect after the death of Dayananda virtually impossible. Moreover, the historical development of the Samaj since the departure of its founder has generally prevented or impeded any significant strengthening of those factors, and the significant diffusion of the Samaj in migrant Indian communities around the globe also works against them. Indeed, it is difficult to see how the Samaj could develop into a sectarian grouping in the foreseeable future. In this respect the Samaj certainly has lived up to the hopes of its founder.

NOTES

1. Cf. *Gazetteer of the Bombay Presidency*, vol. 9, part 1: *Gujarat Population*, Mumbai, 1891, 'Religious Sects', pp. 530-50.
2. *Vedaviruddhamatkhandana*, Mumbai, 1875; *Shikshapatridhwantanivarana*, Mumbai, 1876.
3. *Satyarth Prakash*, 1st edn., Varanasi, 1975, p. 382.
4. Ibid., p. 394.
5. Damodar Sundardas, *Mumbai Aryasamajano Itihas*, Mumbai, 1933, pp. 8-9.
6. Ibid., p.32.
7. See, e.g. Ghasiram, *Maharshi Dayananda Sarasvati ka Jivan-Charit*, Ajmer, 1957, vol. 1, p. 348.
8. For the text of his two wills see *Rishi Dayananda Sarasvati ke Patra aur Vijnapan*, Y. Mimamshak (ed.), Amritsar, 1955, pp. 219, 388.
9. Cf. J.T.F. Jordens, *Dayananda Sarasvati, His Life and Ideas*, Delhi, 1978, pp.196-9.
10. Ibid., p. 204.
11. For an analysis of this process, cf. K.W. Jones, *Arya Dharm, Hindu Consciousness in 19th Century Punjab*, Berkeley, 1976, particularly chs. 6 and 7.
12. For references, Cf. J.T.F. Jordens, *Swami Shraddhananda, His Life and Causes*, Delhi, and New York, pp. 47-9.
13. Jones, p. 167.
14. Ibid., p. 204.
15. Ibid., pp. 94, 113, 205.
16. Ibid., p. 95.
17. Cf. Jordens, n. 12, chs. 3 and 6. See also ch. 11 of this volume.
18. Ibid.
19. For a few examples, cf. the 7 November 1980 issue of the weekly *Sarvadeshik*, *passim*; Jagadish Vidyarthi, *Swami Dayananda Sarasvati, Sachitra Adarsh Jivan-Charitra*, New Delhi, 1971, pp. 3, 5, 6, 7; Prakashchandra Kaviratna, *Dayananda Prakash*, Ajmer, 1973, pp. 3, 4, 12.
20. See ch. 12 of this volume.
21. A number of works on sectarian movements are listed in *The Cultural History of India*, vol. IV *The Religions*, H. Bhattacharya (ed.), Calcutta, 1956, pp. 733-7. For a general overview L. Renou and J. Filliozat (eds.), *L'Inde Classique*, vol. 1, Paris, 1947, pp. 620-61 and R.G. Bhandarkar, *Vaisnavism, Saivism and Minor religious systems*, Varanasi, 1913, are very useful.

Bibliography

BOOKS

Ambedkar, B.R., *Who were the Shudras? How they came to be the Fourth Varna in the Indo-Aryan Society*, Mumbai, 1946.

Bailey, G.M. and I. Kesarcodi-Watson (eds.), *Bhakti Studies*, New Delhi, 1991.

Barz, R., *The Bhakti Sect of Vallabhacharya*, Faridabad, 1976.

Basham, A.L., *History and Doctrines of the Ajivikas*, London, 1951.

———, *The Wonder that was India*, New York, 1954.

Basu, Rajnarayan, *Hindudharmer Shreshtata*, Calcutta, 1872.

Basu, P.S., *Life and Works of Brahmananda Keshav*, Calcutta, 1940.

Bhagavaddatt, Pandit (ed.), *Rishi Dayananda Sarasvati ke patra aur vijnapan*, 2nd edn., Amritsar, 1955.

Bhandarkar, R.G., *Vaisnavism, Saivism and Minor religious systems*, Varanasi, 1913.

Bharatendu, Harischandra, *Bharatendu Granthavali*, ed. by Vrajaratnadas, vol. 3, Varanasi, 1953.

Bharatiya, B. (ed.), *Dayananda-Shastrarth-Samgraha*, Sonepat, 1969.

Bhattacharya, H. (ed.), *The Cultural History of India*, Vol. IV, *The Religions*, Calcutta, 1956.

Brahmo, 'A Punjabi of the New Dispensation', in *The Arya Samaj and a Refutation of its Tenets*, Lahore, 1883.

Brown, W. Norman, *Man in the Universe*, Berkeley, 1970.

Coward, H. (ed.), *Modern Indian attitudes to Religious Pluralism*, New York, 1987.

Chunder, Bholanath, *The Travels of a Hindoo*, vol. II, London, 1869.

Das, Lala Jivan (ed.), *Papers for the Thoughtful*, no. 3, Lahore, 1902.

Dasgupta, S.N., *A History of Indian Philosophy*, vol. 4, Cambridge, 1961.

Dayananda Sarasvati, *Satyarth Prakash*, 1st edn., Varanasi, 1875.

———, *Vedanta-dhvanta-nivaranam*, Mumbai, 1875.

———, *Vedaviruddhmatkhandana*, Mumbai, 1875.

Dayananda Sarasvati, *Shikshapatridhwantanivarana*, Mumbai, 1876.

———, *Rigvedadibhashyabhumika*, Varanasi, 1877.

———, *Satyarthaprakashah*, Ajmer, 1966.

———, *Rigvedadibhashyabhumika*, Yudhisthir Mimamshak (ed.), Amritsar, 1967.

———, *Poona Pravachana arthat Upadesh-Manjari*, Yudhisthir Mimamshak (ed.), Delhi, 1969.

———, *Bhagavata-Khandanam*, Yudhisthir Mimamshak (ed.), Sonepat, 1971.

———, *Sanskarvidhi*, second revd. edn., Yudhisthir Mimamshak (ed.), Sonepat, 1971.

———, *Rigvedadibhashyabhumika*, Ajmer, 1980.

———, *Vedaviruddhmatkhandana*, Delhi, n.d.

———, *Sanskaravidhi*, 2nd edn., Allahabad, 1884.

Derrett, J.D.M., *Religion, Law and the State in India*, London, 1968.

Dobbin, C., *Urban Leadership in Western India*, London, 1972.

Drake-Brockman, D.L., *Muttra: a Gazetteer*, being vol. VII of the *District Gazetteers of the United Provinces of Agra and Oudh*, Allahabad, 1911.

Eliade, M., *Cosmos and History, The Myth of the Eternal Return*, New York, 1959.

Farquhar, J.N., *Modern Religious Movements in India*, rpt., Delhi, 1967.

Forbes, A.K., *Ras Mala*, London, 1878.

Gandhi, M.K., *An Autobiography, or The Story of My Experiments with Truth*, trans. from Gujarati by Mahadev Desai (ed.), Ahmedabad, 2nd edn., 1940.

Gandhi, M.K., *The Collected Works of Mahatma Gandhi*, 90 vols., New Delhi, 1958-82.

Garg, Ganga Ram (ed.), *World Perspectives on Swami Dayananda Sarasvati*, New Delhi, 1984.

Gazetteer of the Bombay Presidency, vol. 8, *Kathiawar*, Mumbai, 1884.

Gazetteer of the Bombay Presidency, vol. 9, part 1, *Gujarat Population*, Mumbai, 1891.

Ghasiram, *Maharshi Dayananda Sarasvati ka Jivan-Charit*, 2 vols, Ajmer, 1957.

Growse, F.S., *Mathura, a District Memoir*, 2nd edn., Allahabad, 1880.

Hay, S.N., *Asian Ideas of East and West, Tagore and his Critics in Japan, China, and India*, Cambridge, MA, 1970.

Jigyasu, Munshiram (ed.), *Rishi Dayananda ka Patravyavahar*, vol. I, Gurukul Kangri, 1910.

Jones, K.W., *Arya Dharm, Hindu Consciousness in 19th Century Punjab*, Berkeley, 1976.

Jordens, J.T.F., *Dayananda Sarasvati, His Life and Ideas*, Delhi, 1978.

Jordens, J.T.F., *Swami Shraddhananda, His Life and Causes*, Delhi, and New York, 1981.
Kane, P.V., *History of Dharmaśāstra*, 5 vols., Pune, 1930-62.
Kaviratna, Prakashchandra, *Dayananda Prakash*, Ajmer, 1973.
Keer, Dhananjay, *Mahatma Jotirao Phooley, Father of our Social Revolution*, Mumbai, 1964.
Kopf, D., *British Orientalism and the Bengal Renaissance*, Calcutta, 1969.
Lekhram, *Maharshi Dayananda Sarasvati ka Jivan Charitra*, transl. into Hindi from the original Urdu by Kaviraj Raghunandansingh 'Nirmal', ed. by Pandit Harischandra Vidyalankar, Delhi, 1972.
Majumdar, B.B., *History of Indian Social and Political Ideas from Rammohan Roy to Dayananda*, Calcutta, 1967.
Majumdar, R.C., *History of the Freedom Movement in India*, 3 vols., Calcutta, 1963.
——— (ed.), *The History and Culture of the Indian People*, vol. V, *The Struggle for Empire*, Mumbai, 2nd edn., 1966.
Marfatia, M.I., *The Philosophy of Vallabhacharya*, Delhi, 1967
Marshall, P.J., *The British Discovery of Hinduism in the Eighteenth Century*, Cambridge, 1970.
Mimamshak, Y., *Rishi Dayananda ke Granthon ka Itihas*, Ajmer, 1949.
——— (ed.), *Rishi Dayananda Sarasvati ke Patra aur Vijnapan*, Amritsar, 1958.
——— (ed.), *Rishi Dayananda Sarasvati ke Patra aur Vijnapanon ke Parishisht*, Amritsar, 1958.
Mitchell, J.M., *Letters to Indian Youth*, 3rd edn., Mumbai, 1857.
Motiwala, B.N., *Karsondas Mulji; A Biographical Study*, Mumbai, 1935.
Mukhopadhyay, Devendranath, *Virjanandacharit*, transl. into Hindi by Ghasiram, Agra, 1918.
Mulji, Karsondas (publ. anon.), *History of the Sect of Maharajas or Vallabhacharyas in Western India*, London, 1905.
Munshi, K.M., *Gujarat and its Literature*, Mumbai, 1935.
Oddie, G.A., *Social Protest in India*, New Delhi, 1979.
——— (ed.), *Religion in South Asia*, New Delhi, 1984.
O'Flaherty, W.D. and Derrett, J.D.M. (eds.), *The Concept of Duty in South Asia*, London, 1978.
O'Flaherty, W. Doniger, *The Rig Veda*, Harmondsworth, 1981.
Parapullil, P.A., S.J., *Swami Dayananda Sarasvati's Understanding and Assessment of Christianity*, Rome, 1970.
Parekh, Bhai Manilal C., *Shri Vallabhacharya: Life, Teachings and Movement* (*A Religion of Grace*), Rajkot, 1943.
Parvate, T.V., *Mahadev Govind Ranade, a Biography*, Mumbai, 1963.
Potter, Karl H., *Bibliography of Indian Philosophers*, Delhi, 1970.

Pyarelal, *Mahatma Gandhi*, vol. I, *The Early Phase*, Ahmedabad, 1965.
Radhakrishnan, S. and Moore, C.A., *A Source Book in Indian Philosophy*, Princeton, 1957.
Radhakrishnan, S., *Indian Philosophy*, vol. I, New York, 1958.
Rai, Lala Lajpat, *A History of the Arya Samaj*, revd. edn., Mumbai, 1967.
Ray, S.N., *Gandhi, India and the World*, Melbourne, 1970.
Reclus, E., *The Universal Geography*, ed. A.H. Keane, vol. III, *India and Indochina*, London, n.d.
Renou, L. and J. Filliozat, *L'Inde Classique*, vol. 1, Paris, 1947.
Report of the Maharaj Libel Case and of the Bhattia Conspiracy Case Connected with it, Mumbai,1862.
Robson, J., *Hinduism and its relation to Christianity*, London, 1893.
Rudolph, L.I. and S.H. Rudolph, *The Modernity of Tradition*, Chicago, 1967.
Shah, J.G., *Shri Vallabhacharya: His Philosophy and Religion*, Nadiad, 1969.
Saletore, B.A., *Main currents in the Ancient History of Gujarat*, Vadodara, 1960.
Sangave, V.A., *Jaina Community, a Social Survey*, Mumbai, 1959.
Sarda, Har Bilas, *Life of Dayananda Saraswati, World Teacher*, 2nd edn., Ajmer, 1968.
Selections from the Records of the Bombay Government, no. 37, New Series, Mumbai, 1856.
Scott, T.J., *Missionary Life among the Villages in India*, Cincinnati, 1876.
Sharma, A. (ed.), *Neo-Hindu Views of Christianity*, Leiden, 1988.
Sharpe, Eric J., *Not to Destroy But to Fulfil*, Gleerup, 1965.
Shastri, D.R., *Original Development of the Rituals of Ancestor Worship in India*, Calcutta, 1963.
Singer, Milton (ed.), *Traditional India: Structure and Change*, Philadelphia, 1958.
Stevenson, Mrs Sinclair, *The Heart of Jainism*, London, 1915.
Sundardas, Damodar, *Mumbai Aryasamajano Itihas*, Mumbai, 1933.
Tagore, Debendranath, *Brahmo Dharma of Maharshi Debendranath Tagore*, trans. into English by Hem Chandra Sarkar, Calcutta, 1928.
Thursby, G., *Hindu-Muslim Relations in British India, a study of controversy, conflict, and communal movements in Northern India, 1923-1928*, Leiden, 1975.
Vidyarthi, Jagadish, *Swami Dayananda Sarasvati Sachitra Adarsh Jivan-Charitra*, New Delhi, 1971.
von Glasenapp, H., *Der Jainismus*, Hildersheim, 1964.
Webster, J.C.B., *The Christian Community and Change in Nineteenth Century North India*, Delhi, 1976.
Williams, R., *Jaina Yoga*, Oxford, 1963.
Zaehner, R.C., *Hindu Scriptures*, London, 1959.

ARTICLES

Barrier, N.G., 'The Arya Samaj and Congress Politics in the Punjab,1894-1908', *Journal of Asian Studies*, vol. 26, 1967, pp. 363-79.

———, 'The Punjab Government and Communal Politics 1870-1908', *Journal of Asian Studies*, vol. 27, 1968, pp. 523-39.

Church, C.D., 'The Myth of the four Yugas in the Sanskrit Puranas; a diamensional study', *Purana*, vol. XVI, no. 1, January 1974, pp. 15-18.

Dayananda Sarasvati, 'Autobiography', *The Theosophist*, vol. 1, pp. 9-13 (Oct. 1879).

Derrett, J.M. Duncan, 'The Concept of Duty in Ancient Indian Jurisprudence: The Problem of Ascertainment', in W.D. O'Flaherty and J.D.M. Derrett (eds.), *The Concept of Duty in South Asia*, London, 1978.

Hay, S.N., 'Jain Influences on Gandhi's early Thought', in S.N. Ray, *Gandhi, India and the World*, Melbourne, 1970.

Heesterman, J.C., 'Veda and Dharma', in W.D. O'Flaherty and J.D.M. Derrett (eds.), *The Concept of Duty in South Asia*, London, 1978.

Hoernle, Dr Rudolf, article on Dayananda in the *Christian Intelligencer* of March 1970, in Lajpat Rai, *A History of the Arya Samaj*, revd. edn., Mumbai, 1967.

Jones, K.W., 'The Bengali Elite in Post-Annexation Punjab: an example of Inter-Regional influence in 19th Century India', *The Indian Economic and Social History Review*, 3 (1966), pp. 376-95.

———, 'Communalism in the Punjab, the Arya Samaj Contribution', *Journal of Asian Studies*, vol. 28, 1968, p. 42.

———, '*Ham Hindu Nahin*: Arya Sikh Relations, 1877-1905', *Journal of Asian Studies*, vol. 32, 1973, pp. 463-4.

Jordens, J.T.F., 'Gandhi's Religion and the Hindu Heritage', in S.N. Ray, *Gandhi, India and the World*, Melbourne, 1970.

———, 'Dayananda and Vedanta: a comparison of the first and second editions of his Satyarth Prakash', *The Indian Economic and Social History Review*, vol. IX, 1972, pp. 367-79.

———, 'Tradition and Modernity: Dayananda Sarasvati's concept of the Vedic Golden Age', *Religious Traditions*, vol. 4, no. 2, 1981, pp. 1-10.

———, 'Dayananda Sarasvati and Christianity', *Indian Church History Review*, vol. 15, no. 1, 1981.

———, '*Yogi ka Atmacharitra*: another nail in the coffin of a fake autobiography', *Paropkari*, vol. 15, no. 1, 1981, pp. 34-47.

———, 'Two Giants look at the Cosmic Man: Dayananda and Ambedkar interpret the *Purusha-Sukta*', *Journal of the Oriental Institute of Baroda*, vol. 33, 1983, pp. 1-10.

Jordens, J.T.F., 'Orthodoxy and Heresy: Reflections on the 1881 Calcutta Pandit Council' in Ganga Ram Garg (ed.), *World Perspectives on Swami Dayananda Sarasvati*, New Delhi, 1984.

———, 'Reconversion to Hinduism, the Shuddhi of the Arya Samaj', in G.A. Oddie (ed.), *Religion in South Asia*, New Delhi, 1984.

———, 'Pilgrimage to the Sources: Dayananda Sarasvati and the Vedas', *The Journal of the Oriental Society of Australia*, vols. 18-19, 1986-7.

———, 'Gandhi and Religious Pluralism', in H. Coward (ed.), *Modern Indian attitudes to Religious Pluralism*, New York, 1987, pp. 3-17.

———, 'Dayananda Sarasvati's interpretation of Christianity', in A. Sharma (ed.), *Neo-Hindu Views of Christianity*, Leiden, 1988, pp. 120-42.

———, 'Modern Critics of the Vallabhacharyas: were they Critics of *Bhakti*?', in G.M. Bailey and I. Kesarcodi-Waston (eds.), *Bhakti Studies*, New Delhi, 1991, pp. 309-28.

Spodek, H., 'On the origins of Gandhi's Political Methodology: the heritage of Kathiawad and Gujarat', *The Journal of Asian Studies*, vol. 30, 1971, pp. 361-72.

PERIODICALS

Indian Evangelical Review, vol. 7, April 1881.

The Leader, 24, 25 August, 23 December 1923; 8 February 1924.

The Theosophist, vol. 1, October 1879.

UNPUBLISHED SOURCES

Graham, R., 'The Arya Samaj as a Reformation in Hinduism with Special Reference to Caste', unpublished Ph.D. dissertation, Yale University, 1942.

Jones, K.W., 'The Arya Samaj in the Punjab: a study of social reform and religious revivalism, 1877-1902', unpublished Ph.D. dissertation, University of California, Berkeley, 1966.

Thursby, G., 'Aspects of Hindu-Muslim Relations in British India: a study of Arya Samaj activities, Government of India policies, and communal conflict in the period 1923-1928', unpublished Ph.D. dissertation, Duke University, 1972.

Index